Monograph 59
THE AMERICAN ETHNOLOGICAL SOCIETY
Robert F. Spencer, *Editor*

*

ESKIMO KINSMEN

Changing Family Relationships in Northwest Alaska

ERNEST S. BURCH, JR.

WEST PUBLISHING CO.
St. Paul . New York . Boston
Los Angeles . San Francisco

To Deanne

COPYRIGHT ©️ 1975 By WEST PUBLISHING CO.
Printed in the United States of America

Library of Congress Cataloging in Publication Data

Burch, Ernest S   1938–
  Eskimo kinsmen.
  (Monograph—The American Ethnological Society:
  Bibliography: p.
  Includes index.
    1. Eskimos—Alaska—Social life and customs. 2. Kinship—Alaska.
I. Title. II. Series: American Ethnological Society. Monographs:
E99.E7B888   301.42′1′097987   75–4972
ISBN 0–8299–0049–7

Introduction

The Eskimos have been as thoroughly studied as any group of people in the world. Articles and books about them number in the several thousands, appearing with increasing frequency over a period of more than two centuries. As Charles Campbell Hughes (1963:452) once put it, "rarely has so much been written by so many about so few." The Eskimos of Northwest Alaska hold a prominent place in this literature, both quantitatively and qualitatively. The anthropologically useful sources for this area alone, consisting of the works of explorers, government officials, and historians, as well as anthropologists, numbers several hundred titles published over a period of nearly two hundred years.

The more specialized literature on Eskimo kinship, although technically beginning with Lewis Henry Morgan in 1871, dates effectively only from the early 1950's. Since then it has flourished, more studies having been published between 1955 and 1970 than had appeared altogether previously. In this more focused literature, contributions from Northwest Alaska again stand out. The work of Albert Heinrich (1955a, 1955b, 1960, 1963) is most notable in this regard, but Leopold Pospisil (1964), Nicholas Gubser (1965), and Robert Spencer (1959) have also made important contributions.

Despite the size and quality of the literature on the Northwest Alaskan Eskimos, certain major gaps remain. One of them is in the area of social change. Although studies of social change have been conducted in the area, they generally have focussed on a relatively restricted range of time. They also have been less concerned with tracing the *sequence* of change than they have been with describing an already changed situation. Most important of all, students of social change in Northwest Alaska have exhibited a remarkable tendency to ignore kinship, while, conversely, students of kinship have not dealt systematically with social change. The present study fills the resulting gap.

A study of both kinship and social change, the present volume deals with a period well over a century in length. A substantial amount of space is devoted to the traditional kinship system, which is defined for present purposes as the one existing in the first half of the nineteenth century. This procedure is necessary in a study of change, because change of any sort cannot be understood without knowing what it was that changed (Levy 1952:45). The account of the "traditional period" thus constitutes a baseline against which changes can be clearly seen, and easily described by way of contrast. The years from 1850 to 1970 constitute the "transitional period," or the era of change. In order to control the sequence of developments over this long period of time, I divide it into early (1850–1890), intermediate (1890–1940), and recent (1940–1970) phases. Because of the great rapidity with which change was taking place in Northwest Alaska at the *end* of the recent phase, the *entire volume is phrased in the past tense.*

Another important difference between the present study and previous works on Northwest Alaska is in spatial coverage. The bulk of the anthropological literature on the area consists of community studies (e. g., VanStone 1962b) and regional (e. g., Spencer 1959) studies of relatively restricted geographic scope. The present volume includes a larger area within its purview, incorporating all of the earlier regional and community studies within a single analytic framework, and including some districts not covered at all in the literature. The territory I have taken as my focus includes the entire area of what is now the State of Alaska west and north of the Yukon River drainage, encompassing an area of some 150,000 square miles. It includes the entire domain inhabited in Alaska by representatives of a single language group, the Inupik-speaking Eskimos (Oswalt 1967:28).

The research on which this volume is based spanned the decade of the 1960's. It included four trips, made in 1960–61, 1964, 1965, and 1969–70, totalling approximately thirty months of active field work.   During these trips I visited or lived in the communities of Anaktuvuk Pass, Barrow, Deering, Kivalina, Kotzebue, Noatak, Noorvik, Point Hope, Selawik, and Shungnak. I interviewed people from practically every part of Northwest Alaska between Norton Sound and the Canadian border, including many districts that were devoid of human population during the period of my research.   During the first two trips I was concerned primarily with a detailed investigation of a single district and a restricted period of time.   During the third, and particularly during the fourth, I strived for more comprehensive spatial and temporal coverage.   The techniques employed in the field covered most of the standard ethnographic repertoire, ranging from intensive participant observation to highly formalized interviews of various kinds.

A legitimate question is how, on the basis of research conducted in the 1960's, I can claim to have reconstructed a kinship system as it existed in 1850.   The methodology employed was complex, and my answer to that question is long enough to require statement in a separate publication (which is currently in preparation).   Briefly summarized, the approach had four main elements.

1.   It depended at the outset on a supply of good informants, individuals who were students of the ways of their ancestors, and who were willing to tell what they knew to an anthropologist. Fortunately for me, Northwest Alaska was well endowed in this respect during the 1960's, and it was my privilege to learn from a number of people who were social historians of the highest calibre.

2.   Secondly, the approach required the acquisition of a large fund of well-documented facts from a limited geographic area, and for a restricted period of time in which the relevant field work was actually conducted.   It was necessary to do this so that the accuracy of the information could be checked thoroughly.

3.   The procedure then involved working back through time and out through space from this core of data, moving progressively from the well-known to the less-well-known.   Both this new information and that previously acquired had to fit together into a single coherent pattern in order to be considered reliable enough to use here.

4. Finally, the approach required the reconstruction of the *total* social system of the peoples concerned. All the information about kinship had to be consistent with a larger body of data about social organization and about historical events in order to be judged reliable. This volume thus presents only a portion of the material taken into consideration in its preparation.

The temporal and spatial limitations of my own field investigations were compensated for by ethnohistorical research. The voluminous and generally reliable literature on Northwest Alaska made it possible to cross-check a number of points made by informants, and it enabled me to write of the traditional and early transitional periods with an assurance that would be unjustified otherwise. Finally, I made full use of the work of anthropologists who preceded me in the field, particularly that of Albert Heinrich and Robert Spencer. Although I take issue with those authors on specific points, I believe that my general findings are consistent with theirs, and I regard the present study as a logical extension of the work they began.

This volume is thus based primarily on the results of my own field studies, supplemented in important respects by literary and archival materials. Accordingly, it contains a greater number of footnotes and citations than are found in the customary ethnographic report. In order to clarify the source on any given topic, two types of citation are employed. Where I am completely dependent on a literary source for my information, the standard anthropological format, e. g., (Spencer 1959:43) is used. Where another investigator and I independently acquired similar information, but from different times or places, reference to the other author's material takes the form of a "see reference," e. g., (v. Spencer 1959:43). Where the information derives exclusively from my own field work, there will of course be no citation at all.

To acknowledge fully the help I received in researching this study would require a volume in itself. The individuals who contributed significant information and material or moral support in the field number in the several hundreds, including literally the entire population of one village, and a substantial proportion of the populations of several others. Since space limitations make detailed acknowledgement impossible, I must restrict myself to a general expression of gratitude to the many people of Northwest Alaska who did so much to help me. I hope they understand why I cannot cite them individually.

A few people must be mentioned by name. James Keating, Daniel Norton, and Lowell Sage saved my life. My debt to their quick action and intelligent care can only be noted, never repaid. I must also acknowledge the help of my wife, Deanne. Her substantive assistance in the research, her moral support under the most trying circumstances, and her constant companionship, have been more than any husband could dare hope for.

The people who contributed directly to the writing of this volume can also be thanked individually. Gary Palmer, Steven Friedenthal, and particularly Dan MacDonald helped in the analysis of portions of the field data. Joan dePena, and particularly Edwin Anderson and Louise Sweet, gave valuable advice and criticisms of preliminary drafts of the manuscript. Thomas C. Correll was an invaluable source of inspiration and ideas. Finally, Sheila MacKie made sure that it all got down on paper, and she saved me from numerous mistakes in the process.

Certain portions of the research were supported by the Department of Anthropology, University of Chicago, the Department of Anthropology, University of Manitoba, and the Northern Studies Committee, University of Manitoba. The Canada Council sponsored the final year of field work, and also defrayed much of the cost of preparing the manuscript for publication. I thank these organizations for their support.

*

Contents

FIGURES

TABLES

*

ESKIMO KINSMEN

Changing Family Relationships
in Northwest Alaska

†

1

The Setting

Northwest Alaska, stretching roughly from Norton Sound to the Canadian border, was occupied in 1800, and probably much earlier, by people who referred to themselves as *Inupiat*—the "authentic people." Traditionally, the *Inupiat* spoke dialects of the so-called (Swadesh 1951–52) "Inupik" Eskimo language. Linguistically, they were distinct from the "Yupik"-Eskimo-speaking peoples in southwestern Alaska and Siberia, and from the Athapaskan-speaking peoples in the Yukon drainage, to the south and east (Oswalt 1967:28ff.). The phrase "Northwest Alaskan Eskimos," like the corresponding Eskimo notion of *Inupiat*, has broad linguistic, cultural, and geographic connotations. It does *not* refer to a specific tribe, society, or other social entity.

The distribution of the Northwest Alaskan Eskimos, as of the first half of the 19th century, is indicated more precisely in Figure 1. During that period they did not occupy all of "Northwest Alaska" (as defined by Armstrong 1971), but they did inhabit most of it. For reasons which are not clear, the north-easternmost portion of the area was not inhabited by anyone on a year-round basis at the time, while the eastern and northeastern shores of Norton Sound, on the southwest, were occupied by Yupik speakers. Thus, the "traditional" homeland of the *Inupiat* extended from the northern coast of Norton Sound to the mouth of the Colville River, and encompassed the entire inland area drained by rivers reaching the sea between those two points.

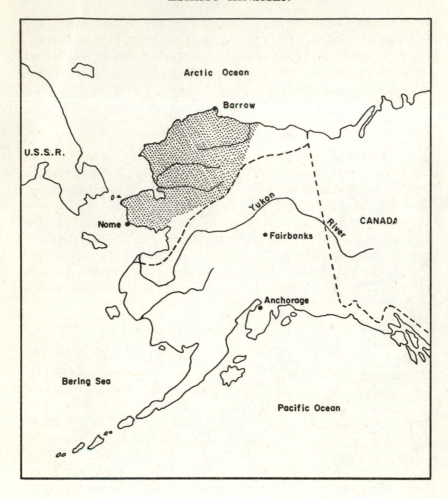

FIGURE 1   Map of Alaska, showing area inhabited by the traditional Northwest Alaskan Eskimos (shaded), and the area designated "Northwest Alaska" by Armstrong (1971) (broken line).

Following the first *protracted* Euroamerican contacts, in the
period 1848–1852, a number of population movements took place.
The previously uninhabited region in the northeast was gradually occupied by Inupik-speaking migrants from the west and
south, while another movement of Inupik speakers took place in
the south, along the eastern shore of Norton Sound.   Some of

the previously occupied inland areas were abandoned during the same period. During the 120-year period covered by this study, therefore, nearly all portions of the geographic area of Northwest Alaska were occupied by *Inupiat* at one time or another, but this occupancy was not continuous in all districts.

The Nonhuman Environment

The vast territory occupied by the Northwest Alaskan Eskimos is divided into a number of physiographically distinct regions (Smith and Mertie 1930; Williams 1958). For present purposes, these will be considered to include the following: the Brooks Range, the northern foothills, the northern coastal plain, the "Southwest Slope," and the Seward Peninsula. The locations of these regions are indicated in Figure 2. (The "Southwest Slope" includes the valleys of the Noatak, Kobuk, and Selawik Rivers; it is these, not the "slope" as a whole, that are indicated on the map).

The best known physiographic region of Northwest Alaska is the complex series of mountain groups that crosses northern Alaska on a roughly east-west axis (Gryc 1958b; Solecki 1951). Known collectively as the "Brooks Range," these groups are juxtaposed to one another in a single chain of mountains in the east and center, but divided into two sections toward the west. One "fork," comprised of the DeLong Mountains, lies to the north of the Noatak River, while the other, consisting of the Schwatka and Baird Mountains, lies to the south. The entire Brooks Range, which is about six hundred miles long, is composed of rugged, glaciated mountains. They rise to about 9000 feet in the east, and between the headwaters of the Noatak and the Kobuk, but most peaks are in the 4500 to 7000 foot range; they are much lower and less rugged toward the west.

Immediately to the north of the Brooks Range lies the area of long ridges and low hills that will be referred to here as "the northern foothills" (Gryc 1958a; Solecki 1951:476). At their junction with the mountains, the foothills range up to 3500 feet in height, but gradually taper off to the north as they approach the Arctic coastal plain. The coastal plain is a huge, flat area having little local relief. Because of the poor surface drainage

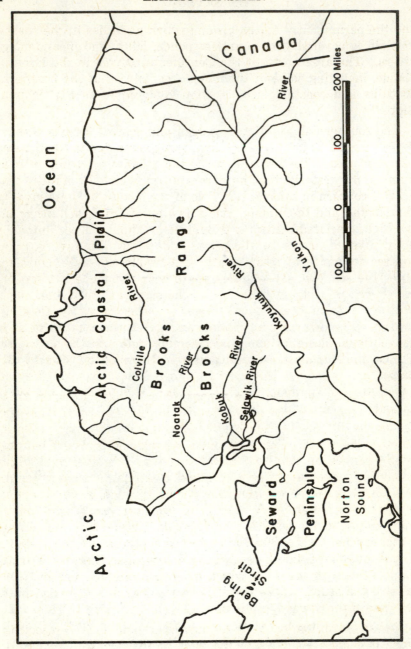

FIGURE 2 Map of Northwest Alaska showing major physiographic regions.

and the permanently frozen ground which underlies it, the coastal plain is covered with countless ponds, lakes, and meandering rivers. The area north of the Continental Divide in the Brooks Range, including some of the mountains, and all of the northern foothills and coastal plain, is often referred to as the "North Slope."

The southern slopes of the eastern and central Brooks Range drain into the Yukon River system, and lie outside the Northwest Alaskan area. Toward the west, the mountains drain into a number of westerly flowing rivers all of which lie within the area of concern in this study. Two of the largest of these rivers, the Noatak and the Kobuk, rise a few miles from each other in the high, glaciated Schwatka Mountains. Their courses immediately diverge, curve to the west, and follow roughly parallel courses for much of their length, and finally converge again to enter the sea just a few miles apart near the modern town of Kotzebue. A range of hills lies to the south of the Kobuk, separating it from the Selawik River, another westerly flowing stream. For descriptive convenience, and in the absence of any conventional designation, I occasionally refer to the area including the Noatak, Kobuk, and Selawik Rivers as the "Southwest Slope."

The Southwest Slope is a topographically varied region that extends from the heart of the Brooks Range (Noatak River), in the north, to the interior basin of lowlands and plains (Black 1958) in the south. The Kobuk and Noatak drainages are bounded by ranges of hills and mountains that are steep and high enough to make the notion of "valley" clearly applicable to them. The Selawik River, in contrast, flows through a wide, open, water-covered plain very similar to the northern coastal plain many miles to the north. The Selawik River enters the sea at Hotham Inlet, just a few miles to the southeast of the Kobuk. The Kobuk and Selawik drainages are separated from the Yukon River system by low hills which gradually increase in elevation toward the south, where they divert the Yukon southward past the base of the Seward Peninsula.

The Seward Peninsula is an irregular land mass projecting some two hundred miles to the west of the Alaskan mainland. Its 20,000 square miles are almost as diverse topographically as the entire mainland region described so far (Collier 1902; Hopkins and Hopkins 1958). Much of it consists of extensive uplands and groups of rugged mountains, but lowland basins occupy much of the interior, there is a wide lava plateau in the northern central portion, and there is an extensive coastal plain on the northwest. The highest point of the peninsula (Mount Osborne, at 4720 feet) is in the southwest, but few other peaks rise above 3000 feet, and the general relief is less than 2000 feet (Hopkins and Hopkins 1958).

Divided into physiographically distinct regions by ranges of mountains and hills, Northwest Alaska is "topographically integrated" by an easily traveled coastline, several navigable rivers, and by a number of mountain passes. These features made extensive inter-regional travel relatively easy even with traditional Eskimo technology, and all the more so with the aircraft, boats, and snowmobiles of modern times. The physiography of Northwest Alaska contributed to the existence of numerous relatively discrete regional ecosystems which constituted natural foci for human activities; at the same time it permitted relatively easy contact between regions.

Climate

Northwest Alaska lies almost entirely within an Arctic climatic zone characterized by long cold winters, short cool summers, and little precipitation; only the southern half of the Seward Peninsula has a sub-Arctic climate (Searby 1968). All of these characteristics are indicated in Table 1, which presents selected cli-

TABLE 1   Selected Climatological Data for Coastal Points

Location	Av. No. Days with Frost	Record Temps. (F°) Max.	Min.	Normal Total Precipitation
Barter Island	311	75°	−59°	6.28 in.
Barrow	324	78°	−56°	4.26 in.
Kotzebue	252	85°	−52°	8.18 in.
Nome	240	81°	−42°	17.88 in.
Unalakleet	235	86°	−50°	no data

Data from Searby (1968) and Environmental Science Services Administration (1970).

matological data for a number of coastal points, beginning with Barter Island in the extreme northeastern corner of Northwest Alaska, and ending with Unalakleet, on the extreme southwest. Comparable data for inland points are lacking. In general, conditions inland are seasonally more variable (warmer in summer, colder in winter) than they are on the coast, while wind speed tends to be lower there except at higher elevations.

The extreme climate of Northwest Alaska limits human activities directly by imposing stringent requirements on clothing and shelter, and also indirectly through its effect on water. Streams and rivers begin to freeze in the mountains in September. The "freezeup" process gradually works its way down the coast, so that by late October, the brackish lagoons behind the barrier beaches are normally frozen even in the southern portions of the area. The ocean, which freezes at a lower temperature than the rivers, is not ice covered until late November to late December, but it stays that way until May or June. The "break-up" process also begins far inland when the snow begins to melt in early May. The first trickles of meltwater gradually swell to a flood, and the ice is gone from most rivers by late May or early June. The sea ice stays solid longer, and it remains in the area for some time after it has broken up. In some years the pack ice off the northern coast may never go very far out of sight of land. The rivers, lakes, and sea are thus ice covered for about half of every year in Northwest Alaska. It is this change between "open water" and ice cover, and not the weather *per se*, that makes for the primary difference between summer and winter in the far north.

Vegetation

Most of Northwest Alaska would appear barren to the casual observer, and so it is when compared with areas farther south. In a more technical vein, only the upper slopes of hills and mountains are "barren" in the sense that they are utterly lacking in vegetation. Most of the so-called "barren" country is actually covered with the more or less continuous carpet of lichens, mosses, short grasses and sedges, and dwarf shrubs commonly referred to as "tundra" vegetation (Britton 1967; Hultén 1968; Wiggins and Thomas 1962). In Northwest Alaska, this tundra vegetation is comparatively rich in plant foods. The most important plant foods were berries, of which several varieties are found, although "Eskimo spinach" (*Rumex arcticus*) used to be eaten in large quantities in many areas, as was "Eskimo potato" (*Hedysarum alpinium*).

A second vegetation zone is the northern boreal forest (primarily spruce and birch), which intrudes into many of the valleys in southern portions of the area, particularly on the eastern end of the Seward Peninsula. Further north, spruce and birch are found in the Selawik, Kobuk, and lower Noatak valleys. In each of these three valleys the trees grow in the higher, better drained areas right along the rivers, and far back on the hillsides; most of the valley floors in-between are covered with tundra.

A third major vegetation area is the "shrub zone," which consists of areas in which willows grow, perhaps along with cottonwoods and alders, but never with spruce. Shrub zones are to be found along rivers and creeks far beyond the limits of spruce, including many of those crossing the northern coastal plain. Although they tend to be smaller toward the north, these "shrubs" often attain a considerable height (20 feet or more) and thickness (4 inches) in the south. The size, abundance, and widespread distribution of these zones of large shrubs along creeks and rivers in Northwest Alaska are in sharp contrast to the situation occurring in the eastern Arctic, and were an important factor in the comparatively high standard of living of inland dwellers in Northwest Alaska. Important primarily for the shelter and fuel they provided, willow thickets were also the major areas in which ptarmigan and rabbits could be found.

Fauna

For a high-latitude region, Northwest Alaska was particularly rich in animal life around the middle of the 19th century (v. Bee and Hall 1956; Burch 1972; Fay 1957; Gabrielson and Lincoln 1959; Hansen 1967; Manville and Young 1965; McPhail and Lindsey 1970). The major elements in this diverse and abundant fauna were bowhead whales, walrus, several species of seals, beluga, caribou, and fish (several species of whitefish, several species of salmon, char, burbot, and grayling). Secondary, but locally or seasonally important animals included several varieties of land (e. g., ptarmigan) and water (e. g., eider ducks) fowl, polar and grizzly bears, Dall sheep, other

varieties of fish (e. g., pike, tomcod), small game (e. g., mar-
mots, rabbits, ground squirrels), and several species of fur-
bearing mammals (e. g., wolves, wolverines, white and colored
foxes, muskrats).

Three general characteristics of this fauna are particularly relevant to an understanding of human life in Northwest
Alaska around the middle of the 19th century. The first is that
all major food species seem to have been at peak population
levels, so that the Northwest Alaskan Eskimos had available to
them a remarkably rich resource base. The second general
characteristic of the Northwest Alaskan fauna in the mid-19th
century is that all of the major resource animals were seasonally nomadic, a fact that put definite constraints on human movements in the area. On the one hand, the people had to be at
the right places at the right times, or starve. On the other
hand if the people *were* in the right places at the right times,
they could live comparatively well. The third and final characteristic of the mid-19th century fauna is that, despite general
abundance throughout Northwest Alaska there were regional
differences in species represented, numbers of animals, and
timing of movements. These regional differences in fauna formed the basis for regional differences in human activity.

The Traditional Northwest Alaskan Eskimos

The "traditional period" is defined as the time when the
Northwest Alaskan Eskimos were operating in terms of an
essentially indigenous system of action. It began at some un-
specifiable time in the past, but definitely included the first
half of the 19th century. Several European exploring expeditions, such as those of Beechey (1831), Franklin (1828), Kotzebue (1821), and Simpson (1843) did visit the area during this
period, but there is no evidence that their brief contacts with
the natives led to major changes in their general way of life.
Trade with the Chukchis, Siberian Eskimos, as well as the
explorers, also brought European goods to the area (Ray n. d.).
For the most part, this was a luxury trade, one whose elimination
would have had relatively minor consequences for the people
in Northwest Alaska (Foote 1965:120; Smith 1968b).

In 1848 all of this began to change. The great English search for the lost Sir John Franklin provided the initial impetus for extensive exploration, and in 1849–50, the H.M.S. "Plover," under Captain Thomas Moore, became the first of several ships to winter in Northwest Alaska (Foote 1965). In addition to the explorers, a few trading vessels also began to operate north of Norton Sound about this time, and American whalers began to visit the area in large numbers (Foote 1964a; 1965:157). The contacts between these outsiders and the Eskimos led to profound changes in the native way of life, and thus marked the end of the aboriginal period in Northwest Alaska. When I speak of "traditional" Eskimo life in Northwest Alaska, therefore, I am referring to the customs which I have reason to believe were characteristic of the period prior to this time of rapid change; for convenience, the date of 1850 will be used as the boundary between the traditional and transitional periods.

The Traditional Societies

The traditional Eskimo population of Northwest Alaska was organized in terms of a set of "societies" (as defined by Aberle *et al.* 1950:101–102; Levy 1952:111ff.; 1966:20). Each of these societies was associated with a particular territory conceived of as its "home" district (v. Burch and Correll 1972; Correll 1972:94). The members of each society were normally within their home district in the fall of the year at about the time of freshwater freezeup. The locations of these territories, and their outer boundaries, are indicated in Figure 3; the labels I use for them and their estimated populations are listed in Table 2 (which is keyed to Figure 3).

The distribution of the members of a society at other times of year varied considerably. The members of some societies stayed within their home territory year-round, moving back and forth between seasonal camps; the members of others moved completely out of their home territory for periods lasting two to three months or more. In any case, the members of each society followed a distinctive annual cycle, one that served to distinguish it clearly from all others in the area.

A third significant feature of the traditional societies was the tendency for each one to be an endogamous unit (cf. Damas 1968a:113; 1969a:126–127). Each society constituted a "deme,"

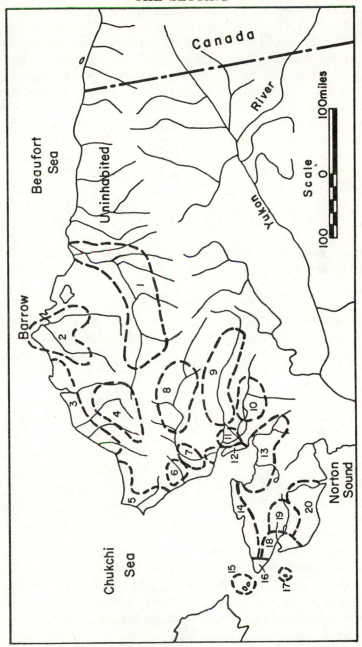

FIGURE 3   Map of Northwest Alaska showing general locations of
traditional societies (mid-19th century).

TABLE 2   Traditional Eskimo Societies in Northwest Alaska

Map Number	Designation	Est. 1850 Population [a]
1	Colville River	575
2	Barrow	700
3	Northwest Coast	475
4	Utukok River	200
5	Point Hope	975
6	Kivalina	350
7	Lower Noatak	300
8	Upper Noatak	450
9	Kobuk River	975
10	Selawik	950
11	Kobuk Delta	275
12	Kotzebue	425
13	South Kotzebue Sound	325
14	Tapqaq	375
15	Diomede Islands	300
16	Wales	750
17	King Island	275
18	Port Clarence	275
19	Kuzitrin River	200
20	Nome [b]	900
	TOTAL	10,050

[a] Rounded off to the nearest 25.

[b] This is the most questionable one in the list. This population may have been divided among two systems of this kind.

in the sense of being a cluster of individuals "partially isolated both spatially and genetically from other similar populations" (Savage 1969:90).   There was no *requirement* of endogamy, and some intermarriage between demes did occur; but for the most part marriages were effected within rather than between societies, regardless of the amount of peaceful contacts between any two of them (v. Correll 1972:94–95).   According to my informants, the farther one goes back in time, the more isolated from each other these societies were in marital terms.

A final characteristic that served to distinguish the members of one society from those of another was that of dialect (Burch and Correll 1972:22; Correll 1972:93, 120, 152–154, 195). Although the Northwest Alaskan Eskimos all spoke the Inupik Eskimo language, regional variation in dialect was pronounced. The several dialects were mutually intelligible— at least to adults accustomed to hearing them—but they were distinctive enough to permit immediate determination of a person's origins when encountered for the first time.

One characteristic a traditional society did *not* have was a distinct name. The Eskimos identified both individuals and groups by referring to their geographic location in space and time, not to their affiliation with a particular society, local group, or other type of organization. *If* the home district of a particular society happened to have a distinctive geographic label, then all the members of that society might be referred to by a single designation, at least for some purposes. The resulting label was not a societal name, even though it might appear to be one. When a home district did not have a single geographic designation, even this spurious correlation would not occur.[1] It is for this reason that the societies are referred to in this study by English rather than by Eskimo terms.

Regional Differences

The traditional Northwest Alaskan Eskimos lived primarily by hunting and fishing, and partly by collecting local plant products. Like all peoples living so close to nature, they reflected in their ways of living the demands placed upon them by the conditions of the specific district in which they lived.

[1] For example, all the members of Selawik Society lived in the geographic region known as "*siilvik*," hence were known as *Siilvingmiut* (people of Selawik). The home district of the members of Barrow Society, by contrast, did not have a single designation; they were referred to variously as *Utqiarviŋmiut*, *Nuwugmiut*, *Kuulugzuaqmiut*, *Ikpikpaŋmiut*, or any one of a number of other names according to where they located their winter houses. In still another variation, all the people who lived along the Kobuk River were referred to as *Kuuvagmiut*, at least for some purposes. For other purposes, they were often divided into *Kuuymiut* (of the delta), *Akunirmiut* (of the middle portion of the river), and *Kuuvaum Kayiarmiut* (of the upper river). In terms of societal membership, however, people living in the second and third areas belonged to one society, while the people living in the delta belonged to a second.

In the approximately 150,000 square mile area covered by this
study, several different environmental situations had to be coped
with; the resulting human adaptations were manifested in regional differences in subsistence base, yearly cycle, and settlement pattern.

A general idea of the nature of the major regional differences can be conveyed through a description of some individual
cases. Four societies, chosen for convenience of presentation,
will serve as examples, these being the Kotzebue, Lower Noatak,
Upper Noatak, and Kobuk River societies. The home districts
of all of these societies were on the Southwest Slope; their location, and the normal *autumn* distribution of the members of
each one are indicated in Figure 4. Each dot on the map represents a local group, i. e., a concentration of people related
by some combination of consanguineal and affinal ties.[2] The
X-mark near the lower left-hand corner of the map indicates
the location of Sisualik, a place that will be referred to frequently in the account that follows.

The members of *Kotzebue society*, totalling some 425 people,
were normally distributed among a number of small communities located along the shore of the Baldwin Peninsula, the northern shore of Kotzebue Sound, and the extreme lower portion
of the Noatak River, about the time of freezeup. They lived
in large, semi-subterranean sod houses, that, for the most part,
were multi-family dwellings. Throughout the fall, the primary
subsistence activity was fishing through the ice for sheefish,
tomcod, and smelt, but the men also did some caribou hunting in
the western portions of the Baird Mountains. As the days grew
shorter and the weather got colder, they would gradually cease
their fishing activities and turn their attention to recreational
and ceremonial activities, and to simply relaxing. Perhaps
some of them would be invited to another district for a messenger feast (Spencer 1959:210ff.), perhaps they would issue
their own invitations, or they might simply stay home and
enjoy themselves, dancing or playing a game similar to soccer.
Unless they had had unusually poor hunting and fishing during
the previous summer and fall, the short days of early winter
were a holiday season for the Kotzebue people.

[2] The demographic and social units represented by one of these dots are
analyzed in Chapter Seven.

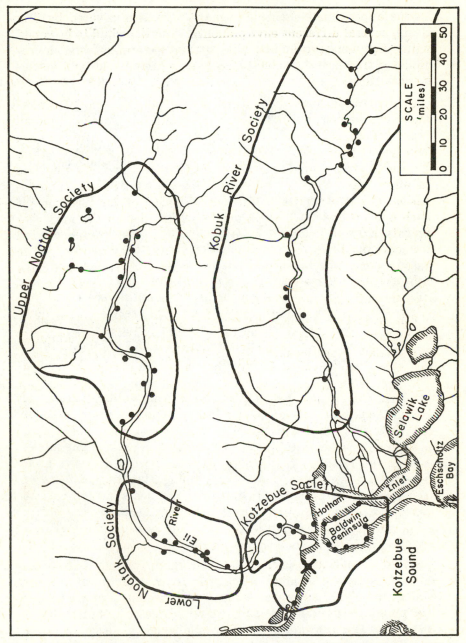

FIGURE 4 Map of "Southwest Slope" showing home districts and major fall settlement locations of four traditional societies.

As the days grew longer again with the approach of spring, some men might venture forth in search of caribou, while others might go to the outer coast to look for seals. In March the emphasis turned to fish again, and much of the population moved to Hotham Inlet in pursuit of the large schools of sheefish that congregate there every spring. Then they would all come in to the main village from the outlying settlements for several days of feasting, dancing, and recreation. This gathering of the general society membership, known as *qatizut*, symbolized and reaffirmed the unity of the society, and its independence from similar units in the general area.

With the warmer days of April, the entire membership of the society would travel to the outer coast, just to the west of their territorial boundary. To make the trip each extended family would carry a thirty-foot, skin-covered boat on one sled, and other paraphernalia on a second. Usually the people moved right onto the ocean at this time, living in snow houses on the still solid sea ice. The men busied themselves hunting seals basking on the ice, while the women spent their time processing the harvest. As the ice grew rotten under the continuous glare of the sun in May, everyone moved into tents on the adjacent shore, but continued the work that they had been doing previously while living on the ice.

In late June, when the ice broke up and moved away from the beach, the Kotzebue people would pack their sun-dried meat and blubber in sealskin pokes, cover their boat frames with new skins, and begin to move south along the coast. The movement began in the north, and the flotilla increased in size as it progressed toward the south, being joined by the members of each camp as it passed. By the time the boats turned east to travel along the northern shore of Kotzebue Sound, the entire membership in the society was traveling as a unit, the flotilla numbering thirty boats or more.

When they arrived at their summer camp ground at Sisualik, they all went ashore and set up their tents in a line parallel to the beach. A bit farther on, the tents of the Upper Noatak and Kobuk Delta people would be in place already; shortly afterwards the Lower Noatak people would arrive and set up their camp also. These societies, represented by virtually their entire memberships, comprised the bulk of the summer population at Sisualik, but small contingents from the Selawik and Kobuk Rivers regularly took part as well. The members of each society set up a camp clearly separated from the others.

Late June and most of July were devoted to the pursuit of belugas. These small whales, reaching a maximum size of about fourteen feet and fourteen hundred pounds, came into Kotzebue Sound in large numbers every summer. They traveled clockwise around the sound, traveling eastward along the northern shore past Sisualik, then turning south to their calving ground in Eschscholtz Bay, in the southeastern corner of the sound. They would stay there for some time, then move out again, generally traveling westward along the southern shore. The men at Sisualik hunted them from kayaks and from their large umiaks, and they must have killed several dozen, possibly hundreds, every summer.

As the beluga hunting season drew to a close, the women finished drying the meat and muktuk (beluga skin and attached blubber) and stored it in pokes. By the end of July, several hundred more people from still other societies had gathered at Sisualik for the great fair (*qatŋut*). This event, which involved the several groups who had joined in the beluga hunting earlier, also drew people from as far away as Point Hope, on the north, and Siberia, on the west and south. It was a major occasion devoted to inter-societal trade, athletic competition, feasting, and alliance making (Burch and Correll 1972:30).

Toward the middle of August people began to leave Sisualik to return to their respective home territories. By the end of the third week of the month almost everyone was gone. The Kotzebue people frequently departed last, since they did not have far to go, but families or groups of men who wanted to travel up the Noatak for a few weeks of caribou hunting before freezeup had to follow a tighter schedule. By the end of August all of the Kotzebue people except the caribou hunters were back at their winter houses. At this time they engaged in salmon fishing, and in hunting the young bearded seals that used to swarm into Hotham Inlet early every fall. These activities and general preparations for winter kept everyone busy until freezeup, at which point the yearly cycle was completed.

The territory of the *Lower Noatak* people comprised the large open basin of the lower Noatak River. Their fall/winter settlements were concentrated for the most part in the forested area between the lower Eli River and the Noatak itself, where they returned each fall to harvest the salmon that spawned there in large numbers. They lived in substantial log cabins or sod houses. By freezeup the salmon fishery had closed, but the Arctic char season was just beginning. The women and children spent their time catching char with hooks, nets, and weirs set under the ice, and setting snares for ptarmigan and rabbits. The men hunted farther afield for caribou. When the short days arrived, the Lower Noatak people, like the Kotzebue people, turned their attention to recreation and feasting, and did not concentrate on subsistence activities again until their supplies began to get low during the winter.

In late March or early April, the Lower Noatak people left their winter homes and moved to the coast to hunt seals, transporting their boats over the hills on sleds. Like the Kotzebue people immediately to the south, they moved right out onto the ice at first, living in snow houses, and moving into tents only later when they returned to the shore. Their spring camps were strung out along the coast between those of the Kotzebue people, to the south, and the Kivalina people to the north. From this time on, the activities of the Lower Noatak people paralleled those just described for Kotzebue. After breakup, they moved to Sisualik for the beluga hunting and then the fair, finally returning to their home territory for the fall fishing and hunting.

The home area of the *Upper Noatak* people was the middle and upper portions of the Noatak Valley, between the treeline and the mouth of the Aniuk River. In the fall they would be spread all over this huge area in small communities of perhaps twenty to forty people. They lived in houses made of willow frames covered with a double layer of moss, or, occasionally, with sod. In the fall, their attention was directed primarily toward caribou hunting, the success or failure of which determined their standard of living until the following spring. If they succeeded in making a large kill in October and November, a good winter was assured; they would spend most of it engaging in feasting and playing soccer, extending the early winter holiday season as long as they could. If the fall hunt was a failure, on the other hand, hard times would follow and they might even have to leave their country and go to some other region in search of game or help from allies. However, in the mid-1800's the caribou population was high, and hard winters were apparently few and far between on the Upper Noatak.

As breakup time approached in May, most of the Upper Noatak people would converge on the river, returning to the spot where they had stored their boats the previous fall. A few people remained behind to hunt caribou all summer in the mountians to the north, but the majority of the population followed the ice downriver to Kotzebue Sound. After stopping in the Noatak Delta for a week or two, while new clothing was made, the Upper Noatak people could move to Sisualik and participate in the beluga hunting and in the fair, according to the pattern described earlier.

The trip downriver, made on the spring flood, sometimes took only two or three days. The return trip was another matter, and it took two or three weeks under the very best of conditions. Accordingly, when the fair was over, the Upper Noatak people were among the first to leave. With their tons of sea mammal products and personal belongings, they had a lot of work to do. If freezeup came early they would be caught short of their destination, and part of their journey would have to be made on foot. When this happened they usually missed the major fall migration of caribou, and they were in for a bad winter. Barring such a disaster, they would return to their country, rapidly spread out again, and repeat the cycle once more.

The *Kobuk River* people spent the fall and winter in comparatively large settlements distributed along the Kobuk, most of them located at or near the mouths of major tributaries. They preferred moss and sod-covered houses, of which as many as ten or fifteen might be situated in a single settlement. The Kobuk people had a diverse and rich resource base in the mid-19th century. In the fall, they hunted caribou, bears, and several species of small game, and fished through the still thin river ice with weirs and hooks. Lean winters were uncommon, and they were usually able to enjoy themselves during the short days, as could their counterparts on Kotzebue Sound and in the Noatak Valley.

In the spring, usually just before breakup, the Kobuk River people would leave their winter quarters, and spread out among spring camps comprised of perhaps three or four closely related families. Here they hunted muskrats and fished while the ice in the rivers and streams broke up. A few people shifted camps again for the summer fishing, but most remained right where they were throughout most of the open water season. A few families on the upper river specialized in inter-societal trade, and they, like the people from the Upper Noatak, would follow the spring flood to Sisualik to hunt for sea mammals and to trade, but the bulk of the membership remained inland. In late July, the men would leave the fishing to the women, and walk north into the Baird and Schwatka Mountains to hunt caribou while the skins were prime for clothing. They would stay in the mountains for much of August, returning to the fishing camps in early September. By that time the women had normally caught and dried hundreds of pounds of whitefish and salmon, and the people were more than ready for the coming winter. Just before, or sometimes just after, freezeup, the people would move again to their fall/winter villages, and the cycle would resume once again.

Inter-Societal Relations

The factors that made traditional Northwest Alaskan Eskimo societies separate social systems did not preclude extensive inter-societal contacts of several kinds (Burch and Correll 1972; Correll 1972:226 *et passim.*). One of these was warfare, an activity that seems to have been very common during the first half of the 19th century (Burch n. d.). But even warfare did not prevent inter-societal relations of a more positive nature; alliances of various kinds typically existed between many individuals in neighboring societies, and often in widely separated societies as well.

The extensive network of inter-societal alliances made it possible for large numbers of individuals to come together in one place for peaceful purposes, particularly at the fairs. The largest fair in Northwest Alaska took place at Sisualik, as indicated in the previous section. Here, in early August, over a thousand people met every summer for two to three weeks of inter-societal trading, feasting, dancing and athletic competition. In addition to virtually the entire membership of four societies (Kotzebue, Lower Noatak, Upper Noatak, and Kobuk Delta), the Sisualik fair drew representatives from Kivalina, Point Hope, the Kobuk River, Selawik, South Kotzebue Sound, Tapqaq, and Wales, and often other societies as well. A similar, but somewhat smaller, fair took place at the mouth of the Colville River, on the north coast, involving people living on the coastal and interior districts of the North Slope. Sometimes people would go to the Kotzebue fair one year and the Colville fair the next (Murdoch 1892:45). Another annual gathering of this sort was apparently held at Point Spencer, on the western end of the Seward Peninsula (Ray 1964:75).

The hundreds of people who participated in the regular summer gatherings spoke different dialects of a single language, and understood the same basic customs. The annual fairs provided an opportunity for people from districts hundreds of miles apart to meet one another, exchange information and ideas (as well as goods), and to establish and reaffirm the various social bonds (Burch and Correll 1972) that connected members of different societies to one another. Personal conduct at the fairs was in striking contrast to that prevailing most of the rest of the year, when inter-societal hostility seems to have been the dominant pattern (*Ibid.*).

Kinship in the Traditional Societies

The twenty traditional societies were actually separate social manifestations of a single culture which existed throughout mid-19th century Northwest Alaska.[3] The regional differences in subsistence base, house type, and yearly cycle described above represented a very general cultural pattern of effective utilization of all available resources; the resources available simply differed to some extent from one region to another. The theme of regional diversity within a more general cultural unity was developed at length by Robert Spencer (1959:6, 126, 131, 454, *et passim.*), and could be elaborated on still further. The emphasis in the present study, however, is specifically on the

[3] See Aberle *et al.* (1950) and Levy (1952) for discussion of how the terms "culture" and "society" are employed in the present study.

general pattern; more specifically still, the emphasis is on the structure of kinship systems as they existed throughout Northwest Alaska. There were, of course, some differences in kinship structure from one society to another, but these differences were so minute as to be scarcely worthy of notice. The basic premise of the present study, therefore, is that the general patterns described below were manifested in each of the twenty traditional societies in Northwest Alaska; as an hypothesis, this proposition can be refuted by contrary evidence from any of the societies concerned.

Each of the twenty traditional Northwest Alaskan Eskimo societies was overwhelmingly kinship oriented, apparently much more so than most Canadian Eskimo societies (Damas 1968a:-116; 1969b:49–50). By this I mean that, both ideally and actually, kinship ties were emphasized at the expense of all others. In traditional Northwest Alaska, kinship formed the axis on which the whole social world turned. As is pointed out in Chapter Six, most traditional "settlements" were in fact kinship units, and no one was ever voluntarily in a situation where no relatives were present.

The emphasis on kinship in Northwest Alaska becomes apparent when one examines the membership in a supposedly *non*-kin organization, such as a hunting crew. Three typical examples of such units are illustrated in Figure 5. The most obvious feature of these "non-kin" organizations is that their memberships can be conveniently represented by genealogical diagrams, (the members being indicated by the black symbols), diagrams that indicate a variety of consanguineal and affinal ties. Most of these relationships are obvious except for that of co-husbands (related through "spouse exchange"), which is represented by the double arrow in Crew "A." The particular crews represented in Figure 5 operated long after the end of the traditional period, but informants said that they were typical of traditional crews in all respects except for the one co-husband relationship. In traditional times exchange marriages rarely occurred between permanent residents of the same settlement, hence co-husbands were rarely members of the same crew.

Robert Spencer (1959:163ff.; 1972:112) argues that membership in a hunting crew was determined on a universalistic, and not on a kinship basis. In other words, a captain tried to

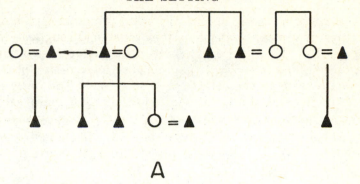

A

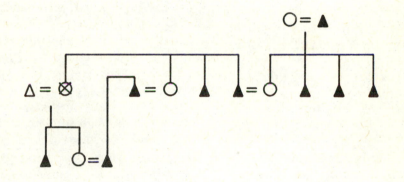

B

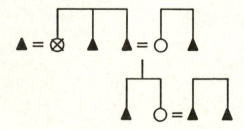

C

FIGURE 5 Diagram showing the composition of three hunting crews.

recruit the best hunters he could get, and family ties were irrelevant. Spencer apparently failed to collect specific examples of hunting crews, accepting informants' statements about
them at face value. With that approach, it is easy to be mis-
led, because the Eskimos do not *think* of hunting crews as
kinship units, and do not describe them as such. But when one
analyzes actual cases, kinship organizations always seem to
emerge, and that is the critical issue. Membership even in
ideally non-kin organizations was actually determined on a
kinship basis most of the time.

The place of kinship in aboriginal Northwest Alaska can be
indicated even more clearly through a consideration of what
other possibilities were available. In other words, what would
happen if one broke his ties of marriage and descent and struck
out on one's own? To state the answer briefly, there were *no*
alternatives. The life of a Northwest Alaskan Eskimo, isolated
—for whatever reason—from his kin was always nasty and
brutish, and often it was short. The miserable fate that befell
a person without kin apparently stems from a complete lack
of provision for such a situation in the general structures of
the traditional societies.

Actually, if not ideally, kinship was relevant in *all* social
contexts in traditional Northwest Alaska. The presence and
support of kinsmen indicated that an individual had people
close at hand upon whom he could call for support. The existence of such people also served notice to the rest of society that
there were people nearby whose responsibility it was to restrain
him from engaging in disruptive behavior. The man *with* kin
was one who could be held effectively responsible for his actions
in an institutionalized way. The man *without* kin was not
such a person; he was a social freak toward whom the other
members of the society had no acceptable way of behaving.

The traditional Northwest Alaskan Eskimos were apparently
more severe in their treatment of isolated strangers than were
other Eskimo peoples (Correll 1972:160, 168; Heinrich 1955a:-
96; 1963b:10; Pospisil 1964:400; Ray 1967:380; Spencer
1959:72–73). The classic case is that of the seal hunter who
accidentally went adrift on the sea ice as a result of wind and
current action. If conditions were unfavorable, he might drift
for days, weeks, or even months before getting back to shore

again, if he did so at all, and his landfall might be tens or hundreds of miles from his home. If he landed near a village (as often happened, since drifting ice frequently runs aground near the points where the larger villages were located), and if he was observed by one of its inhabitants, he was in trouble. Quickly a crowd would gather. Unless he could identify himself—which to an Eskimo meant proving he was related to people known by his inquisitors—he was usually beaten to death in short order. This pattern was universally understood in Northwest Alaska, and when some poor wretch was thus cast ashore, he immediately went into hiding. Instead of seeking the human company he needed to survive, he would try to avoid it until he could ascertain his whereabouts and make an estimate of whether or not he had relatives nearby. Only if satisfied on the latter account would he voluntarily make himself known in a strange region. Otherwise, he would try to return home without getting caught, an extremely difficult task if he had very far to go and/or if he was in a seriously weakened condition. Informants said that they had even heard of men going back out onto the ice when they discovered they were in hostile territory; the chances of survival were greater there than in a region where they had no kinsmen.

The treatment of the drifted seal hunter was probably an extreme case even in traditional times, but it was by no means an isolated one. There are many stories of small groups of men hunting deep in the hinterlands suddenly (and accidentally) encountering each other and having some very tense moments. First, they would try to identify themselves to one another's satisfaction. Failing that, the result varied depending on the relative numbers and condition of the people involved. If the groups appeared to be of equal strength, the tendency was for both sides to withdraw, thenceforth to avoid each other. If one group was obviously stronger, violence of some sort often followed, in which case the fate of the members of the weaker group was often that of the drifted seal hunter mentioned above.[4]

[4] The fairs were striking exceptions to this pattern. A more detailed analysis of the fairs, including a consideration of how many stranger-fearing people could get together peacefully in one place, will be the subject of a separate publication.

Death by violence was not the only possible fate of a person without kin in traditional times. Under certain conditions, survival was possible. Generally, a less disasterous result occurred when children without close kin nearby were suddenly orphaned through some accident or sickness. They might be taken in by a neighboring family, although not actually adopted by them (Heinrich 1955a:48). Usually, the lot of such youngsters was hard. Within the family they were forced to do all the menial labor of the household; they were fed poorly, and clothed inadequately. Even some modern bilingual Eskimos, when translating the English word "slave," will give the Eskimo word for "orphan," which is *iliapaq*. Orphans were often tormented by other children, and even by adults, who could do so with impunity since no one was likely to interfere.

Occasionally an adult might find himself without kin if he belonged to an impoverished kin group whose remaining members were suddenly lost through accident or disease. Or, it sometimes happened that an adult would antagonize his own relatives to the point where they would no longer support him. An outcast was for practical purposes without kin, and was treated accordingly. If such a person were a woman, she might be taken as a wife by a poor man, or more often as a household servant to a wealthy family; but she might survive. If a man, a more tenuous future was in store. He might be able to get along in the village for awhile, usually as a slave living and working in the *qazgi* (social center). But, if he became involved in even a minor dispute, he might be killed.

The Early Transitional Period

During the period 1848–1854, with the Franklin search expeditions and the massive influx of whalers, the Northwest Alaskan Eskimos had their first protracted contacts with Euroamericans. Although one can assume that social change was not new to these people, the changes that began during this period were of a type and magnitude they had never before experienced.

It is useful to divide the transitional period into three parts, according to significant changes in the volume or nature of Euroamerican influence in Northwest Alaska (cf. Damas 1968b;

Helm and Damas 1963). For convenience, I refer to these periods as the "early," "intermediate," and "recent" (transitional) periods, although they are more broadly conceived of as sequential phases of a single era of social change.[5] The early (transitional) period began when the explorers and whalers arrived in Northwest Alaska in considerable numbers. It terminated with the establishment of the first missions and schools. Although there were minor differences from one region to another, the years 1850 and 1890 serve as convenient boundaries for the period.

General Changes

The early transitional period was characterized by a serious disruption of Eskimo life. Most of this disruption related to the demographic structure of the population and not to the social structure; however, the population changes were so great as to cause a complete rearrangement of Eskimo life. The changes were largely the direct result of white contact. The whalers and traders particularly imported liquor and disease which, in combination, had a devastating effect on population size.

The deleterious effects of alcohol and disease during the early transitional period were exacerbated by the drastic decline of the caribou population. The caribou, a primary food resource, and the major source of winter clothing thoughout aboriginal Northwest Alaska, went from a peak population estimated at over 300,000 animals in 1850, to a mere ten or fifteen thousand by the turn of the century (Burch 1972). In short, the caribou supply went from a level of abundance to virtual nonexistence, a change having obvious implications for people so dependent on them for food and clothing. Ironically, the decline in the numbers of caribou seems to have been *unrelated* to European contact (*Ibid.*). The same cannot be said for changes in the walrus and whale populations, both of which were decimated by the whalers (Fay 1957). The same period that saw the intro-

---

[5] This discussion is not intended either as a complete record of events or as a social history of the area, matters beyond the scope of this study. It is a composite picture based partly on personal observation, partly on informant data, and partly on the literature (especially Bancroft 1959; Foote 1964a, 1964b, 1965, 1966; Gubser 1965; Hughes 1965:27–40; Jenness 1962; Ray 1966; n. d.; Rogers 1968, 1969; Sherwood 1965; and VanStone 1962b:17ff.).

duction of alcohol and epidemic diseases thus witnessed the reduction of the subsistence base of the Northwest Alaskan Eskimos, by a factor of perhaps 40–50%.

One unsurprising result of the above developments was a
drastic decline in the number of Eskimos. Foote and Williamson (1966:1046) estimated that the population centered on
Kotzebue Sound declined by 50% between 1850 and 1885. This
figure may not be far off the mark for Northwest Alaska as a
whole.

A second demographic change was a considerable dislocation
of the Eskimo population. This trend began in the 1870's, but
it gained momentum in the 1880's, continuing into the intermediate period. During its early phases, the population movements took people from south to north along the coast. Later,
particularly during the intermediate period, people moved to
the coast from inland regions, and eastward along the north
coast to Canada. An individual who survived this period often
ended his life several hundred miles from the homeland of his
ancestors.[6] The territorial and demographic bases of the traditional societies were virtually destroyed as a result of these
movements.

From about 1880 on, it is meaningless to speak of "societies"
in Northwest Alaska. The basic process involved in the destruction of the traditional societal structure is a simple one
to understand. Large segments of the population of each one
simply packed up and left their homeland, permanently shifting
their residence to a district traditionally occupied by the members of another. These movements were carried out by individual household units, for the most part, although sometimes an
entire local group would move together. The general result
was the mixture of the populations of the different societies.
The district traditionally inhabited by the members of a given
society would become emptied, through death and emigration,
of a large portion of its former population. It would then be-

6 This analysis of population changes is an over-simplification of a very
complex series of events; a more detailed analysis is being prepared for
separate publication. Foote and Williamson (1966), Jenness (1962:7), Rainey
(1941:13; 1947:283), and Stefansson (1909:603; 1951:66) comment on the same
trends, but other writers on Northwest Alaska seem to be hardly aware of
them. Dorothy Jean Ray (1964:62, 63; and in Edmonds 1966:106) goes so
far as to deny flatly that they occurred.

come filled up with migrants from, say, a half dozen different districts, or else it would be abandoned entirely. Contact with total strangers became such a commonplace event that people *had* to learn how to deal with them on a peaceful basis simply in order to survive.

Effects on Kinship

Modifications in the kinship system began at the very outset of the transitional period. Perhaps it is more accurate to say that the traditional kinship system continued to exist in the minds of the people, but their ability to realize the ancient ideals in practice was seriously impaired. It is difficult to place the changes involved into a precise temporal sequence, but they can be assigned definitely to some point in the early period.

The drastic decline in population size, and the dislocation of the population described earlier, had important implications for kinship units. The demographic changes eliminated many lines of descent altogether, either through the deaths of individuals or through simple loss of contact through population dispersal. The coherent network of kinship ties that had characterized each of the traditional societies was greatly disrupted.

The possibility of activities carried out in terms of non-kin organizations was another significant innovation introduced during this period. In general, this meant involvement in organizations that were not only non-kin, but also non-Eskimo. Most often, this change involved men, who were taken on as members of whaling crews on white men's ships or at shore whaling stations. In general, employment of this kind was of a seasonal nature, or for only a limited period, but it was a type of alternative that had not been present at all in traditional times. By 1885, an Eskimo youth could tell his relatives to "Go to the devil," and then join a white man's whaling crew.

Women became involved in ships crews as cooks or sewers from time to time, but their major part in these early changes was as objects of sexual attraction to the white men, who did not bring their own women with them. Prostitution became widespread during this period. Despite stereotypes that hold sexual license to be typically Eskimo, prostitution was something new in Northwest Alaska. It was primarily a symptom of the inability of the Eskimos to cope effectively with the rapid-

g situation. Beyond this, Eskimo women sometimes
⎽hite men—whalers, traders, and trappers, primarily
—and this no doubt had some effect on the wife's own family.
Often such ties were temporary, and lasted only until the
husband involved decided to return to the "Outside," but the
effects were usually lasting as far as the woman and her children were concerned.

The Intermediate Transitional Period

The intermediate transitional period began in 1890, when
mission-schools were established at Wales, Point Hope, and
Barrow. It ended with the rapidly increased government involvement in Alaskan affairs during World War II. For convenience, the boundaries of this period are set at 1890 and 1940.

General Changes

The first mission-schools were established at the largest of
the old native settlements, sites that had been occupied on a
year round basis in traditional times. Between 1890 and about
1910, many additional schools were established at other points,
many of them sites that had not been occupied previously. As
the scale of operations grew, the original combined mission-
schools gradually split into government-run schools, on the one
hand, and church-operated missions on the other, but a close
association between church and school lasted for much of this
period in most districts. Many trading posts were also set
up in Northwest Alaska during this time, often near the missions and schools. These outposts of a foreign way of life quickly became focal points for the native population, and settlements
grew up around each one.

During the first half of the intermediate transitional period,
the two major demographic trends of the previous period—population reduction and dislocation—continued largely unchecked.
Alcohol and disease still took their toll of the native population,
culminating in the flu epidemic of 1918–19. That disaster all
but wiped out the native population of Wales, and many other
communities on the western and southern Seward Peninsula.

The northeast coast, a region uninhabited in traditional times,
was populated between roughly 1885 and 1920 by migrants

from virtually every traditional society in Northwest Alaska. On the other hand, the Upper Noatak, Utukok, and Colville Valleys, formerly occupied by the members of separate societies, became totally emptied of human inhabitants during this period, and the rest of the Brooks Range was depopulated as well.

By 1900, the drop in the price of whale bone, combined with the reduction in the number of whales, had removed most of the whalers from the Northwest Alaskan scene. Their place was quickly filled during the gold rush (Ray 1966:19ff.). The major rush was at Nome in 1899, but nearly a thousand men spent the winter of 1898–99 along the Kobuk River (Grinnell 1901:31; McElwaine 1901:83ff.), and a few dozen prospectors wintered along the Noatak River during the same year (Williamson 1961:77).

By 1905, or thereabouts, the permanently established schools and other new institutions in Northwest Alaska had created a strong impetus for the sedentarization of the Eskimo population. The people generally wanted to be near the missions and stores, and they wanted their children to go to school. At the same time, a shift from subsistence hunting to fur hunting around the turn of the century created a force in the opposite direction, since the effective pursuit of fur-bearing mammals (in the absence of rapid transportation) requires that the human population be spread thinly over a wide area. The decentralizing effects of the fur trade were increased through the establishment of domesticated reindeer herds throughout most of Northwest Alaska. These herds were established by the government in an effort to replace the now nearly extinct caribou. However, effective reindeer herding, like fur hunting, requires that the human population be spread out, not concentrated in sedentary communities.

The conflict between the centralization and decentralization of the native population continued for several decades. On the one hand, the people wanted to settle in the mission-school-store-focused communities. On the other hand, they had to spread out over a wide area in order to hunt for furs and/or look after the reindeer herds. By 1920 the typical villages had a core of permanent native inhabitants, plus another group who spent at least the winters "on the land." The herders and trappers would regularly come in to the village for supplies and for major events, but they had to leave their children with relatives there if they wanted them to go to school. The dilemma was finally resolved in the 1930's by the Great Depression. The bottom fell out of the fur market, and the reindeer, numbering tens of thousands by this time, disappeared even faster than the caribou had a half century earlier. By 1940, virtually all of the native population of Northwest Alaska was concentrated permanently in school-mission-store communities.

Changes in the Kinship System

The intermediate period saw the continuation of the trends begun previously, and some additional ones as well. If the early transitional period was notable primarily for the transformation of the *setting* within which kinship units had to operate, the intermediate period was important for changes in the kinship system proper. These changes were massive, and will be dealt with in virtually every chapter of this book. Only an outline of some of the more general trends will be discussed here.

The explorers, whalers, and miners contributed to social change in Northwest Alaska less by intent than by accident. They were concerned with knowledge or profit, and the Eskimos interested them only insofar as they were relevant to the achievement of those goals. The missionaries and teachers, on the other hand, came with the explicit goal of "saving" the natives, which meant, in practice, the elimination of most of the fundamental values that the Eskimos had. With respect to kinship specifically, their greatest efforts were directed at traditional marriage patterns. The primary targets were polygamy, "spouse exchange," and divorce. Within a few years, the missionaries had succeeded in eliminating polygamous unions altogether, and "exchange marriage" was driven underground. The missionaries also instituted the general American pattern of divorce, which, particularly around 1900, was much more stringent than the corresponding Eskimo custom. All of these changes, and others associated with them, are discussed at length in Chapter Three.

Sedentarization put an end to much of the travel that had been so notable a feature of the traditional yearly cycles. As a consequence, the ties between the now (geographically) distant kin became progressively weaker because there was little effective communication between them even on a seasonal basis. Men still visited neighboring villages from time to time, but the women became highly sedentary. Neither men nor women had much opportunity to see relatives who lived much more than a hundred miles away except on rare occasions.

The intermediate period also witnessed a significant reduction in the number of functions that had been fulfilled traditionally through the operation of kinship units. The first to go were some of the more obvious political functions. A decade or so after the purchase of Alaska, U. S. Revenue Marine (later Coast Guard) cutters began to sail the Northwest Alaskan waters every summer. Ostensibly, these ships were sent to eliminate the illegal sale of liquor and firearms to the Eskimos, but they quickly became involved in the maintenance of law and order generally. Feuding and warfare had been curtailed during the early phase of the transitional period, but they ceased altogether during the intermediate phase. This change began with the direct intervention of U. S. government agents, and through the interference of white men who stayed in the north throughout the winter for trapping, whaling, and/or mining operations. Although warfare had ceased by about 1880, bloodshed related to feuding did not disappear completely until sometime in the early decades of the twentieth century.

The demise of the feud as an operational means of social control signaled the end of the era during which kinship units constituted the ultimate source of power in Northwest Alaska. While the Federal Government of the United States became responsible for law and order on the most general level, newly instituted village councils took over on the local level. It is outside the scope of this study to deal with these changes in detail. It is relevant to note, however, that especially in their early years, the councils functioned largely to mediate or otherwise resolve disputes between the various kin-based factions in the villages.

The intermediate phase of the transitional period also saw a considerable decrease in the number of educational, religious, and recreational functions fulfilled by the operation of kinship units. These changes came about primarily as a consequence of school, church, and organized village activities, all of which were new to Northwest Alaska. Many of the missing functions were not replaced by new ones, resulting in a moral and intellectual vacuum.

Increased opportunity for involvement in non-kin organizations is the final development of the intermediate transitional period that is pertinent here. This trend, which began prior to 1890, expanded considerably subsequently. Schools, churches, stores, and other kinds of organizations offered the Eskimos opportunities for operating in terms of non-kin units to an extent they could not have even considered previously. Furthermore, such participation could now begin at an early age, last a long time, and involve members of both sexes. In addition to changes in the villages themselves, there were increasing opportunities for individuals to leave Northwest Alaska altogether. This process often took men to Fairbanks or to some other major center for summer employment. Hospitilization, too, removed ever increasing numbers of people of all ages and both sexes from the narrow sphere of kin to which they had been restricted previously. This process began as a trickle sometime around the middle of the intermediate period, and swelled to a flood after World War II.

The Recent Transitional Period

World War II marked the end of the intermediate transitional period and the beginning of the recent. The Japanese threat in the Aleutians stimulated a greatly increased awareness of and interest in the Territory of Alaska as a whole, and the northwestern area participated in the new educational, welfare and medical services that eventually resulted. For present purposes, the dates for the period are set at 1940 and 1970, the terminus simply being the final year of field research contributing to this study.

The General Situation

In 1969–70, the Northwest Alaskan Eskimos numbered nearly 11,000 individuals scattered among twenty-eight permanent villages and towns located at various points, most of which were within the territory of their traditional habitation (see Figure 6) (Northwest Economic Development and Planning Board 1969; U. S. Bureau of the Census 1970a). The distribution of

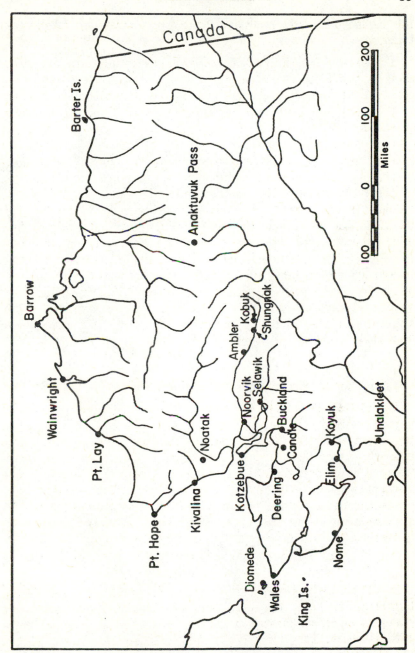

FIGURE 6   Map of Northwest Alaska showing locations of modern communities mentioned in the text or in tables.

the Northwest Alaskan Eskimo population has remained relatively constant since 1940, although the size has increased considerably.   Three new villages (Ambler, Anaktuvuk Pass, and
Kaktovik) were formed, and three old ones (Candle, King Island, and Point Lay) were abandoned, but otherwise the same
villages existed in 1970 that were there thirty years previously.
Although there was substantial migration from the villages into
the larger centers of Barrow, Kotzebue, and Nome (Alaska State
Housing Authority 1971:18; Hippler 1969:20, 35; 1970:48;
Smith 1966:64, 115), the villages remained viable units that
most Northwest Alaskan Eskimos called "home."

The typical Northwest Alaskan Eskimo village in 1970 consisted of a number of wooden houses occupied by conjugal or
(rarely) extended families, a school operated by the State of
Alaska or the Federal Bureau of Indian Affairs, and one or
more churches, which would be sponsored by one of the several
religious organizations represented in the state.[7]   A village
store, usually operated in conjunction with the Alaska Native
Industries Cooperative Association, was a standard feature, as
was an armory of the National Guard.   Finally, there would be
an airstrip, surfaced with corrugated iron matting or gravel,
where planes could land throughout the year.   Stove oil was
the most common heating fuel.   Although gasoline lanterns still
provided light in most of the villages, electrification was being
carried out in many places, and it was scheduled for others.
Beyond this, the details varied.   Kotzebue, Barrow and particularly Nome, were towns of some size, with most of the accouterments—hotels, roads, restaurants, electricity, daily jet service—
appropriate to that status.

The economy of most villages still depended to a large extent
on hunting even in 1970.   Ironically, but fortunately, the recent
period witnessed the re-establishment of a large caribou population in Northwest Alaska as well as a substantial increase in the

[7] During the period 1950–70, a number of community or related studies were
carried out in Northwest Alaska, among them those of Correll (1972), Foote
(1959, 1966), Foote and Cooke (1966), Foote and Williamson (1961, 1966), Hippler (1969), Milan (1964), Saario and Kessel (1966), Smith (1966), and VanStone
(1962b).   Reports prepared by Alaska Consultants (1968a, 1968b), the Alaska
State Housing Authority (1971), and the Federal Field Committee (1968) also
contain a great deal of information about recent Eskimo communities in
Northwest Alaska.

number of moose. Seals and fish continued to be abundant, so that it was possible to make a better living off the land than it had been since the turn of the century. However, the hunting-based economy was thoroughly meshed with that of wages and welfare (VanStone 1960). In most villages the men hunted (and collected unemployment or other welfare checks) throughout most of the year, but worked for wages (if jobs were available) during the summer. In the towns, such as Kotzebue, the emphasis on wages was much greater than in the villages, but a mixture of hunting and cash incomes was essential to everyone in both types of Northwest Alaskan Eskimo settlement throughout the recent period.

The forces of change that were brought to bear on the Northwest Alaskan Eskimos during the recent period were massive.[8] The schools were the most influential of these, but numerous others were involved as well. In 1970 practically every household had a transistor radio and tape recorder, and the generally good mail service (usually twice a week, or more) throughout the area helped bring the outside world to the villages. The massive "wish books"—the Sears and Ward's catalogues—were a greater educational source than most people realize, annually presenting in single volumes, up-to-date, illustrated summaries of a large portion of the entire range of general consumer goods produced in the most highly modernized country in the world. Two or more Whites, usually teachers, had been resident in most villages ever since the schools were founded 50 or more years previously, and in most places the teachers were supplemented by missionaries, storekeepers, anthropologists, and VISTA volunteers during the 1960's. The tourist trade brought numbers of outsiders into the area, although they were concentrated primarily in the large settlements (particularly Nome, Kotzebue, Point Hope, and Barrow). Nome was really a white man's town with a large resident Eskimo population. Although still pre-

---

[8] Various aspects of social change in Northwest Alaska have been described by Anderson and Eells (1935), Brower (n. d., 1942), Burch (1970a, 1971), Chance (1960a, 1960b, 1963, 1964, 1965, 1966), Chance and Foster (1962), Chance and Trudeau (1963), Foote (1964b), Harrison and Morehouse (1970), Heinrich (1950), Hippler (1970), Hughes (1965:27ff.), Jenness (1918, 1929), Nelson (1969), Parker (1964), Rainey (1941), Rasmussen (1934), Smith (1968a), and VanStone (1957, 1958, 1960, 1964). Information on the rapid changes that took place during the 1960's was available through the *Tundra* Times, a native-operated newspaper published in Fairbanks, and edited by a Northwest Alaskan Eskimo.

dominantly Eskimo, Kotzebue and Barrow had many resident Whites of various callings.

The experiences of Eskimos in other areas were at least as important a force for change as the presence of Whites in the villages. Outside Northwest Alaska they were taken into the midst of the world of the 20th century. By 1970, virtually every inhabitant of the area had flown in a plane several times, and the overwhelming majority had visited the larger towns. There they had seen cars and trucks, electricity in every house, running water, self-service stores, movie theaters, restaurants, hospitals, hotels, jet liners, and strangers of all sizes and shapes. Most of the adult men had visited Fairbanks, and Anchorage, or some other large center, in connection with summer employment. Large numbers of people of both sexes had spent some time in the Public Health Service Hospital in Anchorage. Individual Northwest Alaskans had visited every part of the Continental United States, and many had been abroad, particularly during the course of military service. Many young people were going each year to southeastern Alaska or to the Continental United States for high school or technical training, and a few had received university degrees. Beginning about 1960, recruits to the Alaska National Guard were sent to California for six months of basic training.

Kinship

Eskimo kinship in Northwest Alaska was affected more by an acceleration of earlier changes than by major innovations during the recent period. Thus, the gradual loss of the self-sufficiency of kinship units that had begun during the early period continued, but was proceeding at a much faster rate. New opportunities for involvement in non-kin organizations still appeared, but again, at a rapidly increasing rate. Such activities began earlier and lasted longer than they did before, and they were directly affecting an ever increasing percentage of the population.

The entire process was epitomized by the system of formal education. Whereas schooling had started in first grade and lasted from about one to four years for most people during the intermediate period, in 1970 it began with Headstart for many three-to five-year olds, and was mandatory for all children from first through eighth grade. Many youngsters were going on to finish high school, and a few went beyond that for specialized technical training or for university degrees. Inevitably, the process took the young people out of the villages, and away from their homes, at a period of their lives during which even their immediate predecessors had been back within the family fold. Even as late as the 1950's many children left school after a few years to help their parents, but the practice was uncommon by 1970.

During the 1960's a rapidly increasing proportion of Eskimo youth was being sent—voluntarily—to Southeast Alaska, Oregon, Oklahoma, Kansas, or New Mexico (just to name the most frequent places) to continue their education. During this four or five year period, most returned home only for a few months in the summer, and some never got home at all. By the time the high school graduate did return to the village, he was generally much more conversant with the White American kinship system than with its Eskimo counterpart. Indeed, he frequently knew—and cared—little about the sort of kinship that was so important to his ancestors.

By 1970, many a young high school, university, or technical school graduate never returned to the village of his birth. The majority did come back, but increasing numbers were settling down elsewhere, particularly in or near Anchorage and Fairbanks, but also in the Continental United States and abroad (v. Alaska Magazine: 1973). Often their ties with kin and the traditions of their people were broken completely. Of those who did return, many did not know what to do with themselves in the villages. They often drank to excess, and it was not long before they left again for the outside world. This movement away from the villages, and away from Alaska altogether, was stimulated by the voluntary relocation program of the (Federal) Bureau of Indian Affairs, which, during the 1960's, took young people out of many villages and brought them to live permanently in the Continental United States.

Hospitalization on a massive scale was also characteristic of the recent transitional period. This trend began as a crash program by the U. S. Public Health Service to reduce the phenomenally high incidence of tuberculosis in the villages, although it affected the prevalence of other diseases as well. From a strictly health standpoint, the program was highly successful; but it seriously complicated the operations of Eskimo kinship units. Most obviously, it took individuals away from their families for relatively long periods of time (v. Chance 1966:30, 66). If they had not been hospitalized, of course, many would have died.

The important point about hospitalization is, that while absence may make the heart grow fonder, it often made the ties grow weaker. While his wife was away for six months or a year in the hospital, for example, many a young husband found it difficult to restrain himself from seeking other women as sexual partners. In traditional times the kinship system provided means whereby this could be done along lines that were quite acceptable to everyone. During the recent period, sexual relations with someone other than one's resident spouse was adultery, and a serious source of strain in an Eskimo family.

Hospitalization also affected children, removing them from the family context for extended periods of time. While away, the children became accustomed to the soft life of comfortable beds, television, and lots of sweet food. When they returned home, they often had difficulty accepting the comparatively rugged conditions there. The younger children were often catered to in the hospitals. When they returned home they got lost in the usually numerous brothers and sisters who surrounded them there. The parents had more to do than attend to them personally all the time, and returning children often found the home less congenial than the hospital. One of the most frequent complaints of parents of returning children was that they were "spoiled" in the hospital. In this process, which was inevitable if even minimum health standards were to be maintained, the child's opinion of his people in general and his parents in particular often declined significantly. Such an attitude could only result in an unstable family situation.

The above examples are only two among many possibilities. There is no question but that the hospitals saved hundreds, probably thousands, of Eskimo lives. It could be argued that, were it not for the hospitals, there would not be any Northwest Alaskan Eskimos living today. But hospitalization had serious deleterious effects on the operation of Eskimo family units nonetheless.

The hospitals, and the government health program in general, had another, quite different sort of effect on Eskimo kinship, namely a demographic one. The "demographic transition" in Northwest Alaska resulted from the tremendous decline in the death rate which followed the establishment of good medical services in the area. This process began in the intermediate period, but took hold only after World War II. Substantial effects were felt during the 1960's. The demographic change had two main aspects: (1) a very large increase in the number of living children in each family, and (2) increasing longevity, hence progressively more elderly people who had to be taken care of in each family. The latter became significant in Northwest Alaska only toward the end of the recent period, but the former had had serious consequences for the operation of Eskimo family units for some time previously. Both matters are discussed in some detail in Chapter Four.

In view of the truly formidable nature of the forces that impinged on the Eskimo kinship system for nearly a century—and I have mentioned only a few of the most obvious ones—the amazing thing is that *any* of the aboriginal customs could have survived at all. It is a fact, however, that a large number of the traditional ways persisted even into the 1970's. They were not always easy to observe in 1970, for the Eskimos had become expert at hiding them from unsympathetic Whites; but they were there nonetheless.

Interestingly, modern advances in communications systems facilitated a reemphasis of the wider network of kin which had been so important, but which had been largely inoperative since the traditional societal structure was destroyed. Here I refer primarily to two developments: first, the invention of the transistor, which made possible inexpensive, battery-operated tape recorders, and second, the establishment of a network of good airfields and regular air service in Northwest Alaska. Many, perhaps most, Eskimo families owned transistorized tape recorders in 1970, and those who did not could easily borrow them. They used them primarily to make recordings to send to relatives in other villages. Tapes were continually being sent back and forth between relatives who otherwise might not have communicated at all, and sometimes between relatives who had never even met one another.

After World War II numbers of planes had been based permanently in Northwest Alaska, but it was only during the late 1950's that good all-weather airstrips were constructed in most villages. By 1970, the situation had developed to a point at which large numbers of Eskimos could and did travel frequently from one village to another with a minimum of difficulty. A late innovation was to take charter flights. It was not unusual for a group of Eskimos in, say, Kotzebue or Fairbanks, to charter a plane to fly to Point Hope for a major holiday or feast, or for people in Point Hope to charter a plane for travel to Barrow. The 1970 Quarterly Meeting of the Friends Church in Kotzebue brought two whole planeloads of people down from Barrow, and individuals came from points as widely separated as Barter Island and Anchorage. This process permitted the reactivation of large numbers of traditionally based kinship ties that had lain dormant for years. No doubt many of these relationships would have ceased to exist even in theory had not this highly modernized means of communication become possible.

By 1970, kinship no longer had the preeminent position in the life of the North Alaskan Eskimos that it once had. Furthermore, the nature of the kinship of the modern Eskimos was different in a number of respects from that of their ancestors. Nontheless, except in the towns, most Northwest Alaskan Eskimos continued to orient the majority of their activities toward kinship goals most of the time, and those ends frequently involved considerations of a traditional sort. Even in the towns, it was still impossible for anyone to evade kinship obligations *all* of the time, although the patterns there were increasingly non-Eskimo in nature. In 1970, *complete* escape from Eskimo kinship, though possible, could be effected only at the expense of leaving Northwest Alaska and rejecting one's Eskimo heritage altogether.

2

Northwest Alaskan Eskimo Kinship: An Overview

The definition of "kinship" has been a topic of discussion for years, and it was the subject of particularly active debate during the decade in which the present study was conducted. In broad terms, there appear to have been two opposing views on the subject.[1] On the one hand, there was a "conservative" group of authors who defined kinship in terms of biological relatedness and sexual intercourse, although the precise formulations varied from one writer to another. On the other hand, there was a "liberal" group who held that, since there is a great deal more to kinship than biological relatedness and sexual intercourse, any definition of "kinship" cannot be limited to those criteria.

The definition of "kinship" used in this volume lies clearly in the conservative camp. More specifically, it is defined (following Levy 1952:2) as follows:

> that portion of the structures of a society in terms of which
> the membership of the units and the nature of the solidarity

[1] The "conservative" group is represented by Firth (1957:577), Fox (1967:27ff.), Gellner (1957, 1960, 1963), and Malinowski (1930). The "liberal" view has been expressed by Barnes (1961, 1964), Beattie (1964), Buchler (1966), Fortes (1969:49), Leach (1958), Lounsbury (1965), Needham (1960, 1962), Ruel (1962), and Schneider (1964, 1965b). More recently still, Schneider (1972) presented a third, more "radical" view. According to his new position, which is oriented to cultural rather than to social analysis, kinship systems do not even exist.

43

among the members of the units are determined at least in part by orientation to the facts of biological relatedness and/or sexual intercourse.

Like all definitions, the above stipulates only the *minimal* set of characteristics of a class—in this case, the class of any and all kinship structures. In other words, all it does is specify two criteria that serve to distinguish kinship structures from all other kinds of structure. The definition does not presume to indicate what functions are performed in terms of kinship units, what different kinds of kinship units there are, or how kinship organizations operate. Such considerations are problems of analysis, not of definition, a distinction of which the "liberal" authors seem to be unaware. I suspect that every study ever conducted that purported to deal with kinship systems has explicitly or (usually) implicitly focused on organizations distinguished by these two criteria, and not by any others.

The "facts" of biological relatedness and sexual intercourse may be real or assumed. This consideration leads to the distinction between "real" kinship, on the one hand, and "fictive" kinship, or kinship via simulation, on the other (Levy 1965:2ff.; 1966:423ff.). In addition, the facts of a given kin relationship may be morally approved by the members of a given society, or they may be disapproved. Accordingly, there is a second distinction that cross-cuts the first, namely, the one between "actual" kinship on the one hand, and "ideal," or institutionalized kinship, on the other (Levy 1965:5ff.; 1966:426ff.).

Two examples will illustrate how the above concepts will be used in this study. The first is the "customer-prostitute" relationship in contemporary North America. This relationship involves sexual intercourse just as surely as the "husband-wife" relationship does, hence is a kinship unit according to the definition used here. However, the husband-wife relationship is part of the institutionalized structure of United States society, whereas the customer-prostitute relationship is not. This fact does not prevent thousands of customer-prostitute relationships from being established every week. The second example focuses on adoption in North America. The relationship between a woman and her adopted son is not a "real" mother-son relationship, in the sense of the term used here; rather, it is a "fictive" one. It is, however, an institutionalized relationship, i. e., one that receives the moral support and approval of the members of the society at large. In the first example (husband-wife versus customer-prostitute), both relationships are real, but there is a decided difference between the ideal and the actual. In the second example, both relationships are institutionalized, but one is real and the other is fictive.

The Nature of Eskimo Kinship in Northwest Alaska

Descent

"Descent," in the sense used in the present study, refers to kinship based on biological relatedness alone. It is thus the equivalent of "consanguinity" as that term is generally understood. This usage departs to some extent from current conventions in the field, although it is not completely idiosyncratic. For example, Buchler and Selby (1968:69) conceive of descent as the "criteria and the processes by which group membership is determined by reference to one or both parents;" I simply do not specify the kind of "group" that might be involved.

Given the above definition, descent, in the narrowest sense, is a function of procreation. Although they were not aware of all the physiological details, even the traditional Northwest Alaskan Eskimos seem to have understood the basic elements of biological reproduction. Paternity in individual cases might not be known, but the general nature of the process was clear. Descent was recognized bilaterally, and both the male and female lines received equal emphasis.

The traditional Eskimos did not distinguish between actual and ideal descent. All known biological connections between one generation and the next were recognized and considered "good," even when the sexual relations that produced a child were not. The concept of "illegitimate child" did not exist in Northwest Alaska until White missionaries introduced it. Even in 1970 the Eskimos regarded that notion as one of the most ridiculous ideas they had ever heard; the associated idea of "fatherless child" struck many as the ultimate absurdity.

The Northwest Alaskan Eskimos did distinguish between real and fictive descent, however. Real descent, both by definition and in the Eskimo view, existed when the social and biological facts coincided, as when the biological progenitors and the social parents were the same individuals. Fictive descent was everything else. In the Eskimo system, fictive descent included a very large number of possibilities, the most important of which are listed below under the heading of "fictive augmentation."

The difference between real and fictive descent could be indicated terminologically by means of a suffix attached to the regular consanguineal kin term. Real descent was indicated by the suffix "-piaq," whereas fictive descent was indicated by "-saq." Thus *irniqpiaq* is "real son," whereas *"irniqsaq"* might be glossed as "step-son." However, when the ties between a child and both parents were fictive, as in adoption, the term employed was *tiguaq* ("adopted child"). Most of the time, both the traditional and the recent Eskimos did not really care whether or not they were related to someone in a literal physiological ("real") sense. If two individuals operated in terms of a consanguineal relationship, then they were supposed to act the same, regardless of whether or not their membership in it was based on real or fictive membership criteria. The terminological distinction was rarely used except when a technical question about recruitment was being discussed.

The set of individuals related to one another by descent was called *ilagiit*.[2] The term (in this context) is roughly equivalent to the anthropological category of "personal kindred." As defined by Firth (1963:23), this class includes "all a person's cognates, an ego-oriented set of consanguine kin patrilaterally and matrilaterally reckoned, i. e., by ascending and descending relationships." Gubser (1965:142) was correct when he said that,

[2] The term *ilagiit* has a number of different meanings (cf. Graburn 1969:64–66). At the most general level, *ilagiit* are all the people with whom the speaker has a positive association of *any* kind. At the second level, *ilagiit* (kinsmen) are distinguished from *ilauzuat* (friends). It is only at the third level where *ilagiit* (consanguines) are distinguished from affines (*ilagiiksit*). Even this list does not exhaust the meanings of this term, but it should be sufficient to indicate that caution must be employed when using it when speaking to Eskimos.

in Northwest Alaska, the people covered by the term "can be defined only in reference to one person, or, in the case of identical twins, to two persons." *Ilagiit* was not an organization of any kind, but simply a set of individuals related by descent.

Ilagiit were frequently subdivided according to whether they were of higher or lower generations than the person serving as the point of reference. The term *sivuliat* (pl.) denoted individuals in higher generations, and *kiŋuliat* (or *kiŋuviat*) denoted individuals in lower generations. One's oldest living *sivuliaq* (sing.) was the *niaqun* ("head"), and one's oldest known *sivuliaq* was the *sivuliaqput*, or "apical ancestor." Generally, these distinctions were relevant only when people were trying to trace genealogical connections; they did not indicate roles associated with any particular activity or relationship.

Marriage

The second distinguishing characteristic of kinship, by definition, is sexual intercourse. For purposes of this study, a relationship oriented at least in part to sexual intercourse (but not to biological relatedness) will be considered a "marital" one. This "etic" definition corresponds closely with the "emic" one as far as the traditional Northwest Alaskan Eskimos were concerned. The act of copulation, and it alone, established a marriage in aboriginal Northwest Alaska. Conversely, there was no act of sexual intercourse (outside of incest) that could not establish some kind of institutionalized marital relationship. As a consequence, the dividing line between actual and ideal marriage was often obscure, and even the incest taboos were subject to some flexibility of interpretation.

If sexual intercourse was the constant in traditional Eskimo marriage, the residential location and the number of spouses were the major variables. A number of types of marriage were distinguished accordingly. The most common was a residential union of one man and one woman. Two other forms of residential marriage, the fairly common polygynous union, and the rare polyandrous union, also occurred. Finally, there was the non-residential marriage, which usually (but not always) involved sexual relations between members of two residential conjugal pairs who temporarily exchanged partners. The various arrangements are described in detail in Chapter Three.

The forces of social change had had a significant impact on the Eskimos' ideas about sexual intercourse and its implications by 1970. The first innovation to be introduced by outsiders was the idea that intercourse between Eskimo women and White men was subject to a *more permissive* set of rules than was the case for such relations between Eskimos alone (v. Rosse 1883:42; Woolfe 1893:142–143). It was this change which, probably more than anything else, gave rise to the popular notion that Eskimos loaned wives to strangers as a mark of hospitality. As I have argued elsewhere (Burch 1970b:162), this practise was undoubtedly more a form of acquiescence to the powerful newcomers to the region than anything else (cf. Dunning 1962). The whalers, the introduction of liquor, the desire on the part of the Eskimos for American and European goods, and the general state of chaos, acting on a system in which sex with many people was institutionalized anyway, no doubt all played important parts in this process. It was *not* a part of the aboriginal way of doing things. I have heard of several cases of Eskimos "offering" wives to strange Whites—with the wife's permission, but although I have frequently sought information on the matter, I have yet to hear of an Eskimo "offering" a wife to a strange Eskimo as an indication of hospitality.

The government representatives and missionaries who followed the whalers into Northwest Alaska introduced changes of a more conservative sort, at least from a Euroamerican point of view. They waged a relentless campaign against polygamous marriages of both kinds, and against co-marital unions of two men and their wives. The former, probably because they were visible even to an outsider, were apparently successfully eliminated in the intermediate period (1890–1940). Co-marriages, which could be more easily concealed, went "underground," and were carried on in secret for some time. A few unions of this sort were still in existence in 1970, but most of them had been established many years previously.

The Eskimo attitude toward what is proper and what is not in the realm of sexual relations became somewhat closer to general North American standards during the recent period (1940–1970). By 1970, an Eskimo man or woman was ideally expected to have intercourse with one—and only one—person during his or her lifetime. Furthermore, this person was expected to be a spouse with whom one lived only after a church or civil ceremony of the same kinds practised elsewhere in North America. This change did not mean that intercourse outside those limits did not occur among the Eskimos, any less than it does among other people. What it did mean is that such relations were increasingly disapproved of by the other members of the community, and that a distinction between ideal and actual marriage was rapidly gaining force.

The full set of affines (*ilagiiksit*) consisted of one's spouse, all of one's spouse's consanguines, and all of one's consanguines' spouses, at least as a first approximation. However, there were two variations on this basic theme. Heinrich (1960; 1963a:88) has labeled these the "affinal excluding" and "affinal incorporating" structures. In the former, all real affinal kin were sharply distinguished from all real consanguines. In the latter, however, many real affinal kin were "incorporated" into the consanguineal category; indeed, for "affinal incorporators," the boundary between affines and consanguines was often obscure.

The affinal excluding structure traditionally predominated in all areas of Northwest Alaska except the northern interior (Upper Noatak, Utukok River, and Colville River societies), where the affinal incorporating structure was found. During the demographic changes that occurred during the early and intermediate phases of the transitional period, migrants from the interior populated much of the coastal region north of Kotzebue, and the affinal incorporating structure had become dominant there by the beginning of the recent period (Heinrich *Ibid.*).

Affinal "excluders" were often inconsistent with respect to how they classified their relatives. One widespread pattern was to "incorporate" when focusing on older generations, and to "exclude" when dealing with younger ones. For example, a man who regarded his father's brother's wife as a consanguine was very likely to consider his brother's son's wife as an affine; and he definitely would consider his wife's brother's son as one. Whether or not any two technically affinal kin were going to interact on an affinal or consanguineal basis was difficult to predict. My data suggest that active relationships in which the members had a high regard for one another were often carried out in consanguineal terms, whereas relationships lacking those

...acteristics typically had an affinal cast to them. The Eskimos classified the individuals involved accordingly.

The Scope of Eskimo Kinship in Northwest Alaska

The scope of kinship, as defined by the Northwest Alaskan
Eskimos, has been the subject of some disagreement in the literature. On the one hand, Pospisil and Laughlin (1963:187) state
that biological relatedness was thought by these people to cease
at the third ascending and descending generations, and at the
fourth degree of collaterality in ego's generation (v. Pospisil
1964:406–408). On the other hand, Heinrich (1955a:192) claims
that the Eskimo system did not have any institutionalized limits
at all. According to him (*Ibid.*):

> Every consanguineal ancestral connection is utilized to pro-
> vide kinship connections. And as if that were not extensive
> enough, all those connections in the generations above are
> then pursued downward through all of the descendants of
> those relatives that were acquired in the upper generation.

He says further that the Eskimo system did not have any formal
limits, but practical ones only, and that these were usually im-
plicit.

My own data support Heinrich's position. I have not uncovered a single shred of evidence to support the alternative conclusions of Pospisil and Laughlin. Almost all of my informants
had kinsmen outside the limits specified by those authors. The
exact genealogical connections were often unknown or obscure,
but the details were considered irrelevant as long as the existence
of a link of some sort had been affirmed by an older person who
was informed on the matter. Generally in such cases, the relationship in terms of which the individuals operated was the one
appropriate to people of their sexes and assumed generations.
Thus, a woman of fifty, say, and a man of twenty, who were considered to be related (but without knowledge of the exact link)
were likely to operate in terms of the "aunt-nephew" relationship
just because that particular tie seemed to be reasonable under
such circumstances. If the facts of the matter were known, the
woman might turn out to be a "cousin," or a "grandmother," or

even a "great-grandmother," as the Eskimos conceived of such things.

Augmentation

The lack of conceptual boundaries to Eskimo kinship was a logical consequence of four specific characteristics of their system, all of which served to "augment" (Hanson 1971:111) the number of one's kinsmen through time and space. These characteristics were (1) lineal augmentation, (2) marital augmentation, (3) fictive augmentation, and (4) permanence. Each of these characteristics will be discussed separately below.

Lineal augmentation is the process whereby the number of people descended from a single ancestor increases with each passing generation. For example, if my wife and I have two children, each of which has two children, and each of their children has two children, and so on, the number of people related to one another by virtue of their common descent from us increases exponentially with each successive generation. If the number of offspring for each set of parents is limited to two, the process will be faster than if the average is only one, but slower than if the average is only three, four, or more. Because the Eskimos placed no limits on kinship through descent, their system contained the potential for infinite augmentation of this kind. Individuals could be third or fifteenth or hundredth cousins, or whatever, and still be considered "blood" relatives in the Eskimo scheme of things.

The effects of lineal augmentation were compounded by *marital augmentation*. This type of increase in the number of relatives resulted from the pattern whereby Eskimos could establish several successive and/or simultaneous marriages. For example, a man could separate from his first residential wife and take another; he might then take a third in a polygynous union. At any point in the process he and his wife or wives could also become connected to one or more other couples through co-marriage. In all of these situations, which comprised only a few of the many possibilities, the several sets of children of the different women would become fictive siblings to one another, and their offspring would become fictive cousins. Through this process the number of one's "decendants" could be multiplied several times over even from one generation to the next. The same processes operating over the course of several generations could serve to unite hundreds or thousands of people into a single network of consanguineal kin. Each successive or additional residential marriage would also result in the establishment of a whole new set of "in-law" connections (v. Heinrich 1972).

Fictive augmentation increased the effects of both of the other processes, as the above paragraph suggests. Adoption, in which fictive parent-child and sibling relationships were established, was common, but it by no means exhausted the possibilities of augmentation in this realm. Four further possibilities are listed below.

(1) Any person with whom either progenitor *ever* had sexual intercourse could be a parent.

(2) Any residential spouse of any individual ever considered a parent by virtue of (1) could be a parent.

(3) Any child of one's parents, real or fictive, could be a sibling.

(4) Any offspring of any person with whom one *ever* had sexual intercourse could be a child.

In the case of adoption, the establishment of the appropriate relationships was automatic. In the other possibilities it was optional, but most individuals seem to have taken advantage of at least some of the options available to them during some period of their lives. The main point here is that fictive elements could be employed institutionally in such a way as to dramatically increase the number of individuals related to one another in terms of very important relationships, namely, parent-child and sibling relationships.

The seemingly infinite possibilities for augmentation in the number of one's kinsmen were compounded still further by the fourth characteristic, namely *permanence*. The basic rule was a simple one: to the Northwest Alaskan Eskimos, any kinship bond, once established, lasted for the lifetimes of the people involved. Permanence is no doubt an ideal feature of *real* descent relationships in all societies, but the Eskimos in Northwest Alaska carried it over to all other kinds of kinship ties as well, including fictive descent and affinal ties (v. Heinrich 1972:79). For example, when an Eskimo child was adopted, he did not lose his real parents and gain a set of replacements for them. In the Eskimo view, he gained an *additional* set of parents, and usually an additional set of siblings as well. Similarly, when a woman with children separated from her husband and married someone else, her offspring considered both the original *and* the new husbands to be their fathers, and the woman was considered to be married to both of the men.

The various processes of augmentation continued to operate in Northwest Alaska during the recent period, but at different rates than formerly. Lineal augmentation *in*creased because of the great increase in average family size. Marital augmentation greatly *de*creased in significance, partly through the elimination of polygamous unions and co-marriages, and partly through greatly increased constraints on marital separation and "divorce." Fictive augmentation also decreased, partly because of changes in the marriage pattern, but largely through a reduction in the frequency of adoption. The notion of permanence remained in theory, but was greatly reduced in practice. Each of these trends will be discussed in greater detail in subsequent chapters. Their combined effect seems to have been a reduction in the extent of augmentation during the period.

Limiting Factors

The forces of augmentation were counteracted by a number of factors that operated to keep the potentially infinite proliferation of kinsmen at a level far below what was theoretically possible. The primary factors involved were three in number: (1) demographic limitation, (2) cognitive limitation, and (3) deactivation.

Demographic limitation resulted from the small and apparently stable populations of the traditional societies. Continuous exponential proliferation of kinship ties from one generation to the next requires a concomitant increase in the number of individuals in the population concerned. Since this condition was not met, the result was inbreeding, and the multiplication of relationships among a more or less fixed number of individuals. The tendency was reinforced through the custom of adopting children from relatives, rather than from strangers. It resulted in an increase in the number of *relationships* between particular individuals (through multiple connections), but the number of *individuals* related on a kinship basis remained relatively constant. The rapid population increase that occurred during the recent transitional period effectively removed this limitation, but this trend was effectively neutralized by increased rates of both cognitive limitation and deactivation.

Cognitive limitation was the second factor operating to counteract the process of augmentation. By "cognitive limitation" I mean that people simply forgot who their relatives were. In traditional times the Northwest Alaskan Eskimos apparently did not emphasize the retention of genealogical knowledge as much as non-modernized people do in many other parts of the world. Within a society, everyone *assumed* that he was related to everyone else—somehow; but knowledge of the connection, or of some of the possible connections, was often lost as time passed. In the inter-societal context, relationship could never be assumed; it always had to be demonstrated.

The Eskimos required evidence, if not thoroughgoing proof, of at least some sort of genealogical (including marital) connection before they would act as if one existed. The "evidence" consisted exclusively of an expert's (real or assumed) knowledge of the genealogies of the individuals in question. In traditional times, when such information was considered more important than it was in recent times, genealogical knowledge often included lineal ancestors up to the fourth generation in the case of an adult. Interestingly, the breadth was apparently substantial. Many people were likely to know the names of the first cousins of even their great-grandparents, and of their own third or fourth cousins, although knowledge of some of the precise genealogical connections might be lost in the latter case.

In 1970, it was a rare adult who knew who his great-great-grandparents were, and even fewer knew who the first cousins of their great-grandparents were (v. Senungetuk 1971:71). This change was undoubtedly fostered at least in part by the displacement of population that occurred in Northwest Alaska in the second half of the 19th century. The information was lost accidentally when large numbers of people separated and moved away from their ancestral homeland. The apparently high attrition of elderly people—the major repositories of genealogical knowledge—through recurring epidemics and famines in the early and intermediate phases of the transitional period also contributed to this result.

Schneider (1965a:289) points out that White Americans, like the Eskimos, generally did not place any categorical limits on descent. In this respect, therefore, the Eskimos did not have to change to conform to the pattern of the wider society of the recent period. However, White Americans did not consider it important to have very detailed *knowledge* of who their ancestors were beyond one or two generations (*Ibid.* :295). In this respect they differed to some extent from the traditional Eskimos. Northwest Alaskan Eskimo genealogies were still generally deeper than those of most Americans in the mid-1960's, often extending back to the great-grandparental generation, and sometimes to the great-great-grandparent level. Moreover, Eskimo genealogies still presented something of a rectangular appearance on a sheet of paper, since most adult Eskimos knew who their grandparents' first cousins were, and sometimes who their second cousins were. Even young children could list most of their own second cousins.

Deactivation was the final limiting factor on the scope of Eskimo kinship. A deactivated relationship was one whose members were aware of its existence, but who simply ignored it. It was thus a relationship that existed in theory, but not in fact. In some cases the relationship was never put into operation in the first place, in which case the prefix "de-" is misleading. In other cases, deactivation occurred more or less by default, such as when two related individuals moved so far apart that they never came into contact again. More frequent, and more important to the present discussion, were cases in which the members voluntarily deactivated a relationship.

Deactivation of several of one's kin relationships was the inevitable result if the other limiting mechanisms failed to keep the number of one's kin to a manageable level. The basic problem here was sheer quantity. For example, it was almost more difficult for an Eskimo to determine who was *not* a cousin than who was one. Given the all-inclusive nature of the relevant categories, the number of one's cousins could run into the dozens even in one's own local group or village, and into the several dozens when a larger area was considered. But a "good" cousin relationship demanded a certain amount of one's time, since cousins were expected to share, to work together, and to help each other. It would be physically impossible for anyone to have "good" cousin relationships with more than a few individuals even if cousins were the only type of relative in the system. Since they were not, one's obligations to cousins had to be weighed against those to parents, siblings, and children, just to name a few of the more important possibilities. Consequently, an Eskimo was forced to be selective, keeping ties with some individuals permanently active, having others that were only occasionally active, and leaving the bulk scarcely operative at all.

Multiple Connections

By "multiple connections" I refer to the phenomenon of two individuals being related in terms of two (or more) kin relationships simultaneously. As I mentioned above, there was probably a high frequency of multiple connections among the members of each society in traditional times. The reasons for this were numerous, including at least the following: (1) the extreme bilateral scope of recognized descent, (2) the number and variety of marriages, (3) the high incidence of adoption by relatives, and (4) the high level of inbreeding that is inevitable in relatively endogamous populations of such small size.

Genealogical data from the mid-19th century are too sparse to permit detailed analysis of the extent and nature of multiple connections that existed at that time. On the basis of information from the recent period, one would think that the frequency must have been very high indeed. Some of my informants were related to a dozen or more other individuals in two or more different ways. This did not provide them with freedom of choice as to who would be kin and who would not, but it did give them considerable latitude in deciding who would be what particular *type* of kinsman.

The prediction of which of the available alternatives would be chosen in any given instance proved to be extremely difficult. Informants who were aware of at least some of the possibilities in their own cases seemed to use one of three bases of selection. One criterion was that of closer genealogical ties over more distant ones. A second was the selection of "stronger" relationships over weaker ones, as those terms are defined below. Finally, relationships that were established first in time tended to be picked over alternatives which developed later on; however, this rule seemed to hold only where genealogical distance and strength remained relatively constant. I had expected to find consanguineal ties selected in favor of affinal ones, but no such result appeared in my data. Furthermore, there was no clear-cut preference for one of the above criteria over the others; specific individuals used all three inconsistently in different cases. At any rate, once a choice had been made from among the several possibilities it seems to have been retained. Individuals did not switch back and forth between the various alternatives open to them.

Each pair had to come to its own solution to the multiple relationship problem. However, the choice seems *not* to have been the result of conscious deliberation and discussion. Rather, it was arrived at gradually through a process of give-and-take. As long as there was a kinship connection—*any* kinship connection—uniting two people, they had a basis for positive interaction. As the relationship developed through time, it would begin to follow one of the accepted possibilities. Whenever a particular pattern became clear, they began to consciously consider themselves relatives of that specific type.

The mixing of societal populations that occurred during the early transitional period (1850–1890) no doubt reduced the number of individuals connected on multiple bases (v. Correll 1972:-183ff.), but the increasingly sedentary life that came with the intermediate period (1890–1940) reversed this trend. Indeed, during the 1920's and 1930's, many villages became relatively endogamous (v. Milan 1970a, 1970b, 1970c). This development was a function of the tendency for individuals to marry within rather than between communities. However, most villages were not large enough to sustain high levels of inbreeding for more than two or three generations without resulting in an unacceptably high level of first cousin marriages. Before the trend had reached its theoretical conclusion people began to seek mates elsewhere simply because of incest restrictions.

The advent of improved air transportation during the late 1950's, and the adoption of the snowmobile as the primary means of winter conveyance in the late 1960's, substantially increased geographic mobility. To some extent, this increased mobility fostered more marriages between villages than occurred previously. More important was the tendency for large numbers of young people to spend increasingly frequent and prolonged periods in the larger centers of Barrow, Kotzebue, and Nome, and/or in residential schools in southeastern Alaska or the Continental United States. During these visits they became acquainted with many members of the opposite sex from several different villages. The frequency of intervillage marriage increased as a result.

Extensions

The term "extensions" has been applied primarily to the real or assumed practice of "extending" the *terms* for genealogically close relatives to more distant ones. Less often, the term has been used with reference to customs whereby people who are not relatives at all are made kinsmen, usually through some sort of fictive process, such as adoption. It is the second meaning of the word "extension" that will be employed here.

The foregoing discussion of augmentation suggests that the extension of kinship would be either superfluous or else impossible for the Northwest Alaskan Eskimos. If everyone one knows is some kind of relative, how can kinship be "extended" in any meaningful sense? The answer is that it cannot. But it was never true in Northwest Alaska that *all* of a person's acquaintances would be kinsmen. In traditional times the genealogical connections that existed between members of *different* societies were often forgotten after a generation or two. In practical terms, this meant that the people involved were not considered kin. Thus, one obvious possibility for the extension of kinship was to members of another society, and this is the context in which it most often occurred (v. Correll 1972:155).

The Eskimos had a word for the extension of kinship, namely *ilaliuqtuq*.[3] In traditional times this term meant, quite literally, "to *make* (someone) a relative" through a voluntary act, just as one *makes* a house, or *makes* an item of clothing. The specific act required was sexual intercourse. Through intercourse, a man and woman became spouses, and any children either of them *ever* had, before or after, became siblings.

Sexual intercourse was the only way that kinship could be extended in traditional times. The Eskimos did not have fictive

[3] I am grateful to Thomas C. Correll for first bringing this concept to my attention in 1968. Chapter VIII of his dissertation (Correll 1972) contains an excellent account of *ilaliuqtuq* in the Norton Sound area.

marriage, ritual adoptions, or other such devices, and the adoption of children by adults always involved people who were related to begin with. Therefore, *ilaliuqtuq* was the major means by which an individual could enlarge voluntarily the social world in which he could operate on a kinship basis. It was the more binding of the two major forms of inter-societal alliance mechanism, (the other being a trading partnership), and it was systematically employed to reduce danger from outside one's own district. Its particular significance in the inter-societal context has been discussed in a separate publication (Burch and Correll 1972).

The traditional Eskimos did not know how to interact with strangers outside the context of the summer fair, and they usually either avoided them or killed them on sight. During the early transitional period, however, when the survivors of the different traditional societies were being scattered far and wide, strangers were coming into contact in novel situations with increasing frequency, particularly after 1880. Under these conditions, the traditional approach to strangers was neither as feasible nor as desirable in Eskimo eyes as it had been. In order to cope with this new situation, the Eskimos seized on the only traditional means they had of establishing positive relationships quickly, namely, *ilaliuqtuq*.

The *apparent* result of the widespread practice of *ilaliuqtuq* was sexual license, for intercourse sometimes took place between individuals who had known each other for only a few days, or even a few hours. For example, a Seward Peninsula woman was accidentally stranded on board a U. S. Revenue Cutter when a sudden storm blew up, taking the ship to Point Hope. During the day or so that she was in Point Hope, the woman offered herself to any man who would have her, and someone accepted the invitation. Because of the ramifying effects of fictive augmentation, both individuals knew that through *ilaliuqtuq*, they were "making kinsmen," not only for themselves, but for every spouse and every child that either of them would ever have. Because of the widespread population movements that were taking place at the time, they also knew that there was a good chance that at least some of these newly created kin relationships would eventually become operational. My informants cited several cases of this kind. In each one, the principals were engaging in

sexual relations for the explicit and sole purpose of making kinsmen, with particular emphasis on making kin for their children.
In the chaotic circumstances of the time, this was not promiscu-
ity, but a rational means of coping with a difficult situation.

The demographic situation began to stabilize between approximately 1890 and 1910 with the establishment of school/mission
villages throughout Northwest Alaska. As the population movements began to decrease, both in frequency and in magnitude,
people came less and less to encounter strangers in unstructured
situations. Furthermore, through the experiences of the previous half century or so, the Eskimos had become accustomed to
meeting strangers, and the fear and danger involved had been
greatly reduced. And finally, the population movements had been
so extensive, that one could never be sure that a stranger might
not be a close relative of some kind. With families splitting up
and scattering over an area tens or hundreds of thousands of
square miles in extent, one often did not know who even his first
cousins were. Consequently, during the intermediate period, an
interesting new problem developed. It was no longer a question
of establishing kinship ties where none had existed previously,
but a matter of discovering the ties that existed in fact but of
which one was ignorant.

During the intermediate period, *ilaliuqtuq* changed from a
positive act of creation to a passive act of discovery, and the
meaning of the term apparently changed accordingly. As Heinrich (1963a:73, n. 1) has pointed out, "when previously un-
connected [Eskimos] i. e., strangers, meet, the first step in
getting acquainted is a recitation of their respective genealogies."
Eskimos worked their way through a genealogy, their own or
someone else's, individual by individual, reckoning connections
by kin types in exactly the same way an anthropologist would.
For example, the question *sugiviun una*, "What is he to you,"
with reference to a specific person, might yield the response,
arnaqatiga, "My matrilateral cousin." If that was not enough
to satisfy the questioner, elaboration would take the following
form: "He is my mother's sister's son." If the genealogical distance between the two individuals was great, the exercise could
take some time, or it could even be fruitless. But in 1970,
most Eskimos could, through this process, discover at least one
relative in virtually every community between Norton Sound

and the Mackenzie Delta, some hundreds of miles to the north-east (v. Andrews 1939:53; Giddings 1967:19).

The Structure of Eskimo Kinship in Northwest Alaska

The most striking characteristic of Eskimo social organiza-tion is often said to be its "formlessness," or "flexibility" (Adams 1972; Honigmann and Honigmann 1959:119–121; Guemple 1972b, 1972c; Wilmott 1960). Guemple (1972b:3) succinctly summarized what is contained in this view:

> What [flexibility] means is that Eskimo social conventions do not allocate people to social membership in any very un-ambiguous way; and it also means that there are very few prescriptions, either conscious or unconscious, which state how people ought to treat each other once they are allocated.

This feature of Eskimo social organization has been "explained" on various grounds, including (1) an ethos emphasizing relaxed attitudes toward the demands of living (Honigmann and Honig-mann 1959:119); (2) acculturation (Adams 1972), (3) world view, or "metaphysics," (Guemple 1972b), and (4) a lack of "value associated with conventional ways of doing things" (Wilmott 1960:59). Although writers on the subject differ with regard to both the analysis and the explanation of the empirical material, the general impression one gets from the literature is that the Eskimos lived at or near a state of anarchy, a condition that affected even the kinship system (Hoebel 1954:67–68).

David Damas (1963, 1964, 1972), Albert Heinrich (1955a, 1960, 1963a), Leopold Pospisil (1964) and Robert Spencer (1954, 1959, 1972), among others, have demonstrated that the stereotyped notion of Eskimo anarchy is greatly overdrawn. Nonetheless, the view persists that the Eskimos somehow had less structure to their lives than most other peoples. The pres-ent study will contribute to this question of strucure vs. "form-lessness" with specific reference to the Northwest Alaskan Eskimos by showing precisely where the flexibility and where the regularities occurred. Specifically, I will show that there _were_ definite prescriptions about how kinsmen were supposed to treat each other, and that these prescriptions were strongly institutionalized. If there was any flexibility in the content of Eskimo kin relationships it was a consequence of the fact that they were functionally diffuse (Levy 1952:258) to a high degree. The major source of flexibility, and the only really important one in my opinion, was the first to the two listed above by Guemple, namely, the "ambiguous" allocation of individuals among the various positions in the system. Actually, it was not so much a matter of ambiguity as it was one of comparatively broad (but by no means complete) freedom of individual choice regarding the specific people one would interact with on any particular basis. In other words, flexibility lay in the allocation of people among the positions in the system, not in a lack of definition as to how people filling particular positions should behave.

In order to convey an understanding of the structure of Eskimo kinship system, I am going to present the material in such a way as to "build" the system from the "bottom up." Since the basic building blocks of any social system, the roles, are related to one another in particular ways, the logical procedure is to begin with the roles, and then show how they are interconnected at increasingly higher levels of inclusiveness. In the case of kinship systems this procedure is comparatively easy, since kinship roles (e. g., father, mother, parent) characteristically imply particular relationships. After outlining the roles, and describing each relationship in the Northwest Alaskan Eskimo system separately and in some detail in Chapters Three through Five, I will show how the several relationships were combined in the family units that constituted the social context of daily life. The balance of the present chapter will simply serve to lay the groundwork for the analysis which follows.

Kinship Roles

The term "role" is used here to refer to any position differentiated in terms of a social structure (Levy 1952:159). Given this definition, roles are the basic elements of which social systems are built. However, in discussing kinship roles, one must be careful to distinguish carefully between the *roles*, on the one hand, and the *labels* for those roles (and the meanings of those labels) on the other hand (Lundgaarde and Silverman 1972:96). In order to avoid possible confusion on this matter,

I wish to make it clear at the outset that the present discussion is concerned with the former. Labels for roles must be used, however, both by the analyst and by the people involved in the system concerned. Since at least some readers of this account may wish to replicate parts of it, it is both appropriate and necessary to comment from time to time on the usage and meaning of the terms themselves. But this is not a linguistic study, and it should not be mistaken for one.

The conventional way to present information on kinship roles is in the form of a "kinship diagram." The tradition is followed here, but only as a first approximation.

Figure 7 indicates most of the consanguineal roles in the ideal Northwest Alaskan kinship system. The only omission is the position of *qataŋun*, or co-sibling, which is filled by the offspring of a co-marriage. The symbols used are standard for the most part. The only innovations are the use of the square to indicate positions in which sex is irrelevant, and the use of horizontal arrows to indicate that the *pattern* of involvement in the roles concerned extends collaterally beyond the genealogical limits of the chart. The "o" and "y" symbols indicate the ages of ego's siblings relative to ego.

Affinal roles are indicated in Figure 8. One omission from the chart is the role of *nulliq*, which is filled by the respective parents of the members of a conjugal pair. Again in this figure, the symbols are largely conventional. Squares and horizontal arrows are employed as in Figure 7, but the small "o" and "y" in two of the boxes refer to the ages of ego's spouse's siblings relative to that of ego's spouse, not relative to that of ego. The vertical bars are used to separate ego's kin from ego's spouse's kin, on the one hand, and collateral from lineal kin in lower generations, on the other. Finally, it is worth mentioning that, although Figure 8 is an accurate representation of the ideal affinal excluding structure, I never met an Eskimo who actually "excluded" to this extent.

Figure 9, which presents the marital roles, is essentially an elaboration of the relevant portion of Figure 8. In the former, sex of ego and sex of spouse were not distinguished. Here sex *is* distinguished, and the various types of traditional marriage arrangement are outlined. The numbers enclosed in the circles

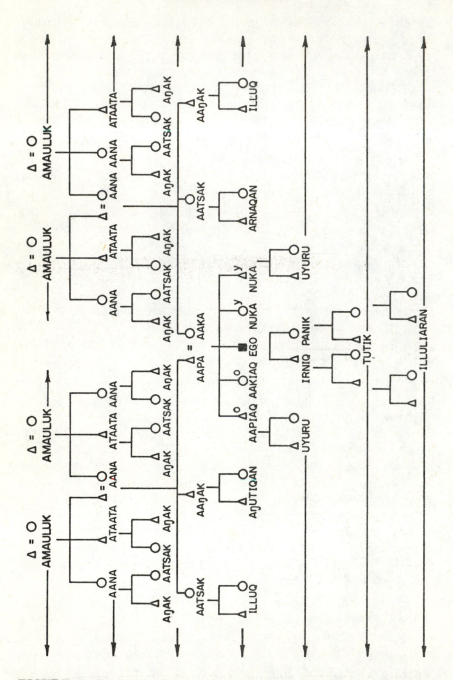

FIGURE 7 Diagram showing Northwest Alaskan Eskimo consanguineal roles, "three-cousin structure," either male or female ego.

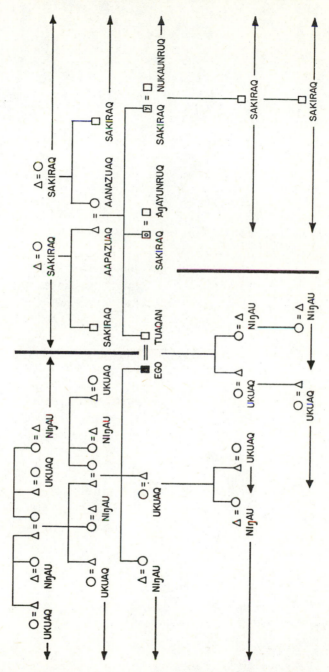

FIGURE 8 Diagram showing Northwest Alaskan Eskimo affinal roles, "affinal excluding structure," either male or female ego.

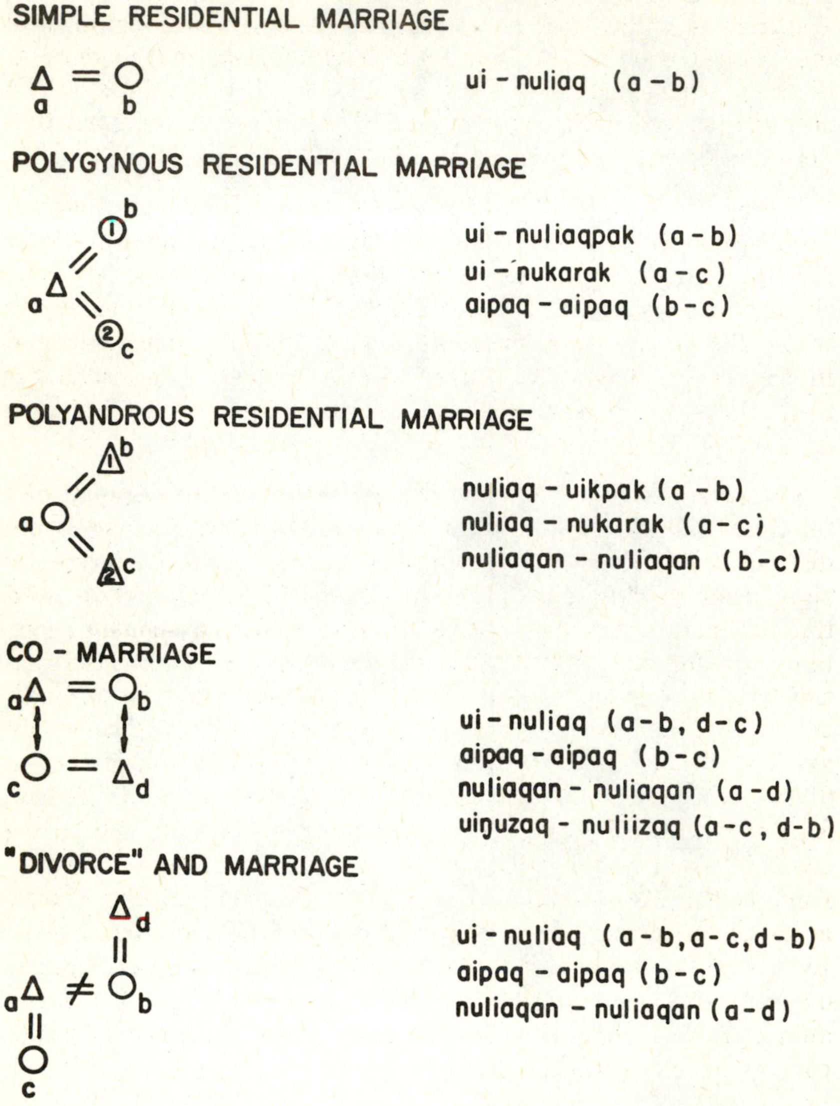

SIMPLE RESIDENTIAL MARRIAGE

$\underset{a}{\triangle} = \underset{b}{\bigcirc}$ 　　　　　　　ui - nuliaq (a - b)

POLYGYNOUS RESIDENTIAL MARRIAGE

ui - nuliaqpak (a - b)
ui - nukarak (a - c)
aipaq - aipaq (b - c)

POLYANDROUS RESIDENTIAL MARRIAGE

nuliaq - uikpak (a - b)
nuliaq - nukarak (a - c)
nuliaqan - nuliaqan (b - c)

CO - MARRIAGE

$\underset{a}{\triangle} = \underset{b}{\bigcirc}$
$\underset{c}{\bigcirc} = \underset{d}{\triangle}$

ui - nuliaq (a - b, d - c)
aipaq - aipaq (b - c)
nuliaqan - nuliaqan (a - d)
uiŋuzaq - nuliizaq (a - c, d - b)

"DIVORCE" AND MARRIAGE

$\underset{d}{\triangle}$
$\underset{a}{\triangle} \neq \underset{b}{\bigcirc}$
$\underset{c}{\bigcirc}$

ui - nuliaq (a - b, a - c, d - b)
aipaq - aipaq (b - c)
nuliaqan - nuliaqan (a - d)

FIGURE 9 Diagram showing Northwest Alaskan Eskimo marital roles and relationships.

or triangles indicate first or second (i. e., subsequent) spouses. The arrows indicate a non-residential sexual relationship, and the crossed equals-sign represents a residential marriage relationship whose members have separated. Finally, it is worth noting that, whereas Figures 7 and 8 employed an ego-oriented network format, the presentation here is fully dyadic.

If one were to visit Northwest Alaska, collect genealogical information from an Eskimo, and then elicit the kinship terms for the various individuals included in that genealogy, the chances are good that he would *never* locate an individual for whom the actual situation conformed to the ideal one presented in Figures 7, 8, and 9. There were a number of reasons for this. It is worth listing them, because they give a good idea of how the Eskimos classified their kin in real life.

(1) *Regional Variations in Classification.* One regional difference, namely, the affinal excluding/affinal incorporating distinction, has already been mentioned. The only other really significant regional variation in classification had to do with the distinction between "three-cousin" and "two-cousin" systems (v. Heinrich 1960:112, 113). In the former, the classification of cousins was based on the sexes of the connecting parents; this is the one that is presented in Figure 7. In the two-cousin system, the classification was on the basis of the sex of the individual cousin, hence "male cousin" (*arnaqan*) and "female cousin" (*aanyaq*). According to Heinrich (1960), the three-cousin system historically had the same distribution as the affinal excluding structure, hence was restricted to the coastal areas and the southern interior (Kobuk and Selawik drainages). By the beginning of the recent period, however, the two systems overlapped a great deal in space. Indeed, some of my informants classified some cousins in terms of one scheme, and other cousins in terms of the other.

(2) *Regional Variations in Terminology.* Although all *Inupiat* spoke the same basic language, there were variations among the several dialects. No attempt is made to describe them since this is not a linguistic study. The forms employed here all come from the Kotzebue area. Some notion of regional variation can be gained from a comparison of the several ter-

minologies available from Northwest Alaska,[4] although many
variations in the literature are due to differences in ortho-
graphy, and *not* to differences in the words employed by the
Eskimos themselves.   The most useful summary of the major
regional variations in terminology is Heinrich's (1955b) report.
I might also mention that informants who had relatives scattered all over Northwest Alaska and who were knowledgeable on
the subject sometimes used the specific terms employed in the
areas in which the different cousins resided.

(3) *Alternative Classifications.*   To some extent there were
different ways to "cut the cake" of kinship, two or more of
which could be employed by the same individual in reciting a
genealogy.   Most of these alternatives simply reflect different
levels of generalization.   For example, an informant might refer to his wife as *tuaqan* ("spouse") rather than as *nuliaq*
("residential wife").   Or, one might refer to all of his brothers
and sisters as *aniqan* ("sibling") rather than by some more
specific term.   The various possibilities were numerous, and it
is not necessary to list them here.   Other alternatives simply
focused on different criteria, the most common one being between a sexual distinction, on the one hand, and the absence of
such a distinction, on the other.   For example, a younger sister
could be referred to as either *nukaraq* ("younger sibling") or
as *nayak* ("younger sister"), and a niece could be classed by
a male either as *uyuru* ("nepotic") or as *nauralautsiaq* ("opposite sexed nepotic").

(4) *Synonyms.*   In many areas the same role could be referred to by two or more terms, the most frequent variable
being the suffix.   For example, in Kivalina, "older sister"
might be rendered *aakiaak, aatauzaq,* or *aakitsiaq.*   As far as
I could determine, such differences were no more significant
than the pail/bucket distinction in English.

(5) *Naming.*   Personal names could sometimes complicate
a genealogy (v. Heinrich 1963b, 1969; cf. Guemple 1965).   If
a cousin was named after one's own father, for example, he could
be referred to as *"aapa"* ("father") rather than by the term for

---

[4] Correll (1972:181–182);   Giddings (1952);   Gubser (1965:134ff.), Heinrich
(1960, 1972), Heinrich and Anderson (1971), Milan (1964:65ff.), Pospisil (1964:401
ff.), Pospisil and Laughlin (1963), Smith (1966:32–33), Spencer (1959:66ff.).   Cf.
Befu (1964).

the role he actually filled. Obvious anomalies of this sort could usually be uncovered by a simple question about them. Responses would take the form, "He's not my *aapa* all right, he's my *arnaqan* ("cousin"); but I call him *aapa* because he is named after my father."

(6) *Substitution*. The Eskimos could substitute one set of roles for another under certain conditions, a matter that will be elaborated on in later chapters. A simple example will illustrate the point. Genealogical cousins who grew up in the same household were often treated as though they were siblings. Although they would eventually become aware of the genealogical details, they would often grow up thinking of each other as siblings and interacting as siblings. Subsequently, they would usually classify each other as siblings except during very technical discussions about recruitment.

(7) *Multiple Connections*. The phenomenon of multiple connections has been described in some detail, and need not be reviewed here.

(8) *Inconsistent Application of the Principle of Affinal Exclusion*. This possibility has been mentioned before, particularly as it affected higher versus lower generations. Most Eskimos incorporated some affines, and excluded others.

(9) *Change in Labels*. By 1970 there had been a certain amount of change in the labels that the Northwest Alaskan Eskimos used for particular roles. For example, a common pattern was to use English labels for "mother" and "father," and to apply the traditional Eskimo terms for those roles to lineal grandparents. It was almost as common for people to employ the traditional grandparent terms for great-grandparents.

(10) *Change in Roles*. By 1970 many Northwest Alaskan Eskimos were operating in terms of a system that was much closer to the White American pattern than it was to the traditional Eskimo pattern. For example, the traditional cousin distinctions had ceased to have any meaning for many individuals, who had replaced them with the comparatively simpler arrangement in which there is just a single position, namely, "cousin." Often one of the old Eskimo words, *aranqan*, was applied to

individuals filling this position, a practice that sometimes complicated discussions of cousin terminology.

To summarize: for purposes of the present analysis, the kinship system of the Northwest Alaskan Eskimos is viewed as being comprised of thirty-three roles. The complete list is presented, this time in alphabetical order, in Table 3. The table also includes a set of English designations for the various roles. It should be kept in mind that the latter are not glosses

TABLE 3 Basic Kinship Roles in Northwest Alaska

Eskimo Label	English Label	Eskimo Label	English Label
aaka	mother	irniq	son
aakazuaq	mother-in-law	niŋau	male in-law
aakiaq	older sister	nuka	younger sibling
aana	grandmother	nukaunruq	junior co-affine
aaŋak	uncle	nuliaq	wife
aapa	father	nuliaqan	co-husband
aapazuaq	father-in-law	nuliizaq	nonresidential wife
aapiaq	older brother		
aatsak	aunt	nulliq	co-parent in-law
aipaq	co-wife	panik	daughter
amauluq	great-grandparent	qataŋun	co-sibling
aŋayunruq	senior co-in-law	sakiraq	affine (spouse's consanguine)
aŋutiqan	patrilateral parallel cousin	tutik	grandchild
arnaqan	matrilateral parallel cousin	ui	husband
		uiŋuzaq	nonresidential husband
ataata	grandfather	ukuaq	female in-law
illuliaran	great grandchild	uyuru	nepotic (niece/ nephew)
illuq	cross-cousin		

of the Eskimo terms; they are simply a set of convenient labels to use when writing for an English-speaking audience. Finally, it should be noted that this list is by no means the only one possible for the Northwest Alaskan system, nor is it necessarily the best in some absolute sense. But it is the one I have found most efficient for the kind of analysis I am concerned with here.

Kin Relationships

The thirty-three roles listed above were interconnected in twenty-seven different ways. The resulting set of relationships is listed in Table 4. The left-hand column in the table presents in pairs the Eskimo role-names that were listed in Table 3. The right-hand column indicates the major categories into which I group the various relationships in the next three chapters for the purposes of analysis.

TABLE 4   Basic Kin Relationships in Northwest Alaska

Singular Labels	Dual Labels	English Labels	General Class
ui-nuliaq	nuliariik	husband-wife	Marital
uiŋuzaq-nuliizaq	nuliizariik	co-spouse	
aipaq-aipaq	aipariik	co-wife	
nuliaqan-nuliaqan	nuliaqatigiik	co-husband	
aapa-panik	panigiik	father-daughter	Parent-child
aaka-panik	panigiik	mother-daughter	
aapa-irniq	irniriik	father-son	
aaka-irniq	irniriik	mother-son	
aaŋak-uyuru	uyururiik	uncle-nephew/niece	Nepotic
aatsak-uyuru	uyururiik	aunt-nephew/niece	
ataata-tutik	tutigiik	grandfather-grandchild	Multi-generation
aana-tutik	tutigiik	grandmother-grandchild	
amauluq-illuliaran	illuliarariik	great GrPa.-great Cr.Ch.	
aakiak-nuka	nukariik	older sister-y. sibling	Sibling
aapiaq-nuka	nukariik	older brother-y. sibling	
qataŋun-qataŋun	qataŋutigiik	co-sibling	
aŋutiqan-aŋutiqan	aŋutiqatigiik	patrilateral parallel cousin	Cousin
arnaqan-arnaqan	aranqatigiik	matrilateral parallel cousin	
illuq-illuq	illuriik	cross-cousins	
aapazuaq-niŋau	niŋauriik	Fa-in-law:So-in-law	In-law
aakazuaq-niŋau	niŋauriik	Mo-in-law:So-in-law	
sakiraq-niŋau	niŋauriik	consanguine:male-in-law	
aapazuaq-ukuaq	ukuariik	Fa-in-law:Da-in-law	
aakazuaq-ukuaq	ukuariik	Ma-in-law:Da-in-law	
sakiraq-ukuaq	ukuariik	consanguine:female-in-law	
aŋayunruq-nukaunruq	nukaunruriik	co-affines	
nulliq-nulliq	nulliriik	co-parents-in-law	

The one remaining column is the second, which presents the labels that the Eskimos themselves used for the different relationships. They could readily specify a relationship through use of the dual number (indicated by the suffix "-ik") and the suffix "-gi". The latter can be glossed roughly as "to be related to someone" in the fashion denoted by the base. Thus, the word *illuq*, which is the label for the cross-cousin *role*, is transformed (with morphophonemic change) into *illuriik*, or the cross-cousin *relationship*. Where the role names differ, however, the name for the relationship is less obvious. For example, the term *aapagiik* (with the base *aapa*, or "father"), could technically refer to either the father-son (*aapa-irniq*) or the father-daughter (*aapa-panik*) relationship. Or, one could turn the whole thing around and, using the base for "son," produce the term *irniriik*. But this term too would be ambiguous, since it could refer to both the father-son (*aapa-irniq*) and mother-son (*aaka-irniq*) relationships.

Damas (1972:40) says that, in the Central Arctic, both designations would be possible, but the one invariably chosen used the label for the subordinate role as the base in the derived term. Thus, "father-son relationship" would always be rendered *irniriik*, never as *aapagiik*, and the context of the discussion would make it clear that the mother-son relationship was not being referred to. In Northwest Alaska, the outcome predicted by Damas was statistically the more frequent, and accordingly is the one presented in Table 4. But the frequency of occurrence in this area was not nearly as high as he says it was farther east.

The Approach

The next three chapters are devoted to a detailed examination of the several relationships listed in Table 4, so there is no need to describe them further at this point. It is appropriate, however, to outline briefly the analytic approach that is used, and to describe the kinds of data that informed the analysis.

The field research on kin relationships was oriented primarily to their *solidarity aspect*, and the presentation in the next three chapters also proceeds from this point of view. The approach was chosen because it seemed to hold the greatest promise of locating patterns in even the most vaguely structured social system, i. e., in the type of social system the Eskimos were supposed to have.

The solidarity aspect is defined (Levy 1952:349ff.; 1966: 220ff.) as the pattern in terms of which relationships among the members of an organization are allocated according to membership, content, sentiment, and strength of those relationships.[5] *Membership* refers to the personnel, i. e., to the individuals who may belong to a relationship. The *content* and *sentiment* of a relationship have to do with the activities involved in the relationship, and the type and degree of emotion with which it is imbued, respectively. Finally, the *strength* of a relationship is the "relative precedence or lack of precedence taken by this relationship over other relationships of its general sort, and over other obligations and committments in the larger social sphere" (Levy 1952:350). Put simply, the analysis of solidarity concerns who interacts with whom, in what way, and under what circumstances.

Most of my information on Eskimo kin relationships specifically was acquired in 1964 and 1965, when my wife and I conducted an intensive study of the subject in one small Eskimo village. The basic information consists of data on 565 individual cases representing all of the twenty-seven relationships in the Northwest Alaskan system. The data were obtained through a combination of direct observation, personal accounts, life histories, genealogies, and informant reports. The case study material was supplemented by interviews covering the same relationship structures, but from a more general perspective. Of particular importance in the interviews was information on the ideal standards of each kind of relationship, and on the changes which had occurred in both the ideal and the actual structures through time.

Both the geographic and temporal coverage of my material were greatly extended when I returned to the field with my family in 1969–70. This time I was interested in seeing how the patterns which had emerged from the previous study applied to other areas, a problem I pursued primarily by means of interviews, partly through observation. The new data confirm-

---

[5] My definition departs from Levy's in that I separate membership from content, and in that I use the word "sentiment" instead of "intensity."

ed the general conclusions of my earlier work, and enabled me
to clarify a number of points.   More importantly, I was able to
widen the scope of my investigation to include a number of
topics I had only touched on earlier.   Of particular significance
here were the structure and composition of larger kinship units
(e. g., families), residence and settlement patterns, and the
more general structure of traditional Eskimo societies in Northwest Alaska.   This information formed the empirical basis for
Chapters Six and Seven of the present work, in which I describe
how the various relationships were connected in terms of the
more comprehensive types of family unit that comprised the
Northwest Alaskan Eskimo kinship system.

3

Marital Relationships

A traditional Eskimo marriage was initiated when a man and woman had sexual relations. As I pointed out in Chapter Two, the traditional Eskimos apparently did not distinguish clearly between institutionalized and noninstitutionalized marriages (outside the bounds of incest) (cf. Heinrich 1963a:84), although their descendents in the recent period were beginning to do so. They lacked any form of fictive marriage in all time periods. The Eskimos, did however, differentiate between residential and nonresidential marriages (Heinrich 1963a:xix, 84).

A residential marriage was undertaken with at least the expectation that it would involve a permanent residential affiliation of the members, and that producing children would be one of its primary objectives. In traditional times, there were three forms of residential marriage, monogamous, polygynous, and polyandrous. *Non*residential marriage occurred when the individuals involved assumed at the outset that any residential association and sexual relations would be temporary or intermittent, but that a number of rights and obligations would bind the members in a permanent relationship. Nonresidential marriage also occurred by default. It occurred when a residential marriage "failed," i. e., when spouses who had intended to live together permanently decided to break the residence tie (*avittuq*), this being the closest thing Eskimos had to divorce. In the Eskimo case,

75

residential spouses who separated were still regarded as husband and wife (v. Heinrich 1972).

Eskimo marriage arrangements can also be classified, for analytic purposes, on the basis of the number of relationships involved. Here the distinction is between "simple" and "complex" marriages. The former occurred when just two individuals and one relationship were involved, namely, in a monogamous union. Complex marriage is a residual category. It included any arrangement involving three or more people, and three or more relationships. Specifically, the category includes both types of polygamous union, co-marriage, and separation-and-remarriage. The simple/complex dichotomy is the more useful of the two classifications for the type of analysis being made in the present study, and it is the basis for the division of this chapter into two main parts.

SIMPLE MARRIAGE

The primary marital relationship of the traditional Northwest Alaskan Eskimos was that of *nuliariik,* or the *ui-nuliaq* ("husband-wife") relationship. This bond obtained between a man and a woman who had sexual relations while living together on a theoretically permanent basis. In this volume, as elsewhere, when one speaks of "Eskimo marriage" without further qualification, it is usually this relationship that is involved. Likewise, when one refers to an "Eskimo wife" without further qualification, one is speaking of a *nuliaq*; a "husband" is an *ui*.

Membership

The traditional Northwest Alaskan Eskimos did not have any institutionalized rules regarding who people should marry. They lacked the levirate and the sororate, and even such broad rules as local group or societal endogamy or exogamy. Consequently, the most general criteria affecting the choice of a spouse were negative ones, namely, incest taboos.

Marriage was ideally proscribed between any two individuals who were related through real or fictive descent (v. Gubser 1965:65; Heinrich 1955a:175; Hennigh 1966; Spencer 1959:62;

but cf. VanStone 1962b:90). This rule was very flexible in its application, however, and genealogical distance was an important variable. Incest restrictions were most stringently enforced at the level of sibling and parent-child relationships, and progressively less so as genealogical distance increased. The marriage of first cousins was regarded as reprehensible, but it did occur from time to time. Second cousin marriage was regarded as inappropriate, but it seems to have been rather common; it was not unusual even in the 1960's. Given the relatively small populations of the traditional societies—most of them numbering less than 1000 individuals—second to sixth cousin marriages must have constituted the majority of cases. Intra-village marriages during the intermediate (1890–1940) and recent (1940–1970) phases of the transitional period also frequently involved inbreeding to a significant extent.

Heinrich (1963a:73 n. 1) says that circumstances played an important part in incestuous relationships, and that Eskimos did not marry cousins "if they [could] help it, but often suitable mates other than cousins of some sort [were] not available." While limitations on the availability of acceptable sexual partners no doubt played an important part in some cases of incest, they were by no means the whole story. I know of no attested cases of incest where other choices were not available.

The data from one district I studied in detail suggest a different possibility. I noticed that despite the significant number of *occasions* on which incestuous relations took place, the total number of *individuals* involved was very small. In other words, the same people tended to be party to more than one such relationship. Some individuals participated in several, and a few attempted even more than they achieved. This leads me to suspect that in at least a few cases, some sort of psychological factor must be involved; just what this factor might be I cannot say. My data do not indicate any changes in either the nature or the frequency of incest between the traditional era and recent periods.

Incest taboos were not the only criteria that influenced the selection of a residential spouse. Parental choice is one that has been frequently reported in the literature (Giddings 1961:154; Gubser 1965:64; Murdoch 1892:410; Petroff 1884:126; Simpson 1875:253; Spencer 1959:77). The published accounts cite everything from mere suggestion on the part of the parents (e. g., Gubser 1965:65) to unions fully arranged by them (e. g., Murdoch 1892:410). All authors who have written on the subject agree that parental influence was a major factor in their children's first marriages, but only occasionally in subsequent ones; in general, my data support this view.

The true "arranged marriage," in the sense of two sets of parents agreeing that their children were going to marry, and then forcing them to do so, did not exist as an institutionalized pattern in Northwest Alaska. It did occur in fact from time to time, but was uncommon. The Northwest Alaskans stand in marked contrast in this respect to the Eskimos of many areas farther east, where individuals were sometimes betrothed while still in infancy. In Northwest Alaska one realistically speaks only of parental *influence*, not of control. Even parental influence had to operate within a context in which the principals ideally had the freedom to make their own choice.

The institutionalized freedom of the individual in choosing a spouse did not prevent parents from trying to *influence* the outcome. One frequent pattern involved parents trying to convince a daughter to accept a particular suitor's advances. This was particularly common in the case of a girl's first marriage, where the initiative was usually taken by the male. Another widespread pattern was for parents to point out an especially suitable girl to their son, and to suggest that he ought to marry her. They would observe that she would make him a good wife, and that they, his parents, would be pleased to have her as a daughter-in-law. It would still be up to the son to go out and win the girl, but the number of times that sons were successful in doing so is remarkable.

A girl's parents could also suggest to a likely young man that their daughter would make him a good wife, and try to persuade him to make advances in her direction. An especially favorable young man (from the parental viewpoint) was sometimes tempted with offerings of gifts of various kinds, such as a boat, if he would successfully woo the daughter. If the man made advances, the parents would put pressure on their daughter to try to accept him as a suitor. There were still other situations in which both sets of parents were in favor of a union, and pressure fell on the potential spouses from both sides. Finally, parental influence took the form of trying to prevent a union of which they did not approve.

A young newly-married couple invariably lived with one or another set of parents. The latter's feelings were thus germane considerations in choosing a spouse. The pressure could become intense if the parents felt strongly about the matter, and it took a great deal of fortitude to resist a parent who had his or her mind made up. Often it was simply a case of parents trying to influence their child to choose one of two or more alternatives both of which were acceptable to the child. The final decision lay with the child, but there was a distinct value attached to following the wishes of one's parents (v. Gubser 1965:64). Besides, a displeased parent could make life truly miserable for a child, and particularly for the child's spouse, if he or she wished to.

Parental influence was strong during the traditional period, but romantic attachments were also made. Spencer (1959:79) says that a love match was generally considered a good risk. My own information indicates that such unions were much more common in the case of second (and subsequent) than first marriages. During the recent period the factor of romance became the predominant one, with a corresponding reduction in parental influence.

Relative age was another criterion that figured in the selection of a spouse in traditional times, and was at least as relevant during the recent period as it had been formerly. Reliable data from earlier periods do not exist. Information on existing marriages in the fifteen villages listed in Table 5 illustrate the recent situation. Of the 380 marriages in the sample, 76 percent (289) were between an older man and a younger woman, while only 15.5 percent (59) were the reverse. The remaining 8.5 percent (32) involved individuals born in the same year, or else were marriages for which the birth date of at least one spouse was missing. The proportions for each of the villages were roughly the same as those for the aggregate population. As long as there was no great discrepancy between the ages of the individuals involved, however, the criterion of relative age was not crucial. Despite the clear emphasis of the general trend, the range of variation was considerable. I recorded one marriage in which the *ui* was some 40 years older than his *nuliaq*, and another in which the *nuliaq* was at least 20 years older than her *ui*.

TABLE 5   Relative Ages of Spouses in Selected Villages, 1969 [a]

Village	Husband Older No.	(%)	Wife Older No.	(%)	Born Same Year No.	(%)	No Data No.	(%)	Total No. Marriages
Ambler	16	(72.7)	4	(18.2)	2	(9.1)	0	(0)	22
Anaktuvuk Pass	17	(89.5)	2	(10.5)	0	(0)	0	(0)	19
Buckland	7	(63.6)	1	(9.1)	2	(18.2)	1	(9.1)	11
Deering	8	(88.9)	1	(11.1)	0	(0)	0	(0)	9
Diomede	9	(69.2)	1	(7.7)	2	(15.4)	1	(7.7)	24
Elim	12	(70.6)	2	(11.7)	2	(11.7)	1	(6.0)	17
Kivalina	17	(70.9)	5	(20.8)	2	(8.3)	0	(0)	13
Kobuk	5	(83.3)	1	(16.7)	0	(0)	0	(0)	6
Koyuk	10	(76.9)	3	(23.1)	0	(0)	0	(0)	13
Noatak	33	(86.8)	3	(7.9)	2	(5.3)	0	(0)	38
Noorvik	36	(73.5)	10	(20.4)	3	(6.1)	0	(0)	49
Point Hope	34	(59.6)	13	(22.8)	3	(5.3)	7	(12.3)	57
Selawik	38	(84.5)	6	(13.3)	1	(2.2)	0	(0)	45
Shungnak	10	(66.7)	3	(20.0)	0	(0)	2	(13.3)	15
Wainwright	37	(88.1)	4	(9.5)	0	(0)	1	(2.4)	42
TOTALS	289	(76.0)	59	(15.5)	19	(5)	13	(3.5)	380

[a] Data from Amsden (1969) and Northwest Economic Development & Planning Board (1969).

The rational evaluation of a potential spouse's abilities in the various pursuits which would devolve upon him (or her) sometimes preceded the establishment of the traditional *ui-nuliaq* bond. Thus, a man might take note of a girl's sewing ability and general industriousness, and a woman might be concerned with a man's potential as a hunter. Such factors seem to have been more the concern of the parents than of the prospective mates, however, at least with regard to first marriages. Parental arguments in favor of a particular match were frequently based on such considerations. Young people seem to have been more concerned with the romantic and/or sexual elements in the situation, although other matters came increasingly to the fore in subsequent marriages.

Considerations other than romantic ones were increasingly relegated to the background during the recent period. Parental control of teenage children was limited—almost non-existent in big families in the larger towns—and young people often had sexual relations with one or more partners before they even thought about getting married. Many marriages during the intermediate and recent periods were legalized only after the birth of the first child.

The Marriage Process

The procedure by which a marriage is founded is an interesting phenomenon, for it symbolizes the significance that marriage has in the society concerned. Most peoples surround the procedure with at least some kind of ritual, often supplemented by taboos, exchanges of goods and services, and other expressions of symbolic and substantive value. Among the Northwest Alaskan Eskimos, however, there was no marriage ceremony whatsoever, and there were no taboos associated with the establishment of a husband-wife relationship.[1] Instead, it consisted quite simply of the parties to the relationship taking up residence together, usually in the house of a relative, having sexual intercourse, and referring to one another with the words *ui* and *nuliaq* (v. Mur-

[1] The Northwest Alaskan Eskimos *did* have a number of ceremonies (v. Lantis 1947) and taboos (v. Stefansson 1951:410ff.) associated with other areas of life, however, so their absence in this sphere cannot be explained away on the grounds that there were no ceremonies or taboos *at all* among these people (see also Ostermann 1952:71–82, *et passim*.)

doch 1892:411; Petroff 1884:126; Spencer 1959:77; Stoney 1900:86; cf. Woodburn 1968:107). Even these conditions did not have to be perpetuated for very long for the relationship to be considered a permanent one.

The complete absence of ritual recognition of the establishment of the basic marital relationship in the traditional society indicates the low position held by the relationship in the Eskimo view of their own social world. Not only was the relationship institutionalized as weak—as I shall argue later—it was regarded as a more or less utilitarian arrangement by means of which the problems of daily existence could be most efficiently handled. Consequently, its establishment did not require the "reorganization of sentiments" and "solemn recognition" (Homans 1960:175) associated with marriage in so many societies. Fortes (1962:8) claims that everywhere in the world, "a person's first marriage constitutes a critical, that is an irreversible change of status, one of the most important in the life cycle." Whatever the case may be from the viewpoint of anthropological *theory*, it seems that traditionally, the Northwest Alaskan Eskimos themselves did not regard it as a very important event. They viewed it as a natural continuation of, not a sharp break with, the past.

If traditional Eskimo marriage was conceptually a simple matter, it was often otherwise physically, for many girls put up strong resistance to it, at least in the case of their first marriage. This stress was apparently associated with the fact that, in the great majority of cases, it meant the loss of a girl's virginity, often under conditions not fully of her own choosing. The unanimous view of my informants was that, in traditional times, and in marked contrast to more recent trends, very few girls had sexual relations prior to the establishment of their first residential marriage tie (v. Simpson 1875:252, 254).

Histrionics on the girl's part do not seem to have been institutionalized. Many girls appear to have been genuinely afraid of marriage, probably because they were relatively young and inexperienced. In contrast to first marriages, subsequent ones seemed to have approached in fact the simplicity that all marriages had in Eskimo theory. They were undertaken at the discretion of the individuals involved, and were devoid of the resistance and emotional displays that so frequently characterized first marriages.

Marriage by capture has also been reported (Giddings 1961:49; Rainey 1947:243; Ray 1885:44; Spencer 1959:77) in Northwest Alaska. Many first marriages no doubt gave the appearance of this sort of thing, but they usually took place with at least the tacit consent of the bride's relatives. Consequently, they are not fruitfully regarded as marriage by capture. Real wife stealing, in the sense of a man literally taking a woman by force, without approval from anyone, also is supposed to have occurred from time to time. However, the cases I have been able to document all consisted of men *taking back* women who had lived with them before, but who had left them; I have discovered no attested instances of first marriages being established in this manner. There are stories from the remote past, though, in which men are said to have abducted women from other societies, women they had never even seen before. This would certainly constitute marriage by capture, regardless of how one might interpret the term. Unfortunately, the evidence for these cases is very tenuous.

The observations of the early explorers generally corroborate the stories of my informants regarding the marriage process. Simpson (1875:253), for example, noted that "a man of mature years chooses a wife for himself, and fetches her home, frequently to all appearances much against her will." But he went on to say that "she manages in a wonderfully short time to get reconciled to her lot," and that is the critical issue. Almost any sort of half-decent man could forcefully abduct a woman, with full knowledge of her relatives, and frequently with their support. If the man had a bad reputation, if he was intensely disliked by the girl's parents, or if he mistreated her once he had her, however, strife would follow. In the Kivalina area alone, there were two instances around the end of the 19th. century in which the fathers and brothers of girls who were being mistreated by men from Point Hope went so far as to murder the offending husbands. Also, since separation could be effected easily in the traditional society, a *nuliaq* would have to be dissatisfied with an *ui* for only a short period before she left him.

Church weddings were introduced into Northwest Alaska early in the intermediate period (1890–1940) by the missionaries. By the end of the period, church and civil weddings were the *only* means by which one could establish a marital relationship through institutionalized procedures. The altered format made it difficult for parents to force a girl to get legally married when she was strongly opposed to it, and made it virtually impossible for a man to abduct a woman according to the pattern described above. However, the transition was gradual. For most of this period couples would get married first according to the traditional Eskimo pattern, and if the relationship proved reasonably satisfactory to the individuals involved, they would have it legalized through a church wedding. The missionaries of course preached against this procedure, but most of them felt it was better to have a church wedding after a brief "trial period" than it was to have no formal wedding at all.

The marriage situation was complicated further by the regulation that a legal wedding could not be performed unless a marriage license had been obtained first. A law to this effect was passed by the Territorial Legislature sometime during World War I (Stuck 1920:135–136). Unfortunately, marriage licenses had to be acquired from a U. S. Commissioner, and those officials were few and far between in Northwest Alaska at the time. The law meant that most couples had the following choices open to them: (1) follow traditional marriage customs exclusively, which meant establishing what was increasingly regarded as a second-class marriage; (2) postpone their marriage until such time as a U. S. Commissioner went through, which could mean a wait of a year or more; (3) ask the local missionary to perform an illegal marriage service, which missionaries were naturally loathe to do; (4) travel two or three hundred miles or more just to get a marriage license, which was usually regarded as more onerous than a common-law marriage; or (5) forego altogether their plans to get married. This unsatisfactory situation persisted for some time. In addition to complicating the transition from traditional Eskimo to contemporary White standards, this law contributed to a general contempt for and disregard of marriage laws that did not start to dissipate until well into the recent period.

During the recent period (1940–1970), and particularly toward the end of it, there was some spontaneous elaboration of the basic legal ceremony, and many girls wore white dresses or even wedding gowns when they got married. The ceremony itself was sometimes followed by a party or a feast, at least if the principals had not been living together for some time previously. That ceremonies were still regarded as something of an imposition from outside is indicated by the fact, as late as 1970, many couples lived together for quite awhile before going through the legal procedure.

Content

The content of the traditional *nuliariik* relationship in Northwest Alaska is most easily understood if one recognizes at the outset that companionship, as such, was irrelevant to it. Except when *ui* and *nuliaq* came together for activities primarily oriented to economic or sexual matters, they did not even see very much of each other. The wife stayed in the house—her own or a relative's—and her husband spent his time hunting, visiting a male relative or friend, or staying in the *qazgi*.

The *qazgi*, sometimes referred to as the "men's house," is accurately thought of as a community social center whose day-to-day activities tended to be dominated by males (v. Correll 1972: 195–220; Heinrich 1955a:96ff.; Senungetuk 1971:50ff.; Spencer 1959:187ff.). In the words of Robert Spencer (1959:187),

> a man spent all his days in the [*qazgi*], whenever he had leisure, and might even choose to sleep there, although this was not the usual custom. A man who stayed in the [*qazgi*] remained for days on end. Their wives cooked food at home and brought it over to the [*qazgi*] in pans and trenchers to feed their husbands. If he were not otherwise engaged, such as in the winter sealing, a man left his house on awakening and went over to the [*qazgi*]. His wife brought food at times during the day, usually in quantity, so that it could be shared with the other men. The man came home at the end of the day to sleep.

In small settlements where there were insufficient numbers of people to justify construction of a separate building for a *qazgi*, the pattern described by Spencer for the large villages was followed in slightly modified form. The men simply used one of the regular dwellings as a *qazgi*; they would bring their work there or spend their idle hours there, while the women and children would congregate in another house. Wherever possible, however, they constructed a separate building to serve the purpose. In summer, when people were moving around and living in tents, the men would turn a large boat on its side, call the area on the leeward side "qazgi," and gather there according to the very same principles. The women would bring the food to the men at the boat, and the men would return to the tents only for sleep and for sex. In good weather, they often slept right there in the open air.

Throughout the transitional period, husbands and wives continued to spend relatively little time together. By the recent period (1940–1970), the pattern had modified slightly; the *nuliaq* stayed in the house, looked after her children, and did household chores. The *ui* too stayed home to work, since there was no longer a *qazgi*, but if he had no work to do and if he was not hunting, he was generally to be found elsewhere. "Elsewhere," depending on the circumstances, might mean visiting friends in the village, talking to other men in the open air, or congregating with the other men in the *"qazgi"* of modern times, which may be the local store in the village, or a pool hall in one of the larger towns. When men were home, it was merely because they had projects to do there, or because they were helping their wives in one of their heavier chores, because they were entertaining visitors, or because they simply wanted to sleep. It was a rare occasion when even a highly acculturated *ui* stayed home simply for the purpose of enjoying his wife's company.

The pattern was beginning to change rapidly during the 1960's, but even in 1970 the trend had affected only young, highly acculturated couples. The emerging pattern was just the reverse of the traditional one. Instead of "going out with the boys," the *ui* either stayed home with his wife, or perhaps took her along when he went out, which was usually to visit another young couple (in the village), or perhaps to go to a movie (in one of the towns).

Childrearing and Sex

The production of children was always one of the primary objectives of residential spouses, and the arrival of a child did more than anything else to cement the tie between the *ui* and *nuliaq*.

The rationale for this emphasis was clear, and explicit. As one man described it:

> My grandpa sure want me to make a kid when I get old enough. "If you don't have a kid, if you get to be old, what you gonna do? You gonna have a real hard time right there! Nobody gonna help you. But if you have kids, they gonna care for you. And the people won't forget you when you die. But if you don't make a kid, if you die, you really lost right there. Nobody remembers you." That's what he told me, and that's why we natives want to have kids all the time.

Many other informants, both male and female, made similar points. By far the greatest emphasis was on the fact that children were the Eskimos' only form of old age insurance. Again and again my wife and I had this formula quoted to us: "If you don't have any kids, who's gonna take care of you when you get old?" The Eskimos could not understand why anyone would want to be married and not have children.

Like everyone except Malinowski's Trobriand Islanders, who reportedly did not understand the process of paternity, Eskimo couples went about achieving the desired goal of children in a most rational way, namely through sexual intercourse. Despite the existence of other socially approved marital associations, the *nuliariik* relationship was the focus of by far the greatest portion of approved sexual relations in the traditional society. It was the *only* relationship in terms of which intercourse had the specific objective of producing children. By the onset of the recent period, it was also the only relationship in which sexual relations were socially approved, hence, ideally, it was the focus of *all* sexual intercourse.

Copulation was, for the Eskimos, a simple straightforward act: the partners would lie facing each other, with the man mounted on the woman. Although the Northwest Alaskans of the 1960's had heard of other ways of going about it, few seemed to be interested in trying them. Sexual stimulation prior to intercourse was minimal between residential spouses (v. Spencer 1959:247). The *nuliaq* was passive, taking little initiative, and generally lying still during the act itself. In most cases the husband simply got the urge and proceeded to satisfy it, regardless of the feelings of his wife. I asked one man if he "would do anything" with his wife if she had a headache, felt sick, or was otherwise indisposed. He replied, "Just when I want to do it myself, I do it. My wife never say anything about it." The only time consideration was given was when the wife was pregnant, and intercourse was stopped fairly soon after the woman began to show her condition. After the child was born, the men were typically impatient, and they frequently tried to resume relations before their wives were ready (v. Spencer 1959:236). There seem to have been few, if any, changes in the general pattern described above between traditional and recent times.

Goods and Services

The economic aspect of the husband-wife tie was considered by the Eskimos to be of equal importance to that of child-bearing in both traditional and recent times. During the interviews in which informants were asked to evaluate specific examples of this relationship, economic considerations were always at the top of the list (the bearing and care of children being taken for granted).

The division of labor along sex lines was sharply drawn in traditional times, and it was most fully manifested in the *nuli-ariik* relationship.[2] The "image" projected by the traditional Eskimo *nuliaq* is that of a skin sewer *par excellence*, and sewing in either a construction or maintenance capacity occupied a great deal of time. She was also in charge of game, practically from the moment a kill was made until the meat was eaten, her duties including retrieving, skinning, butchering, storing, cooking, and serving. In addition, wives brought in a fair amount of small game themselves. They hooked for fish, and snared ptarmigan and rabbits in all districts; along the Kobuk River, they were in complete charge of the crucial summer fishery. Women were responsible for the acquisition and storage of all vegetable prod-ucts—berries, greens, leaves, roots—which constituted a more important resource than most authors recognize. Women were in charge of operating the oil lamps which constituted the only source of light, and the primary source of heat in traditional

[2] For other information on the content of the husband-wife relationship in general, and on the sexual division of labor in particular, see Jenness (1957:45, 66–67, 177), Giddings (1961:138), Gubser (1965:63ff.), Spencer (1959:244–251; 1967/68), Stoney (1900:68, 71) Wells and Kelly (1890:17), and Woolfe (1893:135).

times. It was the *nuliaq* who got the wood for the one cooked meal of the day. She fed and generally cared for the dogs, and she probably drove them more often than her husband did, both when retrieving game and when travelling.[3] Finally, the wife of a rich man or "chief" had a number of important ceremonial obligations to carry out during the course of the year, particularly if her husband was the captain of a whaling crew (v. Spencer 1959:152–155, 177–182, 332ff.).

The traditional *ui* in Northwest Alaska was primarily a big game hunter and fisherman. Much of his time was taken up by hunting and fishing, or in logistic or ceremonial activities related to the chase. Men had to make all their own tools, weapons, and other implements, and were responsible for the construction and maintenance of all household utensils and of the houses themselves. Otherwise, the men spent their time loafing, telling or listening to stories, or participating in athletic pursuits. Warfare was exclusively a male activity.

The substantial increase in the number of children since the turn of the twentieth century reduced practically every child-bearing woman to the position of full-time baby-sitter. During the 1960's almost everything a *nuliaq* did revolved around this central task. Women still cooked, of course, and this activity took up much more of their time than it had formerly, for at least three reasons. (1) Whereas there had been two or three adult women in every house to share the cooking chores for a total of five to ten people, there was normally only one by 1960, and she had just as many people to cook for. (2) Following the general North American pattern, the Eskimos had at least three cooked meals a day, whereas in traditional times they had had one, at the most. (3) The foods and cooking styles of the Eskimo housewife required much more time in 1960 than they had in traditional times. Instead of dried or frozen raw fish or meat for breakfast, they had hot cereal and sourdough hotcakes in 1960; instead of dried or frozen raw fish or meat again at midday, if they ate then at all, they had stew, or soup; and in place of boiled meat or fish in the evening, they had any one of a wide

---

[3] In traditional times most men hunted by walking out from the settlement rather than by driving out with dogs. When they killed a seal or caribou, they would just leave it there and return home. Later, the wife would retrieve the carcass with sled and dogs.

variety of cooked meals. Besides cooking, they had the many dishes and other accessories of the modern housewife to clean, whereas formerly they had had nothing that required daily washing.

Wives had little time for sewing in 1960, the construction and maintenance of parka covers and skin boots being about the extent of it. Most clothing was purchased from the local store or through mail order houses. Clothing maintenance consisted primarily of washing, an activity that did not even exist in traditional times. The quantity of clothing worn by large families made this a burdensome task, particularly since, in most areas, water had to be carried for some distance. Washing machines driven by small gasoline motors alleviated the problem to some extent, and in each of the larger centers, a laundromat was in operation at least part of the time.

Wives ceased bringing game into the village early in the 20th century, the task having been taken over by husbands. Caribou and moose were frequently butchered by the men in the 1960's, and seals, fowl, and small game were the only animals that were generally looked after completely by the women. During the first half of the 1960's, a few wives still looked after the dogs, but men had largely taken over this task as well. Many women never even went near the dogs, and most had limited knowledge of how to handle them on the trail. During the last few years of the decade, there was a substantial shift from dog teams to snowmobiles as winter transportation; women appeared to be driving these more often than they had driven dogs a few years before.

The traditional Eskimo husband had been a big game hunter, but by 1900, most of the big game—whales, walrus, and caribou—had been practically wiped out in Northwest Alaska. The emphasis switched to reindeer herding and trapping. The Depression saw the end of the lucrative fur market and the virtual elimination of the reindeer herds. It also brought the Civilian Conservation Corps, make-work, and welfare into Northwest Alaska, and forced those individuals not already involved irrevocably into the money economy.

The dramatic increase in the caribou and moose populations of Northwest Alaska after World War II permitted the majority of Eskimo men to become big game hunters once again. But a man was also a money earner by this time, and the obligation to work for cash had become even greater than the responsibility to hunt. Some funds could be obtained through hunting (by sale of skins and furs,) but an adequate income usually took men out of the villages for one or two months or more each summer during the 1960's, as long as jobs were available. When they were not working, the men had to fall back on to welfare.

Men were still responsible for the construction and maintenance of the family home, although even here State and Federally supported housing and electrification programs were beginning to take over by 1970. On the whole, husbands bought rather than made hunting implements, tools, and household accessories. Sleds and boats were the only notable exceptions to this rule, but these too were being made by a progressively smaller proportion of the male population every year. Men were still responsible for the maintenance of all of the above items, since the repair services of the city had yet to catch up with the mail-order purchasing methods. In order to make a really good living in the Northwest Alaska of 1970, an Eskimo husband had to be a combination heavy equipment driver (or electrician, or government employee), mechanic (to repair outboard motors, washing machines, and snowmobiles), *and* hunter.

Power and Responsibility

The political aspect was a third focus of the *ui-nuliaq* relationship. In traditional times, the allocation of power and responsibility in terms of this relationship was just as precisely defined as was the allocation of goods and services (v. Heinrich 1955a:134; Murdoch 1892:414; Pospisil 1964:410; Spencer 1959:250). At the general level, the *ui* ideally had authority over his *nuliaq* with respect to the major affairs of life. Decisions on where they should live, when they should move, and how they should deal with any crises and problems that developed were ideally up to the husband. Actually, there was considerable variation from one case to another, and some wives completely dominated their husbands. More often, the pattern seems to have been one of benevolent despotism: the husband reserved the right to make the final decision on matters of major importance, but he usually consulted his wife at some length before doing so. In all of the above respects, there was relatively little change between traditional and recent times.

On more specific levels, authority in discrete spheres was divided between man and wife. Tradition gave the *nuliaq* full authority over the use and disposition of any and all household goods, while the *ui* had similar authority over the use of weapons, tools, and boats. Both individuals were responsible to one another, as well as to other family members, for the effective use of this property. On the specific level, as on the general one, political allocation in terms of *nuliariik* changed relatively little after the traditional period; only the particular goods and activities changed through the course of time.

The institutionalized mechanisms by which a traditional *nuliaq* or *ui* could hold one another responsible for their actions were limited. Neither had recourse to legal sanctions that could be enforced by some more general authority, and conflicts had to be worked pretty much at the personal and family levels. A wife could resort to nagging or more subtle pressures to influence her husband. If this approach did not work, in serious situations, she would call upon her father, brothers, or other relatives for support. The husband could utilize similar techniques, but was normally able to employ physical coercion to some extent to make his wife live up to her obligations.

Pospisil (1964:410) goes so far as to imply that wife beating was institutionally permitted in traditional times. He says that: "Legally speaking, the father had power over his children, and especially over his wife. In the whole Eskimo society it was only the wife who was exposed to serious corporal punishment, which sometimes involved even mutilation." My own data indicate clearly that, while there is no denying that actual cases did occur, wife-beating and mutilation were distinctly frowned upon, even shameful, in traditional times. Every case of wife beating I ever heard of, from any time period, involved men who were either generally acknowledged to be emotionally unstable, or who were intoxicated. If all else failed, both *ui* and *nuliaq* had the right to pack up and leave the spouse, at any time, and at their own discretion.

During the intermediate and particularly during the recent phases of the transitional period, the Eskimo *nuliariik* tie increasingly received the same support from the U. S. legal system that the husband-wife relationship has generally in North America. At the same time, Eskimos lost the freedom of "divorce" that had been one of their traditional prerogatives (Anderson and Eells 1935:170). Consequently, Eskimo husbands and wives lost the one really effective threat they had to keep one another in line, namely the threat of permanent separation.

Sentiment

The traditional *nuliariik* relationship can be described as one characterized by moderately intense positive sentiment, coupled with restrained expression of that sentiment (v. Gubser 1965:139; Spencer 1959:248; cf. Pospisil 1964:404). It was "moderately intense" because, although spouses were expected to be fond of one another, the Western concept of "love" simply was not a feature of this relationship in its institutionalized form. There also seems to have been a pattern of development in the sentiment of the relationship. Relations of a younger couple commonly were rather volatile, swinging back and forth between the poles of attraction and antipathy. As people grew older, these oscillations tended to decrease in magnitude, and eventually reached a fairly steady state. My informants felt that affection between older spouses was expected to be present, but in relatively modest amounts. This traditional pattern of *ui-nuliaq* sentiment persisted until well into the recent phase of the transitional period.

The traditional *nuliariik* relationship was described as "restrained" because, regardless of the nature of the intensity of the sentiment in any given case, spouses were expected to keep their feelings to themselves. Departures from the norm were more common in the display of negative than positive sentiment. That is, when spouses were angry with one another, they were more likely to express their emotions than they were when the opposite situation obtained.

Restraint continued to characterize the *nuliariik* relationship until well into the recent era. In the mid-1960's, when a man returned home after a two-month absence from the village, he was greeted with a big smile and a handshake from his wife, which he reciprocated. He then proceeded to ignore her while making a big fuss over his children and talking to his male friends. The wife would typically step aside and talk to her own friends, or

else go home and make coffee for the multitude likely to congregate there to hear the latest news from outside the village. The
greeting after a long separation was the maximum public display
of sentiment between spouses that one was likely to see. It was
with specific reference to such examples that my informants assured me that spouses were even less demonstrative in traditional times.

The sentiment of the husband-wife relationship began to undergo a transformation during the 1960's, as notions of romantic
marriage began to spread in Northwest Alaska. In the villages,
it was still possible in 1970 for the *ui-nuliaq* bond to be of relatively moderate intensity, and remain viable. In the towns, there
was a pronounced trend in the direction of highly intense sentiment among young couples, and it was becoming increasingly
difficult to maintain a stable marriage in the absence of such
feelings.

The restraint that formerly characterized Eskimo marriage
was also on the wane in the 1960's, particularly in the towns. It
was there that movies, alcohol, and White role models had by far
the greatest impact, and of course the younger couples were the
most affected. Some young Eskimo couples openly expressed affection for one another, walking around town holding hands, kissing in public from time to time, and generally conversing in much
more animated fashion than their parents would have at the same
age. Among older couples, alcohol seemed to be an important
factor in the expression of sentiment. It was not uncommon in
Kotzebue, for example, to hear loud exclamations of either deep
affection or violent displeasure between husbands and wives on
any Saturday night. The behavior of the same individuals when
sober was likely to be strikingly different, much more in line
with the practices of their ancestors.

Strength

The *ui-nuliaq* relationship was a weak one among the traditional Northwest Alaskan Eskimos, a characteristic symbolized
by the fact that the establishment of the relationship lacked not
only ceremonial recognition, but also taboo restrictions of any
kind. At the conceptual level, the weakness of the *nuliariik* tie
reflected the general Eskimo view that all relatives by descent

(as defined in this study) took precedence over all relatives by marriage, including spouses. The concrete illustration of this principle was the blood feud, in which a person ideally was expected to support any consanguineal relative against a spouse if the need arose (v. Hennigh 1972; Spencer 1959:74). On the practical level, the weakness of the traditional *ui-nuliaq* bond was a function of the ease with which a separation could be effected, the details of which are described below in a separate section.

The *ui-nuliaq* relationship became a great deal stronger during the recent period than it had been previously. In large part this trend was a consequence of changing values. These are reflected in the reduction in the strength of consanguineal ties generally, and in the increasing emphasis on the conjugal family as the primary kinship unit. But the change was also due to externally imposed controls on divorce, which became more difficult. By 1960 the full authority of the government stood behind the laws specifying the minimal obligations between husband and wife.

Strains

Every relationship is subject to stress and strain. Indeed, the factors operating to push or pull apart the members of a relationship appear to be just as structured as those operating to bring them together. Consequently, the subject of stress deserves just as much attention as any of the others in a study of the solidarity process. Proceeding from this point of view, I collected a considerable quantity of information on conflict, and, as will be shown, each relationship was indeed characterized by a distinct pattern of stress and strain.

The most common source of marital stress in all time periods covered by this study was infidelity (Gubser 1965:116; Ingstad 1954:43; Spencer 1959:99). In traditional and early transitional times, "infidelity" meant having intercourse with a non-residential spouse without the knowledge and agreement of the residential spouse. Apparently it was extremely common, as might be expected in a system in which virtually any nonincestuous sexual tie could be considered legitimate. Gubser (1965:117) may have been correct when he said that the Eskimos sought "sexual variations in partners rather than in practices." Variation in partners could of course be achieved through institutionalized co-marriage, and when it did occur in this context, was not a source of strain. But when it took place outside of this context, intercourse was typically a source of jealousy and, if perpetuated, often led to the dissolution of the residence tie.

The definition of infidelity gradually became more stringent during the intermediate period (1890–1940). Whereas formerly it had been defined as intercourse with a nonresidential spouse *without* the residential spouse's *permission*, it now became defined as *any* intercourse outside of the residential spouse context. This change was obviously associated with the growing distinction between institutionalized and noninstitutionalized marriage. The change in definition seems not to have affected the frequency of infidelity however, and indeed, the frequency may well have increased. My data suggest that, during this period, practically every adult in Northwest Alaska committed adultery at least once, with some interesting results that will be discussed later under the heading of "co-marriage by default." Sometimes this infidelity led to separation, sometimes it did not, but there were very few cases where it did not lead to jealousy and to considerable conflict between the husband and wife concerned, at least once the wronged partner had found out about it.

During the recent period the trends described in the preceding paragraph continued. Until the early 1960's, it was the rare marriage that was not plagued by sexual jealousy, especially at the start. Most individuals had had intercourse with one or more partners before they got married legally, and their legal spouses knew it. Sometimes jealousy was based on actual behavior, but the *fear* of infidelity seems to have been almost as frequent a source of marital stress. For example, a wife might nag her husband about his former girlfriends, and accuse him of continuing to have sex with them—even when he was not doing so. One man told me that his wife pestered him so much about imaginary infidelity that he felt he might just as well go ahead and indulge in it. The frequency of actual infidelity during the period was difficult to determine. In 1970 I had the distinct impression that it had decreased markedly during

the previous decade, but I did not collect enough data to corroborate my impression.

A second serious source of strain in the husband-wife relationship throughout most of the period covered by this study
was that of failure on the part of one of the spouses to meet
his or her obligations in the economic sphere. When either
spouse was especially lazy or incompetent, very hard times could
fall on a family. This was true because the division of labor
was sufficiently complete as to require major contributions on
the part of *both* spouses if a satisfactory result for *either* one
of them was to be obtained. Once a marriage survived the
initial stages, and particularly after children were involved,
incompetence became increasingly significant as a source of
stress in traditional Eskimo marriage.

During the recent period, the consequences of incompetence
were alleviated through the expansion of the welfare system
in Northwest Alaska. Before, if a *nuliaq* had not made clothes
for her family and/or had not constantly occupied herself with
clothing repairs, it would not have taken too long before the
members of her family would have been wearing nothing but
tattered strips of skin. After World War II, if the husband of
a lazy woman was sufficiently industrious himself, he could
buy the necessary clothes and pretty much eliminate the problem. Likewise, if an *ui* in olden times was too lazy or incompetent a hunter, the family could starve, the husband along with
the rest of them. But in the 1960's, if the husband was too
lazy to do anything, the wife could apply for and inevitably
get from the welfare agencies a cash income that was satisfactory by local standards, and which was certainly adequate
to prevent starvation.

Traditionally, when one spouse was lazy and the other was
working hard, marital trouble was sure to follow, first in the
form of nagging, then with the threat of separation. If the lag-
gard spouse did not rectify the situation, the threat was easy to
carry out in action. In the recent era, not only were the negative consequences of lethargy reduced, but the means of holding a spouse responsible for inactivity became greatly weakened, since separation and remarriage were not as easy as they
had been. Consequently, although laziness was still a source

Burch—Eskimo Kinsmen—7

of strain within the *nuliariik* relationship, it was rarely a cause of separation.

Disputes over child rearing were another frequent source of stress in the *ui-nuliaq* relationship, although this was probably a recent development. Spencer (1959:250), writing about the traditional period in Barrow, says that "a husband and wife agreed on child rearing without question. There is little doubt that the same methods were used in generation after generation," i. e., were traditional in character. It is probably true that the methods of child rearing were agreed upon, but it does not follow that the treatment of *specific children* was a matter of consensus.

During the intermediate and recent periods, at least, favoritism on the part of the parents for just one of their several children was a continuing source of domestic strife. Not infrequently, the preference reached a point where the special child could do virtually no wrong in that parent's eyes, while the unfavored ones could do little that was right. The two spouses rarely regarded the same child as their favorite. When one parent scolded the other's favorite, trouble ensued. For example, one man told me that every time he scolded his wife's favorite, a boy, his wife would start to cry. She would do this no matter how serious the incident for which the boy was being chastised, and I personally witnessed this child get away with behavior that was quite destructive in terms of the Eskimos' own values. Other women, who were not as passive as this one, would be more likely to lose their temper at their husband instead of simply crying. The same sort of thing happened, in reverse, when a *nuliaq* scolded her husband's favorite child.

Marital stress was exacerbated during the transitional period by two additional factors, alcoholic consumption, and the enforcement of certain United States laws. The former became a problem almost immediately upon the arrival of the whalers in Northwest Alaska, i. e., at the very outset of the transitional period (Foote 1964a:18). Drinking facilitated the violent release of tensions which had been present all along, but which had been kept under control. The tendency was increased by the fact that the Eskimos generally regarded inebriated behavior as one thing, and sober behavior as quite another. A person could be held responsible for the latter, but not for the former.

Thus, when drunk, one felt free to express hostility in ways that were scarcely conceivable when sober. And, for reasons that are not clear, hostility toward spouses, more than any other kind, seemed to be expressed under these conditions. Most wife-beating, most public altercations between husbands and wives, and, during the recent period, possibly most infidelity occurred when one or both spouses were drunk.

The enforcement of certain United States laws became a factor in marital stress, apparently during the 1930's, primarily through what is commonly known as the "shotgun wedding." Many young people were not getting legally married, and perhaps not even living together, until after the woman had become pregnant. Once a baby was on the way, there was strong motivation for the man and woman to get together voluntarily on a permanent residential basis. The pattern had evolved of developing the relationship gradually, slowing down the process from time to time (i e., temporarily separating) when the strains became too severe for the individuals to cope with. However, during this period, it became the custom to call in the U. S. Marshall to force a marriage, or to throw the child's father in jail if he refused to marry its mother. The complaint would be lodged by the teacher, the missionary, or even by the village council; it was rarely placed by the parents of the pregnant woman, or by the woman herself. Since most men preferred to stay out of jail, they had to get married, and they usually had to do so fast. When this occurred, the principals were forced to make a sudden and (also under U. S. laws) irrevocable transition to the legally married state. The resulting unions were often unstable for quite some time afterwards. During the 1950's, the representatives of the law enforcement agencies generally softened their stand on these matters, since it became clear even to them that they were not solving problems, but making them worse.

Termination

If the strains in the traditional *ui-nuliaq* relationship became too great, the residence tie was broken (*avittuq*), the initiative coming from either of the spouses. In its institutionalized form, the husband-wife relationship was not expected to contain the strains that were generated within it. If spouses were unable to adjust to one another after a time, they simply parted company, perhaps for a short period, perhaps forever.

The length of the termination depended partly on the seriousness of the strains themselves, and partly on various contextual factors. Included in the latter were such considerations as the availability of other spouses, and the support (or lack of it) from various relatives. If both the *ui* and *nuliaq* were agreed that the residence tie should be broken, the result was assured. If one of them wanted a separation but the other did not, the matter could become complicated, but usually ended in a separation anyway if the disaffected spouse was determined enough.

Heinrich (1955a:170) described the separation process as follows:

> If a woman happens to be living in her husband's house, or one belonging to his consanguinals, she simply picks up her property and leaves. If, with the above form of residence, it is the husband who wants the separation, he throws her possessions out of the house, often literally, and she will have no recourse but to go home to her consanguineal kin. If residence is with the wife or her consanguinals, then it is the husband who must get out, either of his own volition if he is the one who takes the initiative, or unwillingly, if he happens to come home and find his possessions scattered in front of the house.

That such occurrences were commonplace in the traditional period is clear from the statements of my informants, from my genealogical data, and from the literature (v. Heinrich 1955a:170ff.; Murdoch 1892:411; Simpson 1875:253). Generally, the frequency of residential separation decreased with the ages of the spouses, although the presence of young children significantly reduced the likelihood of a permanent break between spouses of any age.

During the transitional period, separation became a much more complicated matter than it had been previously. After the arrival of the missionaries and the American legal system in Northwest Alaska, there was considerable pressure against the dissolution of the residence tie, regardless of the state of a particular marriage. However the main problem was that the residential separation, alone, no longer freed a person to marry someone else. In order to legally marry a new spouse, the old one had to be legally divorced. In order to get a legal divorce, certain legal technicalities had to be observed. These required both time and money, which the Eskimos had little inclination to surrender for this particular purpose. Mere separation was still an easy matter, though, and when the strains became too much for a husband and wife to cope with, they generally parted company. A few married again without observing the legal niceties of the new system. These illegal maneuvers were greatly reduced in frequency by the 1960's, and it was only because the authorities occasionally turned their backs on what was happening that it had not stopped altogether.

The majority of the individuals in the traditional society who lived beyond young adulthood had more than one residential spouse during the course of their lifetime. Generally, only one additional spouse was involved but I recorded one instance of a man who had four different residential wives during his marital career, and one of a woman who had at least five residential husbands. The general pattern seems to have been one or two unstable unions that remained operative for a relatively brief period, followed by one that remained active for many years. The latter sometimes included people who had not been married before, but more often, they consisted of separated spouses who got back together again after a period of separation (v. Murdoch 1892:411; Ray 1885:44).

Even very stable unions were often terminated before too many years had passed by the death of one of the members. Widows and widowers were common in Eskimo villages even in the recent period, although people usually remarried unless they were well into their 60's. In one village, for example, of 28 men living there in 1965 who were or had been married at some point in their lives, eight were or had been widowers. There were also 28 women in the corresponding category, of whom four were or had been widows; one of them had been widowed twice, another three times. By all accounts, similar cases were much more frequent in traditional times, and particularly in the early transitional period (1850–1890), when life was so much more precarious than it was in the 1960's.

COMPLEX MARRIAGE

Polygamous marriage, co-marriage, and separation-and-remarriage are conveniently grouped under the heading of "complex marriage," in contrast to the "simple" residential union of one man and one woman described above. Although the *uinuliaq* relationship was found in each of these more complicated types of marital arrangement, so also were one or some combination of three others, which I refer to as the "co-spouse," "co-wife" and "co-husband" relationships. Before describing these specific relationships, however, it is appropriate to outline on a more general level the four different kinds of complex marital arrangements.

Complex Marriage Forms

Polygynous Marriages

Polygynous unions of one man and two or more resident wives were institutionalized in the traditional period, and numerous actual cases have been attested. The available data suggest that they were more frequent in the large, permanent coastal villages than elsewhere, no doubt because the wealth required to support more than one wife was more easily acquired there. Polygynous marriages have been noted, however, in all districts of Northwest Alaska.

Most polygynous marriages involved just two wives. More were theoretically possible, but rarely feasible. The infamous Aataŋauzaq, a powerful man who dominated Point Hope for many years during the latter part of the 19th century, had five wives living with him at the time of his death (Brower, n.d.; Wells and Kelly 1890:21), but this number was extraordinary. Simpson (1875:254) reported that there were only four cases of polygynous unions in each of the two villages at Barrow when he was there in the early 1850's, and Murdoch (1892:-411) counted a total of six such marriages in the same two villages some years later. Considering the fact that these settlements had populations of two hundred or more each at the time, the frequency seems to have been low even in the major villages.

The above observations make it difficult to account for Pospisil's (1964:410) claim that, among the comparatively impoverished nomads of the northern interior, the frequency of polygynous marriages was high. He reports that one of his informants in Anaktuvuk Pass estimated that, under aboriginal conditions, one out of every six marital unions was a polygynous one. This figure seems far too high, especially when contrasted with the direct observations of Simpson and Murdoch on the coast. In the Kivalina area, for example, which was a much more favorable place to live in than the mountains, I was able to document only two cases of polygyny for the last two decades of the 19th century. I cannot help but suspect that Pospisil's informant was mistaking his idealized conception of the matter for the actual situation.

It is useful to consider what the demographic possibilities might have been, since they would have set limits on possible variation in this respect. The first question concerns the sex ratio in the traditional population: did females outnumber males, was the ratio just the reverse, or was the ratio one to one? After reviewing all available data from the traditional period proper, Foote (1965:215–223) concluded that the ratio of males to females in the population was 13:12, or 52 percent male to 48 percent female. But if males slightly outnumbered females, how could one out of every six marriages be polygynous? One theoretical possibility is that there were a large number of bachelors in traditional times. However, all information bearing on the point suggests just the opposite. Bachelors were apparently extremely rare, the few men lacking co-resident wives at any given time being between spouses, not permanently without them. The demographic problem could also have been solved if polyandrous marriages had been common enough to take up the slack, i. e., if the number of polyandrous and polygynous unions had been comparable. However, as noted below, this was not the case either. Finally, there could have been a disproportionate loss of males during childhood, so that among the population of marriageable age, there would have been more females than males. But Foote's (*Ibid.*) analysis, plus considerations discussed in the next chapter, indicate that this possibility was not realized in fact. Therefore, given the available evidence, it seems reasonable to conclude that, ideals

notwithstanding, the actual frequency of polygynous marriages at any given time must have been very low in the traditional period.

Early census returns from Northwest Alaska support the
above conclusion, and extend its application to the time when
polygynous marriages were being rapidly eliminated in Northwest Alaska due to social factors. The data are presented in
Table 6, which shows the sex composition of the Eskimo popu-

TABLE 6 Sex Composition of the Eskimo Population of Northwest Alaska at Selected Periods

Period	Males	Females	Total
Traditional [a]	—— (52%)	—— (48%)	—— (100%)
1890 Census [b]	1416 (52%)	1313 (48%)	2729 (100%)
1960 Census [c]	2535 (52%)	2326 (48%)	4861 (100%)

[a] Estimates from Foote (1965:223).

[b] Data from Porter (1893:8).

[c] Data on nonwhite population in Barrow and Kobuk census districts only
(U.S.B.O.C. 1961:3–36, Table 27).

lation of Northwest Alaska at selected periods ranging across
virtually the entire time period covered by this study.[4] The
figures indicate a remarkably consistent pattern which scarcely
departs from the 52:48 ratio for a span of well over a century.
They indicate clearly that there is no demographic basis for a
high frequency of polygynous marriages in any time period
for which information is available; indeed, all available demographic data indicate a result just the opposite of that required
for such a marriage pattern.

[4] The total figures are certain to be on the low side, although they are
accurately indicative of the tremendous population decline that had occurred
in Northwest Alaska since 1850. But the point at issue here is unaffected
either by errors in the total, or by errors in "tribal designation," since the
figures presumably represent the sex composition of the population actually
observed by enumerators in Northwest Alaska.

Polyandrous Marriages

According to Heinrich (1960:119), "polyandry as an approved, structured kinship form" did not exist in Northwest Alaska. Spencer (1959:543), echoing the same theme, suggests that polyandry among the Northwest Alaskan Eskimos was more apparent than real, being in fact a matter of the "husbands allocating his sexual privileges to his friend or partner." My own data indicate that both authors are incorrect.

Actual cases of polyandrous unions have been attested in Northwest Alaska, and there definitely was a place for them. It is true, however, that they were extremely rare. This conclusion is indicated by the fact that one of the two cases I learned about was also recorded by Stefansson (1914:206) half a century earlier. Apparently the majority of the population looked on such marriages as being stupid or amusing, but that is not the same as saying that they could not or did not exist. Furthermore, with reference to Spencer's point, an Eskimo husband did not "allocate" sexual access to his wife. If any "allocating" was done, it was accomplished with at least the tacit consent of the woman involved in any situation short of rape. Abuse of the woman's rights by her husband, in this, as in other matters, was likely to result in a separation of the spouses except in the most unusual circumstances.

Polyandrous unions, although theoretically possible, were uncommon in fact because of certain overwhelming strains that were inherent in them. In the first place, given the institutionalized division of labor in the society, it would have taken an extraordinarily capable woman to be able to cope with the burdens involved in being married to two hunters. Either that, or the men involved would have to have been very poor hunters, which itself would have been a source of instability. Furthermore, the difficulties involved in giving two men equal and continuous access to one woman were considerable, especially given the high value that the Eskimos attached to male sexual prowess. The Eskimos themselves were aware of all of these problems, and simply avoided getting into what, for them would have been an obviously unsatisfactory state of affairs.

Co-Marriage

The primary form of non-residential marriage among the traditional Northwest Alaskan Eskimos was what I refer to as "co-marriage," but which is known elsewhere as "wife-exchange," "wife-trading," and "exchange-marriage," to name only the most common labels.[5] It consisted of the union of two conjugal (i. e., resident husband-wife) pairs into a larger marital unit via the mechanism of sexual intercourse between each man and the other's wife. The execution of the "exchange" which established a co-marriage varied according to the circumstances under which it occurred. One pattern was described by Heinrich (1955a:135) as follows:

> The transfer of marital partners usually lasts for a week or several weeks, but one night would be sufficient to set up the relationship. The usual procedure is for the males to exchange homes at night and return to their respective homes for the day, and again, at night, to exchange sleeping places, but one night's residence at the other's house would be acceptable.

This procedure was generally followed only when the principals all lived in a single village. However, in traditional times, co-marriages were frequently established between couples living not only in different settlements, but in altogether different societies.

There is reason to believe that the basic emphasis then may have been on co-marriages between, rather than within societies, this institution being one of the most effective alliance mechanisms the Eskimos had (Burch and Correll 1972; Correll 1972:-175, 195). Under those conditions, the setting in which the exchange occurred was quite variable. It often had to take place at a fair or messenger feast, the only two occasions on which individuals from different societies met with any regularity. In any case, once the union had been established, it continued for the lifetime of the members, regardless of whether or not sexual relations that established it were ever repeated.

5 For other analyses of and information on co-marriage in Northwest Alaska, see Burch (1970b), Green (1959:45ff.), Gubser (1965:67–68), Heinrich (1955a:133–140; 1955b:79, 80; 1960:115; 1963a:80–83), Hennigh (1970), Pospisil (1964:410–411), and Spencer (1959:83–84; 1968).

A variety of factors leading to co-marriage have been suggested (v. Guemple 1961:23ff.). The most common is that it was a purely lustful arrangement decided upon by the men, without regard for their wive's feelings on the matter. With respect to this position, it is difficult to argue with Guemple (1961:26) when he says that *if* a purely hedonistic explanation of the institution was tenable, then

> we should be hard put to explain the fact that exchange relationships, once brought into being, remain intact throughout the lifetime of the principals and their descendents *whether or not sexual relations are periodically renewed.* (italics his)

Furthermore, as Heinrich (1955a:135) has shown, "any of the four people primarily involved can initiate the union, and any of the four people that would enter into the union can prevent its occurrence." In its ideal form, a co-marriage was established as a *permanent union* with the mutual understanding and consent of *all four* participants. The sexual relations simply got it started.

Rainey (1947:242) reported that the "old women say that they did not like wife exchange." It is true that there were cases in which women were pretty much bullied into a co-marriage by their husbands. But, to conclude that this pattern was general is to ignore certain facts. The most important of these is that there were strict limits on how far a wife could be pushed around by her husband before she simply packed up and left him. Also, there are known cases where the wives were the major initiating force behind a co-marriage. I suspect that Rainey's informants, who were probably speaking through an interpreter, felt that they could not say anything else to a member of a society in which such a practice is so overwhelmingly frowned upon, regardless of how they actually felt. It might also be true that Rainey's informants, who had long since become Christians, might have looked back with sincere distaste on practices that they had thoroughly enjoyed many years previously.

Another motive for engaging in co-marriage was suggested by Spencer (1959:84), who said that it frequently supplemented the ties already existing between "partners" (*niuviriik*), a conclusion in which Gubser (1965:67) concurs. This position seems eminently plausible to me, yet my own informants in several districts absolutely denied any connection between the two. Since I had already read Spencer's repeated references to the double connection, I pursued the point at some length in the field. As far as my informants were concerned however, partnership and co-marriage did not mix, either conceptually or concretely.

Gubser (1965:68) proposed a third possibility. He says that the specific act of exchange marriage "was regarded as a vacation—a source of diversion and relief from the ennui of months of trapping and hunting or sewing and collecting firewood." Heinrich (1955a:133) apparently agreed with this view when he said that exchange marriage served "as a tension reducing device, as a vehicle for reducing some of the interpersonal psychological problems that would naturally crop up in closely knit communities." Unfortunately, this explanation does not account for the fact that the union persisted even when sexual relations were never repeated. It indicates why sexual activities might be indulged in from time to time in an *already existing relationship,* but I find it an inadequate explanation of why such a union would be established in the first place. A co-marriage imposed many important obligations on the individuals involved in it, and I doubt that many people would have been willing to assume them just for a bit of recreation.

Ray (1885:44) raised another possibility when he said that "when a man is obliged to take a long trip and his wife from any cause is unable to accompany him, he will exchange (her) with some friend who has an able-bodied wife, each entering upon their new relations with the greatest cheerfulness." Similar situations were reported by Murdoch (1892:413), Spencer (1959:84), and my informants. Once again, however, because of the mutual obligations that devolved upon co-spouses, it seems likely that this explanation would more adequately account for the activation of already existing co-marital relationships than for the establishment of new ones. Nevertheless, if the people involved were all good friends in the first place, the need for a capable woman on a long trip may have acted as a precipitating stimulus for a co-marital union.

A fifth factor was suggested by my informants, and, was emphasized by them. They pointed out that in the old days, a

person without kinsmen was a person whose days were numbered; the people in the traditional period were acutely aware of
this fact.   Co-marriage was just about the best way in which
people could increase the number of their relatives in a short
period of time.   Paul Green (1959:45), himself an Eskimo from
Northwest Alaska, put it this way:

> In early days ago, Eskimo change wife in Arctic of Alaska
> to make big family and have lots of relatives. Suppose, here,
> man and wife from Kotzebue and man and wife from Point
> Hope. Them men they exchange wife, they agree everything
> among themself, and they claim their children just like one
> family. And when them children grow up, parents told their
> children they have half brother or half sister at Point Hope
> or Kotzebue.

This account supports my contention that co-marriages were
more common between societies than within them, although in-
tra-societal arangements did exist.   In traditional times, co-
marriages seemed to have functioned primarily as inter-regional
alliances, created and maintained through the mechanism of
kin relationships.

Co-marriage came under immediate attack from the missionaries and other Whites when the new social order began to be
instituted in Northwest Alaska, between about 1890 and 1910.
It quickly changed from an overt to a covert custom, and eventually died out—at least in its traditional form.   Some interesting traces of co-marriage still remained in 1970, however.
I refer here to the phenomenon that I call "involuntary co-
marriage" or "co-marriage by default."   This occurred when one
man engaged in clandestine sexual relations with another man's
wife, thus establishing between them the co-spouse relationship
without the consent or knowledge of their respective residential
spouses.   From the modern point of view, this was simply marital infidelity; from a more traditional point of view, it was
more complicated.

Casual sexual liaisons between adults could not be kept secret in a small village for very long, especially if they were
repeated with any frequency and/or over any length of time.
The interesting part came when the spouses who were being
"two-timed" found out about it.   The jilted spouses were faced

with a three-pronged dilemma, the alternatives being those of rejecting, ignoring, or accepting the situation. If they rejected it, they could find themselves suddenly without a residential spouse. If they ignored it, they were likely to find themselves appearing as fools in the eyes of the community as a whole. If they accepted the situation, however, they could find themselves thrust into an ancient form of relationship requiring close cooperation, but with a person of whom they were extremely jealous.

Cases of rejection were the most obvious to the outside observer, because a great deal of heat was usually generated, with wife beating, fistfights, and protests to the village council. Sometimes the relationship between "co-spouses" was so strong that either or both of them threatened to divorce their residential spouses if they made any objection. If the jilted spouse was not very fond of his (or her) husband (or wife), separation often followed. Often, however, such a threat caused him (or her) to remain silent about the whole thing, even though he (or she) was deeply upset by it.

Cases of acceptance were the most interesting from the viewpoint of the present discussion. In terms of frequency they apparently fell somewhere between the ignoring and rejecting alternatives. They are very difficult to explain as anything but *de facto* cases of co-marriage. For example, in one case I know of, it is certain that the husband did not father one of his wife's children, and, for various reasons, there was little doubt about the identity of the real father. Everyone in the village knew who the genitor was, although the husband claimed that the child was really his own. His wife's "boyfriend" however, was extremely affectionate and attentive toward this child, which everyone could see. It just so happens that he and the husband got along very well together too, the "boyfriend" frequently helping the husband in a variety of activities. This looked suspiciously like a co-husband relationship in action, and it was not a unique case.

More frequent was the situation where three, but not all four of the parties in the "involuntary co-marriage" situation fully accepted it. One of my informants told me of a case he was personally involved in.

Informant: One time when Henry and I was drinking, we talk about that, and what I did to his wife before.   So I tell him, "You'd better go over to my wife and do the same thing."   So he try, alright, but my wife sent him away. When he come back he said he's scared of my wife.

Anthropologist: What would you have done if he had gone to bed with her?

Informant: I wouldn't say nothing, just because I did it first myself.

Anthropologist: Did you send him over when you were staying in his house?

Informant: Yeah!   His wife and I was laugh and laugh at him that time!

Here we see a case of acceptance on the part of everyone but one of the wives, her solution being to ignore the situation (of which she was fully aware).   This particular union was not always so calm, though.   For years, the husband of the "girlfriend" had been violently opposed to her relationship with my informant. Gradually he came around, and by the time that I came to know them the two were extremely close friends—true co-husbands.

Separation-and-Remarriage

The second way in which a non-residential marriage was created was when one spouse left the other and married someone else.   The critical factor here was the traditional Eskimo notion that all kin relationships, marital or otherwise, were permanent.   A relationship could be inactive for long periods of time, but in their view, there was no such thing as a complete dissolution of any kinship tie.   Thus, separation (*avittuq*) in the traditional Eskimo sense, meant the breaking of the residence tie, not (necessarily) the end of the relationship *per se*. The husband-wife bond so affected then moved into another stage, which Heinrich (1963a:80) has called "marriage in lesser degree."   When the separated individuals remarried, which they virtually always did, they retained the connection with their first spouse, but added another husband-wife relationship to it.

When separated Eskimos married new partners, they did not lose *any* of the connections they had established through their first marriage. Instead, they added a whole new set of relationships to the first (Heinrich 1972). Furthermore, the two men involved, the first and the second husband of the same woman, automatically became co-husbands; the first and second wives of the same man became co-wives; and finally, the offspring of the first and second marriages became *qataŋutigiit*, or co-siblings. In each of these respects, separation and remarriage produced a set of relationships identical to those occurring in the other forms of complex marriage. Although these relationships sometimes lay dormant for years, they were always there in theory, and they could be activated whenever the individuals involved chose to do so.

Co-Wives

The "co-wife", or *aipariik* relationship, was the most common of the three relationships resulting from complex marriages. It obtained between any two women who had ever had sexual intercourse with the same man. Normally, it occurred in three different contexts: (1) between the two (or more) women in a polygynous residential marriage, (2) between the two women in a co-marriage, and (3) between the two women in a separation-and-remarriage. The content, strength and sentiment of the relationship varied somewhat according to the particular context in which it occurred.

In the non-residential context, the content of the *aipariik* relationship was so vaguely defined as to preclude detailed specification. A woman was expected to "help" and "support" her *aipaq* (singular) but the precise details were left to the discretion of the parties concerned in any concrete situation. With respect to sentiment, the relationship was institutionalized as one involving intense positive affect on the part of both members. Informants repeatedly stressed that co-wives were "supposed to love each other," and that in the ideal case, they were to be "just like one woman." The relationship was apparently relatively unrestrained, and co-wives were expected to engage in active conversation, gossip, and mild joking with one another (v. Pospisil 1964:403), at least when the husband(s) was (were) not present.

The most interesting aspect of the *aipaq-aipaq* relationship was its strength. It ranked behind the ties to consanguineal relatives, but apparently was stronger than the *ui-nuliaq* (husband-wife) relationship, and it definitely took precedence over the relationship between co-spouses. The relationship of co-wives seems ideally to have taken precedence over all other relationships except those between consanguineal kin.

The ideals of *aipariik* were most closely approached when the relationship was established through a co-marriage. In the case of separation-and-remarriage, the relationship was often inactive. This means that, although the relationship was there in theory, and although the mutual assistance and support obligations were still incumbent on the women involved, the members simply had little or nothing to do with each other. Under normal conditions this was expected; under crisis conditions, the women were supposed to help each other regardless of their feelings.

In the polygynous context, the content of the co-wife relationship was defined to a much greater extent than it was in the other two situations.[6] This is perhaps to be expected, since polygynous co-wives always lived in the same household, hence were in continuous contact with one another. In other marital situations, *aipariik* might come together only occasionally, if at all.

There was a clear-cut division of labor between residential co-wives. The first wife, the *nuliaqpak* of the husband, was normally in charge of the children. The second wife, the husband's *nukarak*, was left to do practically all of the rest of the work, i. e., the cooking, sewing, wood gathering, butchering, and all the other work that fell to women in the traditional period. The *aipariik* relationship was also a hierarchical one in this context, the second wife being subordinate to the first. When the first wife gave an order, the second was expected to obey it. Ideally, the *nuliaqpak* was supported by the husband in case of a dispute with the *nukarak*. The differential allocation of authority was supposed to obtain regardless of the relative ages of the women concerned.

[6] For additional information on the co-wife relationship in the polygynous context, see Gubser (1965:67), Pospisil (1964:411), Ray (1885:44), Simpson (1875:252), and Woolfe (1893:134–135).

Despite the hierarchical nature of the relationship, both women were expected to treat each other's children exactly as they did their own. The children normally called both women "mother," and both women referred to one another's children as "daughter" or "son." Aldrich (1889:33) even claimed that, "should two wives have children about the same time, they nurse either one, whether it be their own or not."

The strains in the *aipariik* relationship were often considerable in the polygynous setting. Abuse of her authority by the first wife, or disobedience by the second, would lead to trouble, as would mistreatment of each other's children. One of my informants, who grew up in a polygynous household, told me what could happen:

When we stayed above Uivaq, near Cape Lisburne, that's the time my father was sick. We had a hard time on food. My father had a younger brother living with us, but he was not a very good hunter. This is while I was a little kid. My mother, the *nukarak*, was the cook for the family. And one time her *aipaq*, named *Kuunruq*, said that when my mother cooked she always hid some of the meat. Then she told my mother not to feed me anymore. (I was so young that my mother was still packing me on her back that time.) My mother was very sorry that *Kuunruq* didn't want me to be fed; and anyway she had never taken anything without asking first. And she started to worry about me. When she looked around, everything was handy to steal all the time, but she never took anything. She never took anything without asking the owner about it. But then the family found about *Kuunruq*. She had taken some meat for herself one time when she was cooking, and she blamed my mother for it. My mother never let me off from her back that time, because she was afraid for me. Later she told me that whenever she started to talk, I would reach around with my hand and grab her mouth because I was so hungry; I guess I thought she was chewing food to give to me. That's the way my mother took care of me, and I got through it all right. When my father got well again, we started to move north, and *Kuunruq* started to babysit for me again.

Many other stories about jealously and intrigue between co-resident *aipariik* were cited by my informants. It seems that, in this context, the ideal patterns of the relationship were often honored in the breach, particularly during hard times.

The open, active relationship of co-wives, in any of its forms, was a thing of the past by the 1940's. Like all of the institutions of complex marriage, it began to disappear early under the impact of White influence. Sometimes the missionaries persuaded men to "divorce" one of their wives, but more often, one wife would die in an epidemic, and she simply would not be replaced (v. Johnshoy 1944:159).

Covert cases of *aipariik* still existed in Northwest Alaska as late as 1970, but only in highly restricted circumstances. Some of the older people continued to operate in terms of co-wife relationships established many years previously, but any individuals so related were obliged for a number of reasons to keep secret the nature of their association. On the surface they were just "friends." The few active relationships of this sort which I learned about were established through co-marriage. Polygynous unions had been non-existent for many years, and I never heard of any ties established in this context still in existence in 1970.

Co-Husbands

The relationship between *nuliaqatigiik*, or "co-husbands," existed between any two men who had ever had sexual intercourse with the same woman. Like the relationship of co-wives, this one occurred in three different contexts: (1) between the two (or more) men in a polyandrous marriage; (2) between the two men in a co-marriage, and (3) between the two men in a "divorce" and remarriage.

The relationship of co-husbands was more difficult for me to get information on than any other in the entire Eskimo kinship system. Part of the problem stemmed from the fact that there were almost no concrete instances of this relationship in a polyandrous context even in traditional times. Furthermore, the relationship seems to have been inactive in the context of separation-and-remarriage in the majority of cases, which leaves co-marriage as the only situation in which active *nuliaqatigiik* relationships operated with any frequency. Here, the relationship seems to have been functionally diffuse to such an extent as to be nearly devoid of any prescribed content. Like its female analogue, the co-husband relationship involved "friendship," "assistance," and "support," three vague prescriptions that could mean a wide variety of things in specific cases.

The Northwest Alaskan Eskimos had an active sense of humor, one often tinged with a finely honed blade of cynicism. If one asked an Eskimo informant to tell how people "should" act in a given situation, one was likely to be told that there is no sense talking about *that* because people never behave as they are supposed to anyway. Nowhere in my experience was this cynicism more apparent than in the case of the co-husband relationship, especially when men were talking about it. Consider the following excerpt from an interview:

> *Anthropologist*: How are *nuliaqatigiik* supposed to be to each other?
>
> *Informant*: Well, they should love each other [laughter] and help each other. That's the way some of them used to do. But sometimes they hate each other too [laughter].
>
> *Anthropologist*: But are the good ones supposed to love each other?
>
> *Informant*: Yeah! When a man agrees with another man about that, and they become *nuliaqan*, they should love each other like brothers, and the kids call each other "brothers" and "sisters."

At least two points are apparent in the above exchange. The first of these is that my informant did not think that the ideal was very often realized, as indicated by his laughter. The second, more important point, is that he felt that the relationship was supposed to involve considerable intensity and strength —it was just "like brothers."

My analysis of the co-husband relationship is based partly on such brief exchanges as the one cited above, and partly on the assumption that it paralleled in at least its general characteristics the relationship between co-wives. On this basis, I conclude that the relationship was functionally diffuse, responsible, and relatively unrestrained. Whether it was egalitarian or hierarchical I simply cannot say. The relationship was ideally a strong one, probably the equivalent of that between co-wives,

MARITAL RELATIONSHIPS   **117**

perhaps even stronger. Documented cases of this relationship were extremely strong, but the sample is small.

Most of the remarks made about the co-wife relationship in the recent period apply to co-husbands. The only difference is the extent to which cases of infidelity led to active, positive, co-husband relationships. Men apparently considered ignoring such situations as an unacceptable alternative. They either lost their temper and caused a lot of trouble, or they established close ties with the other man involved. Sometimes they did both, but in sequence. That is, they lost their tempers first, but subsequently established positive relations. On the surface, instances of the latter seemed to be unexceptional cases of friendship, which is just how those concerned wanted them to appear.

Co-Spouses

The *nuliizariik*, or co-spouse relationship, involved couples who had sexual intercourse *outside* the context of permanent residential affiliation. In traditional times, this intercourse ideally took place only in the context of co-marriage. More recently, it also occurred in what I call "co-marriage by default." As described above, this occurred when an individual had sexual relations with someone else's spouse without the permission of either co-residence spouse; it amounted to only half of the institutionalized co-marriage.

The sexual intercourse involved in the co-spouse relationship differed from that in the relationship between residential spouses with respect to both objectives and procedure. In the co-spouse (*nuliizariik*) relationship, the sex act *per se*, not the production of children, was the primary focus of the individuals concerned. Accordingly, intercourse between co-spouses involved greater activity and pleasure than it did in the case of *ui* and *nuliaq*. Whereas the *nuliaq* was generally a passive sexual partner for her husband, the *nuliizaq* was not. She frequently took the initiative in getting things going, kissing and hugging her partner (the *uiŋuzaq*), and sometimes manipulating his genitals. Even before they had progressed to the gradually increasing physiological stimulation that culminated with intercourse, co-spouses characteristically talked together for some time. Such behavior was rare between an *ui* and a *nuliaq*.

One informant described the difference to me as follows:

> When I had a *nuliizaq* myself, I never do it right away. I
> just talk to her, and talk, and pretty soon, when she gets real
> lively, I ask about it. When I try to kiss her, and she starts
> to be real kindly when I start to kissing at her, that's the
> time I catch it quick! But my wife—we never do anything.
> I never try to make her lively. She'll be ready anytime, just
> when I want to do it myself.

Sex was an exciting experience in the context of the co-spouse
relationship, but a commonplace event between *ui* and *nuliaq*;
it was executed accordingly by the individuals involved.

The content of the co-spouse relationship was minimal outside the sexual context. Also except for sexual intercourse, it
was very vaguely defined. In traditional times, of course, the
members usually derived from different societies—or at least
from different communities in the same society—so they did
not even see each other very often. But even when they happened to be in the same community, it was the two men, on the
one hand, and the two women on the other, who spent most of
the time together, the former in the *qazgi* or out hunting, the
latter remaining behind in the house. The content of the relationship was no greater in the case of "co-marriage by default," since in this context the members attempted to keep the
connection a secret, or they tried to ignore it, or they were not
even aware of its existence.

The sentiment institutionalized in the co-spouse relationship
was positive, and often relatively intense. My information
is limited on this score, but what I have suggests that the emotions with which this relationship was imbued were often greater than those characterizing the residential spouse relationship. It would appear that this relationship was one in which
the cliché, "absence makes the heart grow fonder," had some
meaning. In public, co-spouses had to be just as circumspect
in expressing their sentiments as *nuliariik*. In private, however,
they were less restrained, often engaging in animated conversation, and caressing and nuzzling one another.

Ideally, the co-spouse relationship was a very weak one, certainly weaker than that of residential spouses, and probably the
weakest in the entire Northwest Alaskan Eskimo kinship sys-

tem. This meant that whenever there was a conflict, one's obligation to every other type of relative, including one's residential spouse, had to take precedence over one's obligations to the co-spouse.

The contrast between the relatively great emotional intensity on the one hand, and the institutionalized weakness on the other, was a source of instability. When the discrepancy became too severe, conflicts between residential spouses particularly, but also between co-husbands and co-wives, sometimes led to what might be called "co-marital separation." In other words, the two conjugal pairs simply had nothing more to do with one another. Another possibility was for one of the two residential couples to separate, with one set of co-spouses becoming residential spouses, and the remaining man and woman going their separate ways. A third possibility was for *both* of the co-spouse relationships in a co-marriage to become imbued with significantly greater intensity of sentiment than *either* of the residential spouse ties. In this case, the "exchange" could be made permanent (v. Murdoch 1892:413; Spencer 1959:84). Under such circumstances a former *nuliizaq* would become the *nuliaq*, and the role of *nuliizaq* would disappear. This procedure was a very straightforward way of bringing the actual situation back into line with the ideal one simply by re-assigning roles among the individuals involved; it was a procedure that was characteristically Eskimo, and apparently rather common in traditional times.

The co-spouse relationship nearly disappeared as an institutionalized marriage form in Northwest Alaska after the turn of the twentieth century. A few relationships originally established in terms of traditional patterns were still in existence in 1970 between people then well along in years. They perforce operated as co-spouses only in secret, and were presented to the world, including other Eskimos, as something else altogether. For the most part, the *nuliizariik* relationship degenerated into "co-marriage by default" during the recent period, and was rapidly changing into the Eskimo equivalent of an "extra-marital affair." As such, the relationship had lost its traditional significance, and the terms *uiŋuzaq* ("boyfriend") and *nuliizaq* ("girlfriend") had acquired pejorative connotations.

*

4

Other – Generation Relationships

"Other-generation relationships" is a convenient label with which to designate the entire set of bonds connecting kinsmen of different generations. These included the parent-child, nepotic, grandparent-grandchild, and parent-in-law–child-in-law ties. Each of these general categories, in turn, was further divided into several specific patterns in terms of which individuals interacted.

To analyse all the other-generation relationships in a single chapter is more than just a descriptive convenience. Grouping the relationships concerned in this way highlights the feature of the Eskimo system known as "substitutability" (Heinrich 1963a:71ff., 100ff.).

Substitutability is the process by which individuals lacking a certain top priority relationship in their network of kinsmen could fill the gap by substituting a lower priority relative in the vacant position. For example, someone without any siblings might recruit a cousin to interact with him on a sibling basis. Through this mechanism, the Northwest Alaskan Eskimos were able to keep the realities of their social world reasonably close to the ideal pattern by employing what was basically a fictive kinship procedure.

Heinrich (*Ibid.*), the only other writer to note the phenomenon of substitutability, focused his attention exclusively on relationships within the same generation, and within the consanguineal sphere. In fact, substitutability occurred also in the realm of other-generation consanguineal relationships, and it even affected affinal relationships under certain conditions. Same-generation consanguineal changes were certainly the most common form of substitution, but they were not the only ones; and they were not necessarily the most important ones either.

PARENT–CHILD RELATIONSHIPS

The core of the other-generation category consisted of the parent-child relationships. They were basic in two respects. First, and most obviously, parent-child relationships had to exist before any of the others could exist. Second, and less obviously, the parent-child relationships were the top priority ones for which others were substituted. When a person's father was living in some other district, or after he died, an uncle or grandfather, or perhaps a father-in-law, would typically fill in to discharge the missing functions *vis á vis* affected individual. If a person's mother died or lived elsewhere, an aunt or grandmother, or possibly a mother-in-law would act as surrogate. Through this process, until one reached an age when members of older generations were all dead, one normally had either parents or parent-substitutes living in close proximity virtually all of the time. Similarly, if one's children were all dead or living elsewhere, one recruited a child-substitute from among one's nieces, nephews, or grandchildren, or, to a lesser extent, one's children-in-law. Thus, by one process or another, the parent-child pattern characterized at least some relationships in virtually every local group in aboriginal Northwest Alaska.

Membership

A parent-child relationship was known as *qitunrariik* (dual). At the level of analysis employed here, there were four such relationships: (1) *aapa-irniq* (father-son), (2) *aapa-panik* (father-daughter), (3) *aaka-irniq* (mother-son), and (4) *aaka-panik* (mother-daughter).

Every traditional *nuliariik* relationship that was active for any length of time had children accruing to it. If no children were born biologically to a couple, they were adopted, or else the spouses would separate (v. Thornton 1931:64). Childless couples, in the literal sense of husbands and wives who never had offspring (through either procreation or adoption) simply did not exist among the traditional Eskimos, and they were still very rare in the recent period (post-1940).

In addition to "same-family" children, most traditional Eskimo couples had one or more sets of "other-family" children (Heinrich 1963a:153). These consisted of children who had been adopted out, as well as the offspring of plural marriages, co-marriages, and separation-and-remarriages. All of the individuals recruited through one or another of these means operated in terms of one of the same four basic patterns.

Procreation

Traditionally, a Northwest Alaskan Eskimo child entered the world in stark surroundings, primarily because of the extensive taboo restrictions surrounding birth. Typically, a small hut—a snow house in winter, a tent in summer—was built some distance away from the family dwelling. When her time came, the prospective mother had to move into the hut and give birth to her child without help from anyone (v. Brower n. d.:380; Nelson 1899:289). In the case of a first-born, more experienced women would coach her some time beforehand, and they might stand outside the hut for moral support; but inside, the mother was always alone. The dietary and other taboos associated with the event were voluminous.

The ideal pattern was modified when the people concerned were travelling, but it was still adhered to as closely as possible. When the pains indicated that birth was imminent, a hole was hastily scooped out of a snowbank and lined with skins, or else a tent was erected. When the party was travelling on foot, it might continue on its way, leaving the woman on her own. Stoney (1900:70) described an instance in which a group travelled another three miles after leaving an expectant mother in a hole in the snowbank; that evening, the woman walked into camp with her baby, having received no help whatsoever during the entire process.

The traditional approach to childbirth was a severe strain on the mother. Accordingly, it was abandoned readily under the influence of teachers and missionaries (v. Nelson 1899:289). Knapp (1905:877) reported that some women in Point Hope were still having children in parturition huts as late as 1905, but by 1910, the practice had virtually ceased in most districts. Subsequently, female relatives, and even husbands, were allowed to help, as were other, more experienced women, if needed. In the 1930's, a few women in most villages were trained as midwives, and from that time on, one or two such women were normally present during childbirth.

With the more recent establishment of modern hospitals in the larger towns—Barrow, Kotzebue, and Nome—the Public Health Service tried to get all women to come to the hospital to have at least their first child (v. Chance 1966:20). In the 1960's, all women who were anticipating complications of any kind were taken to the hospital. Pre-natal care was still not up to general American standards, though, especially in the villages. This was partly because the Public Health Service could not get all the pregnant women into town for the necessary check-ups, and partly because a villager's diet was usually deficient in various respects. However, in 1970, it was a rare normal pregnancy that resulted in the death of either the mother or the child at childbirth.

Numbers

Traditionally, the Northwest Alaskan Eskimos wanted to have as many children as they could. Despite the ideal, the average number of children per conjugal pair throughout the entire 19th century seems to have been just two, with the range being one to three (v. Foote 1964b:2; 1965:205; Jenness 1957: 172; Murdoch 1892:38–39; Nelson 1899:29; Petroff 1884:12; Ray 1885:44; Rosse 1883:34; Simpson 1875:254; Stefansson 1956; Thornton 1931:150; Woolfe 1893:137). Since having children was highly valued in the traditional scheme of things, it is important to understand why they actually had so few.

The conclusion that traditional family size was small is based on the number of (living) children actually seen by early observers; it had nothing to do with birth rate itself. Statistics on the latter are lacking, but Stefansson (1956) was under the impression that this figure too was relatively low, one birth about every three years for each woman being the norm. My own data support this view. It is important to determine whether the apparent low rate was a result of conscious planning on the part of the adults involved, or whether it was due to factors beyond their control.

The Northwest Alaskan Eskimos had very few means of birth control in traditional times. According to my informants, they failed to employ even those techniques, such as *coitus interruptus*, available to them (v. Anderson and Eells 1935:177; Chance 1966:19), although both Howe (1909:453) and Stefansson (1914:201) claim that abortion through violent massage was practiced. Stefansson (1956) attributed the low birth rate to the fact that the Eskimo mothers did not wean their children for several years, a custom that apparently reduces the frequency of ovulation even if it does not prevent it altogether. Another possibility is that the frequency of spontaneous abortion during the first few hours or days of pregnancy may have been unusually high in traditional times due to the heavy physical labor that constituted part of every woman's daily activities.

The number of *living* children could have been limited by infanticide. Weyer (1962:131ff.) claims that this technique of population control was practiced by Eskimos generally, and it had been well documented (Balikci 1967; 1970:147ff.) for at least the Netsilik Eskimo population of Northern Canada. The critical question for the present study, however, is whether or not infanticide was practiced in Northwest Alaska; if it was, to what extent, and on what basis?

Infanticide was definitely practiced in Northwest Alaska; my informants and the literature (Howe 1909:453; Jenness 1957:41, 139; Klengenberg 1932:320; Simpson 1875:250; Spencer 1959:-87, 92; Stuck 1920:250) attest to that fact. The extent to which it was practiced is another matter, however, and documented cases of successful infanticides are extremely rare (v. Seeman 1853:66; Thornton 1931:25). Most of the time both the literature and my informants cited cases of *attempted* infanticide, but most of them were attempts that failed. Indeed, at least three of my informants claimed to have been the subject of infanticide efforts by their parents, but each had managed to live for more than seventy years despite that fact.

How can one fail to kill a newborn baby if he really wants to do the job? Obviously, one could not fail, which suggests that the Northwest Alaskan Eskimos did not go about it very seriously. Instead, they used something of the "baby-on-the-doorstep" approach so often depicted in cartoons. They would wrap the baby in skins, and leave it near a trail, or another settlement. If no one found it, the baby died. If someone did find it, on the other hand, the chances were good that they would take it, and either keep it themselves or give it to some other couple. The most common form of "failure" in infanticide attempts seems to have been of this type.[1] The second type of "failure" was a change of heart on the part of the parent, or perhaps on the part of some other relative who was present at the time.

Infanticide seems to have been successful in a high proportion of cases *only* when starvation was general in a district. It was rare even then, being regarded by the people themselves as an unfortunate means of coping with disaster by eliminating a strain on their meagre resources. It was *not* a deliberate means of limiting population size, but a technique of family survival (cf. Freeman 1971b).

In sum, the small number of children which characterized the traditional Northwest Alaskan Eskimo family was apparently a function of non-social factors. Foremost among these probably was a low birth rate, and a high infant mortality rate due to natural causes. Planned fertility control was probably uncommon. Population reduction through infanticide was sufficiently rare as to have little or no effect on average family size.

Women began to have larger families during the intermediate period (1890–1940) than they had had previously despite the fact that they continued the traditional practice of delayed weaning. The change appears to have started about the time the population became relatively sedentarized around school/mission villages (although there are not enough data to demonstrate this definitively). However, substantial numbers of people still died before

---

[1] Interestingly, an unsuccessful attempt to kill a baby did not necessarily terminate the relationship between that child and its parents. Informants who were subjected to attempted infanticide, but who were found and kept by other adults, subsequently learned who their real parents were and interacted with them as "other-family children."

they had children of their own (v. VanStone 1962:130).   The rise in the birth rate was so dramatic, however, that the average number of live offspring per conjugal pair began to creep upwards anyway; a poor 50% survival rate still would leave 6 children out of twelve live births, or twice the number of a large conjugal family in traditional times.

The most dramatic upsurge in the birth rate did not come until the recent period, probably not until the Public Health Service had substantially reduced the hazards of tuberculosis in the late 1950's (v. Chance 1966:17).   By 1960, the percentage of the population under 20 years of age had increased to 57%, up from an estimated 43% in 1910.[2]   In 1964–65, it was a rare woman over 30 years of age who did not have six living children, and many had a lot more than that (v. Chance 1966:19).   Some women in their twenties at that time faced the very real prospect of having fifteen or twenty *living* children by the time they finished their procreative activities.   Only systematically applied birth control techniques could have reversed such a trend.

Birth control information and materials began to be distributed quietly by the Public Health Service during the early 1960's.   By 1970 they were available to every native woman who requested them.   As a consequence, the decade of the 1960's witnessed what might be called a "fertility revolution" in Northwest Alaska (cf. Freeman 1971a).   The change is clearly indicated in the crude birth rate figures of the period 1950–1970; these are presented in Table 7, where they are compared with the average for the United States as a whole.

The figures presented in Table 7 indicate two important birth rate characteristics in the population during the relevant time period.   The first is the very high birth rate in this area compared to the United States generally, the Northwest Alaskan rate being approximately double the national rate for most of the period.   The second important characteristic is the remarkable drop in the birth rate during the 1960's.   In 1968 and 1969 the crude birth rate in Northwest Alaska was more than 50% lower than it had been just a decade earlier, and it was even beginning to approach the rate for the nation as a whole.

[2] The 1960 figures are based on data in U. S. Bureau of the Census (1961:3–36, Table 27).   The 1910 figures are based on data in U.S.B.O.C. (1913:1137).

TABLE 7   Birth Rates, 1950–1970:   Northwest Alaska
(compared with U. S. total)

Calendar Year	Northwest Alaska [a] Births per 1000 Population	United States [b] Births per 1000 Population	N.A. % of National Rate
1950	46.7	24.1	194
1951	48.4	24.9	194
1952	47.0	25.1	187
1953	45.9	25.0	184
1954	47.0	25.3	186
1955	50.8	25.0	203
1956	49.2	25.2	195
1957	49.2	25.3	194
1958	49.7	24.5	203
1959	49.5	24.0	206
1960	47.9	23.7	202
1961	44.4	23.3	191
1962	45.3	22.4	202
1963	41.5	21.7	191
1964	41.3	21.0	197
1965	43.0	19.4	222
1966	36.8	18.4	200
1967	31.6	17.8	178
1968	24.4	17.5	139
1969	22.9	17.7	129
1970	27.2	18.2	149

[a] Data from Rogers (1971:17).

[b] Data for 1950 through 1956 (U. S. Bureau of the Census 1960:23); for 1957 through 1962 (U.S.B.O.C. 1965:4); for 1963 through 1968 (U.S.B.O.C. 1970b:48); for 1969 and 1970 (National Center for Health Statistics 1971:1).

Rogers (1971:10) claims that the drop in the birth rate in the 1960's "can be attributed to public programs which had this as their objective," but he expresses surprise that the "programs appear to have had such immediate and dramatic results." The results are not surprising to me, however, because the most striking feature of this "revolution" was that the major impetus came from the Eskimos themselves.

The Public Health Service made birth control programs available, but the Eskimos made them work. During the early 1960's many Public Health Service personnel in Northwest Alaska were *extremely* hesitant to promote or even offer a birth control program, because they had tried it earlier on some Indian reservations in the Continental United States, and had been vehemently attacked there for "trying to wipe out the Indian population." Embittered by that experience, the doctors were very cautious in Alaska. But the Eskimos, particularly the women, were ready for birth control, and accepted it readily. Significantly, a major factor in the success of the program seems to have been the support of older women. Many of them put considerable pressure on their daughters to limit the size of their families—they did not want their daughters to have as many children as they had had themselves. Six living children were enough in any family, the older women argued, and their daughters apparently agreed.

Adoption

Adoption was widespread among the traditional Northwest Alaskan Eskimos, and it was still relatively common during the recent period (v. Gubser 1965 :146, 155; Heinrich 1955a :149, 150; Jenness 1918 :95; Milan 1964 :62; Murdoch 1892 :419; Spencer 1959:74, 91). In traditional times particularly, the practice functioned to distribute children in such a way that the mean, the median, and the mode figures for the number of children living with each conjugal pair were probably virtually identical, namely two.

When an Eskimo child was adopted, it became a full-fledged member of the adopting family. At the same time it continued to retain *all* its connections with the family into which it was born. Incest taboos applied to both sets of kin. For these reasons, a child adopted out became an "other-family" offspring of the donor family. The child would have two sets of parents, a real set of "other-family" parents and an adopting set of "same-family" parents.

The Eskimos commonly adopted children already related to them. Until well into the recent period, they *always* adopted the offspring of people *known* to them. Most frequent were adoptions by grandparents in the Eskimo sense of that term, i. e., by consanguineal relatives of the second ascending generation (regardless of whether they were lineal kin or not). The most common pattern seems to have been for relatively young grandparents whose own children were at or approaching maturity to adopt their first grandchild, the child simply staying with them when its parents decided to move out of their household. Adoption by relatives other than grandparents was also common, particularly by same-generation consanguines who apparently were not going to have any living children of their own.

A child who was adopted by people who were already related to him became connected to them in terms of two (or more) relationships simultaneously. As far as the principals were concerned, the initial connection was always replaced by the appropriate parent-child relationships, thus strengthening the tie between the individuals concerned (v. Dunning 1964). For the other relatives, the resulting relationships were amenable to a certain amount of manipulation. The final solutions were usually the ones most appropriate to the relative ages, sexes, and generations of the people involved, regardless of the facts. There were many possible variations and permutations all of which were discussed in Chapter Two under the heading of "multiple connections."

When sequential adoptions occurred, the picture became even more complicated. For example, a child who was orphaned in its infancy might be adopted by, say, its mother's mother. Later on, it might be taken in by one or another of its parents' siblings (and family). If the child liked more than one of its parent's siblings, it might move back and forth from family to family, and end up considering the whole set of uncles, aunts, and cousins, as parents and siblings. In cases of this sort, stronger relationships were substituted for weaker ones; that is, people changed from cousins to siblings, and from uncles to fathers, rather than *vice versa*.

Multiple adoptions seem to have been particularly common during the intermediate period (1890–1940). Schools were established in most villages, and most parents wanted to have their children attend. At the same time, trapping, reindeer herding, and general subsistence requirements, forced many families to spend the greater portion of the school year some distance away from the village. Children whose parents were "on the land" lived with relatives in the village so that they could attend school.

They often became integral members of those families in the process. Over the years a youngster might live with more than one family, and eventually come to regard several adults as parents, and several sets of children as siblings.

An interesting possibility in the Eskimo system was adoption at the initiative of the child. Spencer (1959:90) described a typical case.

> In one such instance, a boy, apparently well into adolescence, made a connection with a family not related to his own. He became so fond of them, and they of him, that he left his own parents and went to live with the family of his choice. This was viewed as true adoption, inasmuch as he employed kinship terms in referring to his foster parents. Having called the daughter of this family "sister" he could not have married her.

Even very young children could make arrangements of this kind. If the child felt strongly enough about it, there was very little that the natural parents could do to prevent an adoption, short of taking the youngster right out of the district. In traditional times, one would adopt oneself out only to relatives; the case described above by Spencer derives from a much later period.

Legal adoption (under United States law) became operative in Northwest Alaska during the intermediate period. It was often regarded as a technical nicety by the Eskimos, but less so with each passing year. By 1970, most people who had the money to pay the fee did their best to secure legal adoptions. For the most part, these followed traditional patterns. Accordingly, they were usually obtained, since all that was required, in addition to payment of the fee, was the written consent of the donor parents. This was easily acquired, since all parties were well known to one another, and usually already related. Interestingly, the Eskimos appeared to be more desirous of legalizing adoptions than they were of legalizing divorces or even marriages. This was probably due to the fact that, under the new system, the real parents could reclaim a child if they changed their minds about it—*if* the child was not legally adopted. Traditionally, if parents changed their minds after an adoption had been effected, they would have had a very difficult time getting the child back again unless the child himself settled the issue in their favor.

Content

The traditional Eskimo approach to infant care is aptly characterized by a single word—intense. Except while an infant slept,
someone was constantly occupied in looking after it. If an infant
started to cry, it was cleaned, if dirty; if hungry it received the
breast. If neither of those approaches worked it was placed on
the mother's (or some other female relative's) back inside the
parka, and rocked until it quieted down. When a crying child
was old enough to pay attention, parents would try to distract
it with various objects or ruses. Eskimos absolutely could not
stand to hear an infant cry.

Basic training began early, but was not forced. Toilet training, for example, was begun before a child could walk. It consisted in the parent holding the child over a small pot and telling
it to urinate. The rate of progress was up to the child, but
toilet training seems typically to have been in the advanced stages
by the time a child could walk with any competence. Weaning
was likewise a gradual process. Demand feeding continued until
a child was capable of eating meat chewed by the mother and
passed to its mouth from hers. Solid food gradually replaced
milk and chewed food as the bulk of the child's diet, but as a
rule, a child was not refused the breast until the next one came
along. If another child did not follow, weaning was sometimes
delayed for several years.

The general pattern of infant care changed relatively little
between traditional and recent times. One difference was that,
in the latter period, children were rarely breast fed beyond the
age of four years, and bottle feeding was normally begun within
the first year. Bottle feeding seemed to be less a source of nutrition than a means of pacification, however. At night the mother
prepared a number of bottles, and every time the baby cried, it
was given one. By the time children reached the age of three
or four they would still be drinking from bottles from time to
time, but they were just as likely to be drinking Kool-Aid as
milk.

The responsibility for infant care devolved primarily upon the
mother. In traditional times, when children were outnumbered
by adults in most households (v. Foote 1965:228), mothers had a
great deal of assistance. In those days, even the demanding

Eskimo approach to infant care placed a very modest burden on the mother. As the number of live offspring per female increased during the intermediate period, babysitting took up progressively more of a woman's time. By the 1950's, when large families were the rule, most mothers were hard put to find time to do anything but look after the younger children, even though they often pressed older children, grandparents, husbands, and even hired babysitters into service.

Education

The education of children was traditionally the obligation of the parents. Although other relatives, particularly grandparents and nepotics, normally made important contributions, the responsibility for seeing that the requisite education was carried out still rested on the parents.

Normally, mothers focused their attention on daughters, fathers on sons. When one of the parents was dead, however, teaching duties sometimes crossed sex lines. For example, I have heard of widowers teaching their daughters how to sew, work skins, and cook. In another case in which the children were all female, the widower taught his oldest daughter how to hunt, and she became quite proficient at it.

The traditional Eskimo theory of education placed very strong emphasis on the "watch, then try" approach. Even in the 1960's, one often heard the admonition to "learn by doing." The child was not subjected to lectures on how to do this and that. It was expected to follow the appropriate role model (i. e., same-sexed parent) around, observe, and then try things for itself. The child was expected *not* to ask questions. When a child made a mistake, it might receive a few suggestions; then it had to try again, and again, and again—until it had mastered the problem. Through this process children learned how to learn by watching, a skill that began to be acquired at a very early age. The ability to learn by watching apparently developed their visual memory to a very high level (Kleinfeld 1971).

Where the trial and error approach involved physical danger to the student, such as in sea-ice hunting, there was usually an older, experienced person along to guide the trials, and to minimize the significance of errors. For a long time, a son would simply follow his father and watch. Gradually he would be permitted to try easier things for himself. Eventually he would do everything himself, while still under the watchful eye of the father. In districts where sea ice is continually in motion, such as in the Bering Strait area, sons often had to follow fathers for many years before they had mastered enough knowledge of ice, wind, and current to set out safely on their own.

Education through admonition and instruction was largely restricted to the inculcation of moral standards. This aspect of education was achieved primarily by means of the countless comments and observations on right and wrong that were scattered throughout normal conversation, and partly by means of stories with moral overtones. Lectures on morals were also employed from time to time, however, with the instructor serving as the example. One of my informants described how his own father did it.

> The old man was strict. Every once in a while he would make us get together, and he would talk for a long time about doing the right way. He taught us mostly about himself. He talked about himself all the way through. He said he did this thing wrong, and he did that one the right way.

Using other people as illustrations seems to have been frowned upon in a discourse on values, although the Eskimos were by no means reticent in pointing out both good and bad attributes in others during the course of normal conversation.

The education aspect of parent-child relationships underwent drastic changes during the intermediate period (1890–1940). The schools, of course, were important in many of these changes. One major consequence of schooling was in the demands it made on a youngster's time, taking up a great deal of that formerly occupied by "watching and doing." A second major influence of the school was shifting the emphasis from learning by "watching and doing" to learning vicariously, through reading and instruction. The third major impact of schools vis á vis the parent-child relationships specifically was in the realm of expression. Traditionally, youngsters were expected to be present in most social contexts, with their eyes and ears open but their mouths shut. However, the children's restraint was a source of great frustration to the White teachers, since their approach to education required that children speak up. By 1970, after decades of competition, the teachers seemed to be winning out: children were not as quiet around the house as they had been formerly, and they were also more responsive in school.

The large increase in family size had an even greater impact than the schools on education carried out in terms of parent-child relationships. Where formerly a father might have one or two sons to teach, by 1950 he had three, four, or more; I know of one woman who had eight daughters to look after. Instructing each child to the same extent would have been a full-time task in itself.

In the traditional era, each child of the same sex went through the same educational process. In the 1960's, the coverage was extremely uneven. Only a few children still received a significant amount of parental instruction, which required either that they leave school early, or that they do so promptly at the end of the eighth grade. Others acquired an absolute minimum of knowledge from their parents. The common pattern during the recent period was to concentrate on one child, and hope that the others would pick up the necessary knowledge on their own.

The selection of the specific child on which to focus parental attention depended on a variety of factors. Generally, emphasis was on the eldest child of the appropriate sex. When parents continued having children after the older ones were grown up, the next ones to receive a significant amount of attention were those who came of age just when the parents were anticipating a decrease in their own activity as a result of advancing age. Sometimes, when the oldest child reached his or her teens while the parents were still in their prime, it was ignored in favor of a younger one. Another factor that seemed to be important was the degree of interest expressed by the child. A child who really wanted to learn something, and who followed a parent around, watching and requesting to "try it myself," would normally be given the opportunity in due course.

The breakdown of the traditional system of education was accompanied by a tremendous decrease in the amount of technical knowledge required in order to survive. In the 1960's, the element of survival was no longer a factor. Expertise was relevant only with respect to how *well* one lived. Modern technology and the welfare system in Northwest Alaska had so reduced the need for training in subsistence techniques that few parents made any special effort to get their children to learn them.

During the 1960's, most young men and women were left more or less on their own as far as these things were concerned— until they got married. Then, suddenly, the full responsibilities of being a spouse and parent were thrust upon them, and they had to learn everything fast. At this stage, parents were not always available to instruct them, and parents-in-law were often a major factor in a young adult's education. Fortunately for the people involved, most of the major tasks of adults in the modern era could be learned to a reasonably adequate degree within a year or two, especially by young people who had been exposed to these activities for much of their lives. However, youngsters who went to high school, and who did not spend any winters at home for four or more consecutive years, often found that they had quite a bit to catch up on when they returned permanently after graduation.

Political Allocation

The ideal allocation of power and responsibility in terms of parent-child relationships was absolutely clearcut: from the birth of the child until the death of the parent, the latter wielded authority, and the former bore responsibility. The general ideal changed little between the traditional and the recent periods.

My informants were in unanimous agreement that the prime virtue of any child *vis á vis* its parents was that of obedience. Obedience was regarded as an end, not as a means. If a child was caught doing something that he was specifically told not to do, it was the fact of disobedience and not the act itself that was of primary concern to the parent. Stealing, for example, was regarded as very bad—in its own right. But if, after a child was told not to take things without asking for them, and he was later caught doing so, he would be chastised first for disobeying, and only later scolded for stealing. The sex of either parent or child did not affect this basic pattern.

The scope of parental authority was ideally all-inclusive, hence very vaguely defined. The areas of child accountability corresponded in equal measure. In theory, a parent had authority over his children in just about everything except the child's relationship with his own children; and there the matter was ambiguous.

The ability of a parent to enforce his or her authority was considerable while the children were still young. Punishment usually took the form of a scolding. Physical punishment was considered unpleasant, but when a child was particularly offensive, and contrary to the Eskimo stereotype, it was slapped or spanked. This became rather common during the recent period. There are cases on record of parents hitting children with sticks, and lashing them with dog whips; until late in the intermediate period, there was no effective check on the extent to which a parent could go in this direction. Physical coercion was actually condoned, however, only when it involved the restraint of youngsters attempting to engage in activities likely to result in bodily harm to themselves, such as playing near water. Something parents *never* did to punish children was withhold affection or food from them.

Adult children theoretically were still subject to parental authority, but there was limit beyond which parents could not go in attempting to get their own way with a recalcitrant adult offspring. I know of one case, for example, where a parent tried to hit a son with a stick, only to be thrown bodily out of the house and told to stay there. In any case, parents could wield authority effectively only in close residential contexts. When parents abused their power, adult offspring could always move away from them.

Economic Allocation

The basic rationale for having children was that they were needed to help the parents during their old age. Parents attempted to inculcate the appropriate values early, and children were not very old before they were pressed into some sort of service.

During the 1960's boys chopped wood, helped feed the dogs, got water, ran errands, and dumped the slop; girls babysat for younger siblings, washed dishes, and helped clean the house. In traditional times the specific tasks were different, but the same general pattern of assistance with minor chores prevailed. In the recent period, most children did not start to take on adult tasks until their late teens or early twenties, often not until they had established households of their own. Traditionally most people were able to shoulder a full burden of adult work by the time they were in their mid-teens.

Economic factors were the main reasons why parent-child relationships often reached the stage of their most satisfactory development as children matured into adulthood, and as parents moved on into middle age. This was so because both parents and children were normally physically active and technically competent at these stages of their life cycles, and the burdens placed on both were considerably alleviated as a result. Daughters had children of their own to look after, but they could get babysitting help from their own still active mother. The mother could also help the daughter with sewing and the various other tasks that fell to Eskimo women. The daughter, in turn, could assist her mother when someone brought home an especially large quantity of game, and she could help her with most of the other work of a heavier sort. Fathers and sons both hunted, but if some equipment was broken, the father could stay home and repair it. By this point, the son could deal completely with the hunting chores by himself, and both equipment and the fruits of the chase passed freely between them.

During the recent period, the Eskimos developed a procedure whereby adult sons went away to work for cash in the summer, while the father and younger sons stayed at home to hunt. This arrangement could be quite profitable to all concerned. Actual cases varied widely, of course, and differences in residential arrangements alone could greatly alter the picture. However, the situation I have just described was a major goal that most Eskimos seemed to be aiming for, and the recent pattern seemed to be little changed in this general respect from the traditional one.

Parents gradually gave over the heavier work to their sons and daughters as they began to age, busying themselves in the lighter activities of logistic support. Aging fathers tended to stay home (or in the *qazgi*) and spend their days making and repairing tools, nets, and other equipment, while their sons hunted.   Similarly, mothers increasingly limited themselves to watching over infant grandchildren for their daughters, and assisting them with lighter tasks, such as sewing.

After the advent of old age pensions, elderly Eskimos were able to make another major contribution to the welfare of the family.   In the 1960's, for example, many a son obtained cash for ammunition and other items from aged parents, supplying them with food in return.   In cases where the parents and the children were living in different villages, it was at this time that the responsible son or daughter would either send for aged parents, or else would go get them and bring them to live with or close to them.   Sometimes they would move themselves, with the members of their family of procreation, to the village where their parents lived.

Sentiment

Traditionally, parent-child relationships were ideally characterized by positive sentiment of great intensity, probably to a degree exceeding that of any other relationship in the entire social system.   This general rule applied to all parent-child relationships, regardless of sex, and was supposed to hold throughout the lifetimes of the members.

The degree to which individuals were permitted to express sentiment in terms of parent-child relationship varied according to the sexes of the members, and particularly according to the absolute ages of the members.   Infants of both sexes were treated in a most unrestrained manner by both fathers and mothers.   Parents hugged their babies, cuddled them, rubbed noses with them, made faces at them, played with them, talked to them, and continually carried them around; even fathers sometimes packed crying children on their backs if nothing else would quiet them down.   As the children grew older, parent-child relationships were ideally marked by increasing restraint, and the number of intimate contacts between parents and their offspring decreased in frequency.   This trend, which began when the child was roughly three or four years of age, increased gradually until it reached puberty.

When the child reached puberty, there was an abrupt change in the direction of increased restraint. The sex of the members also became more important. The father-son and mother-daughter relationships, while no longer intimate after the children reached puberty, remained open and direct in the sense that the members were permitted to look one another squarely in the face. The mother-daughter relationship remained relatively unrestrained as well, and adult daughters and their mothers were permitted to smile and talk animatedly to one another. The father-son relationship, on the other hand, became rather restrained. An adult son was expected to maintain an attitude of quiet respect in his father's presence, and to listen, not talk; any conversation between them was expected to be conducted in quiet tones and to focus on matters of moment, not on trivia (v. Cantwell 1887:44). The father-daughter relationship also became relatively restrained, closely resembling in this respect the relationship between father and son. The relationship between adult sons and their mothers became restrained to the point of avoidance. They were expected not to talk at all unless it was necessary, and then to converse only in a monotone. An adult son was permitted to look his mother in the eye, but to do so conveyed an attitude of disrespect, hence was avoided whenever possible.

The traditional ideals of sentiment between parents and their children had been reduced only slightly by the 1960's. Similarly, the expression of that sentiment had become only slightly less restrained than it had been traditionally. Two interesting developments had complicated the actual situation, however.

The first change affecting parent-child sentiment was the adoption of two different patterns of expression. One pattern, the traditional one, was employed in contexts in which only Eskimos were present. The other, modeled on the less intense and less restrained American pattern, was often employed in the presence of Whites. By 1970, many Eskimos were very sophisticated in these matters, and could switch abruptly back and forth between the two patterns with the competence of professional actors.

The second major change in parent-child sentiment was connected with favoritism. Ideally, Eskimo parents were supposed to view each offspring with equal affection, and *vice versa*.

In fact, parental sentiment was frequently allocated differentially among children, one or two being favored over the others. In the majority of cases, the child favored by the mother was not the same one favored by the father, although favoritism did not otherwise correlate with sex. In addition, each parent pressured the other to treat his or her favorite in an approved way. In traditional times, when most couples had only two children living with them, the net effect was that the overwhelming majority of children were favored by one parent or the other, hence were treated very well.

Both the traditional ideal and actual patterns persisted throughout the transitional period. That is, a parent ideally treated all offspring the same, but actually favored one over the others. With the great increase in the number of children per family, however the result was a marked distinction between a few favorites, on the one hand, and many non-favorites on the other. Upon the favorites were bestowed the best clothes, the most and best food, and the greatest attention, by the favoring parent. A favorite child could do just about anything and get away with it. Non-favored children, especially those who were truly rejected, were treated quite differently. They had to run errands, do the dirtiest chores, wear the ugliest clothes, and eat the worst food. Rejected children could do the least little thing wrong and get a severe scolding or thrashing for it.

Children in an unfavored position did not appreciate their lot one bit. During the recent period, hostility toward parents by unfavored children was widespread, and had become a major source of stress. However, there was no guarantee that a favored child would live up to the ideals of a parent-child relationship any more than an unfavored child would. Some of the former turned out to be the worst ones from the Eskimos' own point of view, while some *un*favored children—ones who overlooked their poor treatment—grew up to be exemplary. Consequently, some parents eventually had second thoughts on the matter, and realigned their sentiments later on in life.

Just why certain children were favored and others were not is unclear. The Eskimos themselves had a number of explanations, and they are probably as good as any.

One explanation of parental favoritism was the "identity of name" theory (v. Heinrich 1963b; Jenness 1957:15; Spencer 1959:286ff.). According to this view, children who were named after one of the parent's parents would be accorded favored status almost automatically. This theory *does* account for several of the cases that I observed. On the other hand, there were many more cases where it did not apply at all. Indeed, the identity of name theory, all by itself, was not very useful in predicting just how a child would be viewed by his or her parents. For example, one girl who was born while her father was away from the village was named after his mother by the midwife. The father had been an unfavored child himself, and his mother had treated him very badly for most of his life. So, he decided that he would *not* treat his daughter—who had the same name as his mother—in the same way that his mother had treated him. The result was that this daughter was his favorite child. The same man had a son who was named after his wife's father. In this case, the wife decided that she was going to treat the son exactly as his namesake had treated her. This meant that the boy had to do a variety of menial chores, such as serve everyone coffee before they got out of bed in the morning. In the latter case, the parent treated the child *just the same* as the namesake had treated her; in the former, the parent treated the child *just the opposite* of the way that the namesake had treated him.

The Eskimos had several other theories about parental favoritism. According to one of them, the position of a child in the birth order was said to affect their choice. Either the oldest or the youngest one was supposed to be favored, with a slight preference for the latter. Adopted offspring were also said to be favored over real offspring. Still another explanation held that, in a family with only one daughter, the girl would be the favorite, as would the son in a family with only one boy. These theories did account for many of the cases I recorded, but they did not tell why a factor was operative in one instance and not in another, and they did not explain the numerous exceptions.

Strength

The parent-child relationships were the strongest bonds that existed in traditional Northwest Alaska, at least from the child's point of view. This strength was related to the allocation of power, and was a consequence of the fact that the parents were the locus of the greatest authority in the traditional society. Institutionally, a child could not disobey a parent, regardless of what might be involved in a particular situation. This fact guaranteed that parent-child relationships took precedence over all others, again from the child's point of view.

A parent, of course, was usually beholden to his own parents as long as they were alive. Just what happened when an adult's parents were dead is not quite certain. I suspect that in such circumstances the parent-child relationships then became the strongest from the parental point of view as well. However, I am not sure what was supposed to happen if a person ever had to choose sides in a dispute between a sibling, particularly an older one, and a son or daughter (v. Gubser 1965:140).

Parents were no longer the wielders of maximum authority in the villages of the 1960's. They were superceded in those respects by the legal institutions of the United States and the State of Alaska. If an Eskimo had to choose between conflicting obligations to a parent, on the one hand, and say, the United States Government on the other, he would probably have followed those to the government, not out of any sense of moral commitment, but because he was afraid not to. He would probably have suffered guilt feelings in the process, feelings he would *not* have experienced if he had *dis*obeyed a government order in favor of his parents.

Parent-child relationships were still preeminent *within* the kinship system in 1970. Whether or not any one of the four was institutionalized as being stronger than the others I cannot say. As far as the ideal situation was concerned, there was no evidence for any distinctions between or among them. In actual cases, there was considerable variation. This was influenced to a high degree by the type and quantity of sentiment with which particular relationships were imbued by their members. Thus, the relationship between a parent and a favored child very often took precedence over one between the same parent and an unfavored child, at least from the parent's point of view. Likewise, the tie between a father and son, or a mother and a daughter, sometimes grew to be especially strong after years of cooperation that had been highly satisfactory from the viewpoints of both members.

Strains

Many of the strains to which traditional parent-child relationships were subjected resulted from the failure of one or both
members to live up to the ideal prescriptions of the relationship
concerned. There were several common variations on this basic
theme. Along the political axis, a relationship was strained to
the degree and in the respects that the child disobeyed the parent,
or to the extent that the parent abused his authority over the
child. From an economic viewpoint, failure to live up to the
ideals of mutual cooperation and support was the major source
of conflict. Stinginess, particularly with food, seems to have
been especially irritating in the Eskimo view. In these general
respects, there seems to have been little change between traditional and recent times.

Many of the conflicts resulting from failure to live up to be-
haviorial ideals in recent years were associated with favoritism.
Often, a youngster who was in the unfavored category was repeatedly mistreated (according to Eskimo standards) by one or
both parents throughout his childhood and adolescence. If he
was an especially good child, he would overlook this treatment.
If he was merely a normal child, he would keep his feelings to
himself, and forget nothing. By the time the child reached adulthood, he might have a lengthy list of grievances stored away in
his memory. If enough resentment had built up, an apparently
trivial incident, or alcohol, could be sufficient to unleash a violent
reaction.

Drinking was often a factor in the release of pent-up resentment over mistreatment by parents. For example, when a son
got intoxicated, he sometimes went "looking for his father," because he suddenly "remembered" all the mistreatment he had
received as a boy at his father's hands. Normally, relatives
would go to considerable lengths to keep someone bent on this
kind of revenge from finding the parent concerned. This was for
both the child's and the parent's sakes. On the one hand, the
child was usually capable of giving the parent a severe beating
by this stage of his or her life. On the other hand, if the child
succeeded in locating the parent and beating him (or her) up,
he (or she) was likely to suffer agonizing guilt after sobering
up. Usually this proceeded to the point of extreme depression

and withdrawal, and occasionally went as far as a suicide attempt. No matter how serious the strains in a parent-child relationship became, alcohol-stimulated vengeance inevitably compounded them.

"Third party interference," or conflicting obligations to different people, seems to have been almost as common a source of stress in traditional parent-child relationships as failure to live up to the ideals of parent-child behavior. For the most part these conflicts were between one's parent(s), on the one hand, and one's spouse, on the other. Ideally a child was supposed to defer to the parent over the spouse without question. Actually, it was rarely that simple, particularly when all the parties to the conflict were living in the same house. What does one do when one's mother (or father) is tormenting one's wife (or husband)? In concrete situations, the Eskimos did not find solutions to this problem any easier to come by than other peoples do. And, like many other peoples emphasizing extended family households, traditional Eskimo women tended to boss around co-resident daugthers-in-law, and the men often tended to treat co-resident sons-in-law in an equally authoritarian manner. Such behavior could lead only to stress between parent and child, or to stress between husband and wife, or to both.

Strains resulting from "third party interference" still affected parent-child relationships in Northwest Alaska in the 1960's, but not to the extent that they had traditionally. A major factor in the change seems to have been the transition from extended family households to extended family neighborhoods that occurred during the intermediate periods, a change that will be described in greater detail in Chapter Seven. "Third parties" were still around in 1970, but not in such close proximity as they had been 50 years previously. Also, the emphasis had changed. In the 1960's, parents were regarded as a source of marital strife; in the traditional period, spouses had been regarded as a source of conflict between parents and their children.

Termination

There was no acceptable way that a parent-child relationship could be terminated in traditional times, short of the death of one of the members. No matter how severe the strains might become in any given case, the individuals involved were expected to work things out.

Actually, parents often became separated from a child when it married and moved away to live with its spouse. When the marriage was within the same society—as it usually was—the parent and child concerned normally got to see one another at least once or twice a year during the seasonal round, and might even live together for a particular season every year. When the child married into another society, the contacts were far less frequent and much more irregular. However, in the reasonably well documented cases I have of inter-societal marriage under aboriginal conditions, the child still brought his (or her) family to spend the winter with his (or her) own people every few years. Accidentally permanent separations, which one *might* expect to have been common in such a nomadic population, seem to have been rather unusual during the traditional period because of the territorial integrity and highly structured annual cycle of each society. During the extensive population movements during the last quarter of the 19th. century, however, many children were separated forever from their parents while both still had many years of life ahead of them.

The traditional view regarding deactivation of parent-child relationships persisted into the recent period. Youngsters often moved to other villages when they got married, but tape recorded "talking letters" continually passed back and forth between them and their parents. Related families who did not get to see one another periodically as part of the normal course of events tried to save money for a visit at least once every year or two.

The only people who became permanently and absolutely separated from their parents in the 1960's were those who moved to the continental United States and deliberately disappeared into the general population, or those who moved to Fairbanks or Anchorage and participated in the skidrow existence that was possible there. Another recent variation on the traditional theme was when an aged, and ill or senile parent had to go to the Public Health Service Hospital in Anchorage to be properly looked after. Such circumstances typically produced ambivalent feelings in the children, who were thus freed from a tremendous burden, but who also were unable to live up to their basic responsibilities as children.

The death of a parent was a sad event for an Eskimo. As a young Point Hope man told VanStone (1957:210): "Yes, it is hard to make a living, but worse to go without parents. It is easy to find food and fuel, but hard to find parents after they have passed away." These sentiments were echoed almost verbatim by informants in other parts of Northwest Alaska.

Histrionics and loud expressions of anguish were considered inappropriate upon the death of a parent, no matter how fond of the deceased a child had been. The older a parent was at the time of death, the less emotion the children were supposed to express. In the case of a very aged person, everyone, including both the child and the parent, had long been aware of the impending event; the children normally passed through it with scarcely a break in stride (v. Gubser 1965:216ff.; Spencer 1959:149, 252). The death of a child evoked a greater expression of sentiment than the death of a parent. There was some variation here too, however; the loss of a child in an already large family seems to have occassioned less of an emotional response in the parents than would the death of a child in a family of only two or three.

Inheritance

Traditionally, children inherited those personal possessions of a deceased parent that were not left with the body, and that had not been promised by him (or her) to someone else. Items typically left with the body included weapons, clothing, tools, and household utensils. Amulets and magic songs were most often willed (*qiuvaanaqtuq*) to specific individuals, apparently more often to grandchildren than to offspring. The goods that figured most prominently in parent-child inheritance, therefore, were houses, boats, dogs, sleds, and nets, and occasionally caribou corrals and whaling equipment. Land, of course, was a "free good" in Northwest Alaska, hence was not subject to any rules of inheritance.

Inheritance varied considerably from one case to another. The details depended on several factors, such as the age and sex of the deceased, the age and sex of the surviving spouse(s) (if any), the ages and sexes of the surviving children (if any), the quantity of goods left behind, and the specific residence situation of the deceased and the survivors at the time of death. Frequently invoked formulae were the following:

(1) Spouses normally received an inheritance before children, at least if they were not advanced in age. Often, especially if the oldest survivor were a widow with children, the inheritance was to be held in trust by her for the children until they reached maturity, and used for the benefit of all.

(2) Goods were inherited by offspring of the same sex as the deceased parent rather than by those of the opposite sex.

(3) The oldest surviving child of the appropriate sex normally received precedence over his or her juniors, but was often expected to share the inheritance with them and/or use it for their benefit.

(4) The child(ren) residing with the parent at the time of death received consideration before those who were living somewhere else.

The actual details were worked out by the survivors, depending on how relevant these formulae were to the circumstances of the case, and depending on the presence or absence of specific stipulations by the parent concerned. Often a parent who felt his end approaching would dictate who would get what, especially if the circumstances differed significantly from those presumed by the formulae outlined above.

The general inheritance patterns outlined above were still followed in the 1960's. One innovation was for older people to make up written wills and deposit them with the local school teacher or missionary. Written wills usually contained provisions of a traditional sort, but they were less subject to dispute than word of mouth. Although oral stipulations still prevailed, people who had acquired substantial assets, and who expected to be survived by several adult offspring, were increasingly attempting to preclude disputes with written statements.

Gerontocide

One stereotyped notion about Eskimos is that they used to abandon their aged (Howe 1909:453; Stuck 1920:249, 250). The general picture most people seem to have is that the Eskimos used to leave their aged parents behind to starve when they abandoned a camp, or else placed them in some situation they could not possibly survive, such as on a drifting pan of ice. Since widespread practice of such a custom would contradict the view of parent-child relationships presented so far, it is appropriate to comment on it at this point.

Gerontocide has been documented for the Northwest Alaskan Eskimos. Both the literature (e. g., Spencer 1959:92) and my informants agree that it did occur. However, as is true of infanticide, Eskimo "gerontocide" has been grossly misunderstood (v. Jenness 1918:95; cf. Lee 1968:35–36). My information makes it clear that aged parents were abandoned *only* under conditions of the most extreme hardship, and it was rare even then (Hooper 1881:57; Klengenberg 1932:316–319; Seeman 1853:66; Simpson 1875:245, 249, 250). In every case that has come to my attention except one, abandonment occurred in situations in which old people had to be sacrificed or everyone would have starved to death. In the exceptional case, the individuals did abandon their parents; they came to be regarded as deviants as a consequence, and were subsequently treated as outcasts.

Old people were not left behind to die. If they were left behind at all, it was so that the younger, more active members of the family could travel more quickly to where food could be procured, and *then return* (v. Spencer 1959:92). Most cases which appear to have been abandonment were actually desperation measures designed more to save parents than to get rid of them. In every case that I was able to record except the one mentioned above, the children rushed back to their parents once they had obtained supplies.

An ancient custom that might *appear* to have been gerontocide was related to taboos about living in a house in which a death occurred. According to this pattern, the occupants of such a house had to abandon it forthwith, and in mid-winter they were understandably loathe to do so. Consequently, when someone was sick to the point of death, and regardless of his age, his housemates would place him in a little snow house or tent to die there by himself (v. Stefansson 1914:283, 284). The practice varied considerably from district to district. In some regions they had no custom of this kind at all. In others, just the house had to be abandoned when somebody died inside. In still other areas the people not only had to abandon the house, they had to destroy the clothes they were wearing at the time. In mid-winter this could be disastrous for everyone involved. In terms of the

Eskimo world view this practice is best conceived of as self-protection, and not as a deliberate removal of the weaker members of the population.

NEPOTIC RELATIONSHIPS

Membership

"Nepotic" is a convenient term for referring to any relationship connecting collateral consanguineal relatives one generation apart, the degree of collaterality being left unspecified. Among the Northwest Alaskan Eskimos, there were two nepotic relationships at the most general level, these being *aaŋak-uyuru* (uncle-nephew/niece), and *aatsak-uyuru* (aunt-nephew/niece). The positions of *aaŋak* and *aatsak* were filled, respectively, by all male and female collateral consanguines of the first ascending generation without any collateral limitation, and by fictive siblings (*qataŋun*) of one's parents. The term *uyuru* denoted individuals in the corresponding lower generation positions, but did not specify sex.

An important variation in the basic scheme outlined above is a fourfold division into ortho- (or same-sexed) nepotics and hetero- (or opposite-sexed) nepotics. In the Kivalina-Kotzebue Sound terminology, the relationships were as follows: *aaŋak-uyuru* (uncle-nephew), *aaŋak-nauralautsiaq* (uncle-niece), *aatsak-uyuru* (aunt-niece), and *aatsak-nauralautsiaq* (aunt-nephew). In terms of this set of distinctions, the term *uyuru* referred to the junior ortho-nepotic, and *nauralautsiaq* referred to the junior hetero-nepotic. The fourfold terminology was common throughout Northwest Alaska in traditional times, but seems to have been stressed in some districts (e. g., around Bering Strait) and deemphasized in favor of the twofold pattern in other areas (e. g., in the northern interior). Regardless of the terminology used in a given district, the fourfold pattern was the one that actually guided people's behavior.

The discussion so far as been based on the premise that one's uncles and aunts were roughly the same age as one's parents. However, among a people where a woman could have her last child some twenty or thirty years after her first, the situation was often not so clear-cut. It was not unusual among the Northwest Alaskan Eskimos to have an *aaŋak* or an *aatsak* actually be younger than an *uyuru;* members of the senior generation were frequently close in age to the members of the junior generation. In such situations, the ideal patterns of nepotic relationships were usually set aside. The individuals involved normally operated either as siblings or as cousins, depending on situational factors, such as residence.

Just how close in age two people had to be before the same-generation relationships were substituted for the nepotic ones is difficult to say. A crude rule of thumb, based on a number of observations, is that about ten years of age difference was the cut-off point. If an *aaŋak* and an *uyuru* were over ten years apart, the likelihood was that they would interact on a nepotic basis, at least if it was the former who was the older one. If they were less than ten years apart in age, they would generally interact in terms of sibling or cousin relationships. What happened in a case where the "nephew/niece" was ten years older than the senior I cannot say, never having observed or heard about such a situation.

Content

The traditional nepotic and parent-child relationships were virtually identical in content. They differed, however, in the degree or moral obligation to live up to the appropriate standards of behavior. Parents were primarily responsible for the education of their children, but aunts and uncles were expected to help out a great deal. Parents and children were expected to share with and assist one another, and so were nepotics, but to a lesser extent. As parents had authority over their children, so uncles and aunts had authority over their *uyuru*, but not as much as parents did. The pattern of "similar but to a lesser degree" covered all of the activities appropriate to the relationships concerned. Aunts and uncles were like parents held "in reserve" until needed.

During the transitional period, the content of nepotic relationships did not change very much. The only difference seems to have been that the frequency of interaction decreased considerably as extended family households gave way to conjugal ones, and as people became primarily occupied in looking after their own offspring.

The reserve status of nepotic relationships *vis á vis* parent-child relationships was one of their most significant features. Individuals who were theoretically related on a nepotic basis often interacted in parent-child terms under circumstances in which, or in the respects that, the latter were inoperative or deficient for some reason. For example, when a woman died, her sister might undertake to teach a surviving daughter how to sew, scrape skins, and cook; when a man died, his brother might teach a surviving son how to hunt. Sometimes an aunt or uncle became a surrogate parent at the initiative of the *uyuru* while the real parents were still alive and living in the same community. Usually this happened when the strains in the parent-child relationships had become too much to bear. The *uyuru* would move in with the aunt and uncle simply to escape intolerable parental domination.

When the parents were absent, the decision to effect a "functional replacement" usually rested with the aunt or uncle, with or without the consent of the *uyuru*. For example in 1964 a young man came to Kivalina from Kotzebue with several bottles of whiskey, got thoroughly intoxicated, and created havoc in the village. After he had sobered up, his oldest uncle in the village took him aside, and gave him a revealing lecture.

> As long as your parents aren't around here, I have to be your father. Anyway, I did a lot to help bring you up. When you misbehave it's like my own son misbehaving. When your parents aren't here, I don't want you to bring any whiskey up here! If you do that again you are going to get into plenty of trouble. So don't do it *no more*!

Sentiment

Nepotic relationships ideally ranked behind both parent-child and sibling relationships in intensity. Actually there was wide variation. Many individual nepotic ties were extremely intense. Aunts and uncles, like parents, often had favorites, but nepotic favoritism rarely approached the extremes that characterized many parent-child relationships. Informants told me that aunts and uncles tended to favor *uyurus* who were not favored by their parents, and the observational data I have on the matter support this contention.

A major difference between parent-child and nepotic relationships was in the area of expression. It will be recalled that expression in terms of parent-child relationships changed from extreme openness and intimacy to reserve and mild avoidance as the children matured. Nepotic relationships too were characterized by unrestrained expression of sentiment at the start, but they stayed that way from the senior point of view. From the viewpoint of the *uyuru*, however, they became increasingly restrained. The process sometimes went so far as to be intimate and demonstrative from the senior perspective, while avoidant and restrained from that of the junior.

Gubser (1965:149) once observed "an uncle tease a young nephew and niece to the point of tears—something unthinkable for a parent to do to his own child." I saw this happen many times. For example, a whole boat-load of teenagers, all originally from Kivalina, arrived back in that village for a visit from Kotzebue, where they were living at the time. They had numerous aunts and uncles in the village, but their parents were all in Kotzebue. Within five minutes of the arrival of the boat, there was a large crowd on the beach. The uncles and aunts were walking around making a huge fuss over their *uyuru*. How big their *uyuru* had grown! How was the *uyuru* doing in school? Uncles interrogated their nephews on the details of their sex life, saying that they had heard thus and so about their nephew and his new girlfriend. The uncles and aunts were talking loudly, gesticulating, and laughing. The *uyurus*, by contrast, were standing around staring at the ground or at the sky, not saying a word. Some adults even ducked down so as to make an *uyuru* who was staring at the ground look them in the eye, only to burst into laughter when the *uyuru* turned his or her head aside.

Strength

Determination of the strength of nepotic relationships is difficult, partly because the Eskimo ideal was ambiguous, and partly because there was wide variation from case to case.[3]

---

[3] These statements are not made on impressionistic grounds, but follow from detailed analysis and reasoning. A preliminary version of this reasoning can be found in my doctoral dissertation (Burch 1966:253 *et passim.*).

Clearly they ranked behind parent-child and sibling relationships, and ahead of cousin and all affinal ties. They were situated in a middle ground that also included grandparent–grandchild relationships. In concrete situations, the relative precedence of relationships between specific individuals varied according to genealogical distance, the "interactional distance" of residential separation, and the sentiment with which the relationships were imbued. In the recent period the same pattern held, except that the husband-wife relationship had become much stronger than any nepotic tie.

MULTI–GENERATION RELATIONSHIPS

Membership

"Multi-generation" refers to those relationships in which two or more generations separate the members. In Northwest Alaska there were three such relationships: *aana-tutik, ataata-tutik*, and *amauluq-illuliaran*. The role of *aana* was filled by all female consanguineal relatives of the second ascending generation, and *ataata* was the corresponding role for males. The reciprocal position, that of *tutik*, was filled by all consanguineal relatives of the second descending generation without reference to sex. The *amauluq-illuliaran* relationship obtained between consanguineal relatives three generations apart; sex was not distinguished in either the senior or the junior positions. In all of the multi-generation relationships, lineal relatives were not distinguished from collateral ones, father's relatives were not distinguished from those of the mother, and genealogical distance was ideally not a factor (although it often was actually).

Multi-generation relationships constituted a very small proportion of the entire set of kin relationships in Northwest Alaska in traditional times. This was the case for two reasons: (1) family size was small and (2) average life expectancy was short. An *amauluq* (great-grandparent) must have been a very rare individual. The medical revolution of the recent period (1940–1970) had a great impact on both the youngest and the oldest age groups, which are the ones affected in the case of multi-generation relationships. In 1910, the individuals estimated to be under twenty years of age comprised 45% of the population, while those judged to be 50 and over constituted only 8%. By 1960, the first category had grown to an estimated 57%, where it held steady for the subsequent decade. The over-50 category had increased to slightly more than 10% of the total population by 1960, and was approaching 12% by 1969.[4]

These demographic changes, along with the all-inclusive nature of the membership criteria, combined to push multi-generation relationships from the least to the most numerous type of kin relationship in Northwest Alaska. By 1970, many grandparents could count several dozen grandchildren, and many youngsters had half a dozen or more living grandparents and great-grandparents. By this stage of life an *amauluq* could be related to practically every child in a village. Simply because of the numbers involved, most multi-generation relationships which existed in theory were inoperative in practice.

Content

Like nepotic relationships, the traditional multi-generation relationships were very similar in content to the parent-child relationships, but in lesser degree.[5] There were a few important differences however, particularly in the area of education and in the provision of certain services.

The primary obligation to see that youngsters were properly educated in traditional times, as noted previously, fell upon the parents. The *execution* of this duty very often devolved upon grandparents, however, for two reasons: (1) they were the primary repositories of wisdom and knowledge, and (2) they usually had more time for the purpose than the parents did. Although parents took the primary part in teaching children how to harvest natural resources, grandparents usually led

[4] The 1910 estimate is based on U. S. Bureau of the Census data (1913:1137), and the 1960 estimate is based on U. S. Bureau of the Census (1961: Table 27). Estimates for 1969 are based on Amsden (1969) and the Northwest Economic Development and Planning Board (1969).

[5] Great-grandparent–great-grandchild relationships did not differ in content, sentiment, or strength from those obtaining between grandparents and their grandchildren, hence the two will be discussed simultaneously.

in the instruction of manufacturing techniques (v. Pospisil 1964:412). Thus, a father would teach his son how to hunt, and a grandfather would show him how to make bows and arrows. Instruction in the games, rituals, taboos, and the ancient traditions of their people was normally done by the grandparents, for few parents were their equal in the task.

The education aspect of the multi-generation relationships became significantly reduced in importance after World War II. The changes were even greater in these relationships than they were in the parent-child relationships. There are several reasons why this was so. First, as mentioned previously, there were too many grandchildren for a grandparent to devote much attention to more than a small number of them; their problem was even more difficult in this respect than it was for parents. Second, the knowledge of the old people was largely irrelevant to contemporary conditions, and both the grandparents and the grandchildren knew it. Third, the school had usurped many of the educational functions of the family in general, and of the multi-generation relationships in particular. Finally, in many villages, a language barrier had grown up between old people (who could speak only Eskimo) and their grandchildren (who could speak only English), with the result that the information which the former could convey to the latter was very limited in scope.

Traditionally, a number of services, in addition to education, were performed in terms of multi-generation relationships. While individually most of these services were of comparatively minor significance, their cumulative effect was often considerable. Furthermore, in contrast to the essentially one-directional flow of teaching activities, these additional services were characterised by a high level of reciprocity.

The details of the miscellaneous services performed in terms of multi-generation relationships varied according to the ages of the individuals involved. While the grandchild was an infant, it was looked after much of the time by a grandparent, usually, but by no means exclusively, by the *aana*. By the time that the *tutik* was perhaps five or six, it had begun to perform many chores for the grandparent, particularly if the latter was getting on in years or else was an invalid. Aged grandparents always had one grandchild more or less "in tow," following them around, or playing in their immediate vicinity so as to be readily available should their assistance be required. This grandchild would help the grandparent check the net or snares, assist them over rough spots in the path, run errands for them, and do innumerable other chores. The grandchild in question was either one assigned the task by its parents—the children of the grandparent—or, more often, one who had formed an especially close attachment to that grandparent while still a youngster. When this grandchild passed into adolescence, his place might be filled by another, much younger sibling or cousin. The traditional ideal changed little in the recent period, except that the requirements of going to school prevented most youngsters from carrying out these tasks most of the time.

Old people traditionally also performed a number of incidental but very useful services for adult grandchildren. Thus, an *aana* might twist caribou sinew into thread, or willow bark into line for a net, for a granddaughter, and an *ataata* might make a bow or a war club for a grandson. Equally important was the performance of magical services by the grandparent for the grandchild. Magical ability was not restricted to old people in the traditional society, but they seem to have had more of it than anyone else. Thus, a sick grandchild might be healed without fee by a grandparent who had the necessary ability. Or, when a young person suffered an injustice at the hands of a non-relative, a grandparent often offered "to work it," i. e., to achieve revenge for their grandchild through the application of magic. Finally, magic songs, amulets, and techniques for manipulating the nonempirical environment (v. Burch 1971) were characteristically passed on from grandparent to grandchild rather than from parent to child.

Most of the traditional services were no longer performed by grandparents by the 1950's. The tremendous increase in store-bought goods eliminated the need for old people to make things, and the new mechanical and electrical skills required to maintain most items by 1970 were for the most part beyond their competence. With the arrival of Christianity around the turn of the century, old people began to refuse to perform magical services, and they also stopped transmitting their magic songs, amulets, and techniques to grandchildren.

Sentiment

The sentiment with which traditional multi-generation relationships were imbued was ideally of great intensity. This sentiment was expressed rather openly when compared to many of the other relationships in the kinship system (v. Gubser 1965:148; Jenness 1957:129; Milan 1964:62; Spencer 1959:-236). The change between traditional and recent times was minimal in both respects. Grandparents, especially the *aanas*, fondled their young grandchildren, kissed them, and hugged them. They often gave pet names to favorite grandchildren which, once given, were used by the old person for the rest of his or her life. A grandparent might still call a grandson "funny-looking little man" (*ayutigiilak*) well into the latter's maturity. Except for the "joking cousins" (*illuriik*) tie, the multi-generation relationships were the only ones in the entire Eskimo kinship system where nicknames of this kind were considered appropriate.

The grandparent-grandchild relationships remained relatively demonstrative throughout the course of their existence. Always, the least restraint was shown by the grandparents, especially by the *aana*. When the grandchild reached adulthood, he was relaxed in the presence of his grandparents, and could converse freely with them. Although he could face a grandparent directly, the *tutik* was expected to speak in quiet respectful tones, both when addressing grandparents, and when speaking in their presence.

Sentiment was ideally allocated equally among one's grandchildren or one's grandparents. In traditional times, this ideal may have been achieved in fact in a high proportion of cases. In the recent period, the ideal became impossible to attain simply because of the numbers involved. Consequently, there was pronounced favoritism, usually between a grandparent and a grandchild who had been named after him (or her). The pattern here was similar to that of parental favoritism, although it rarely involved the rejection of non-favorites, which parental favoritism, often did. Instead, it was a matter of the selection of one or a few grandchildren (or grandparents) for special attention. Children favored by a parent were rarely viewed with the same sentiments by a grandparent.

Strength

In terms of institutionalized strength, the multi-generation relationships were somewhere in the middle ground along with nepotic relationships. Thus, they ranked between parent-child and sibling relationships, on the one hand, and all other kin relationships on the other.

In fact, there was wide variation in strength from case to case. The actual situation depended on residential arrangements, the absolute ages of the members (particularly of the grandparents), and the sentiment with which a particular relationship was imbued. For example, the relationship between a youngster and a resident grandfather who was young and dynamic enough to dominate the household, and who was particularly fond of the child concerned, was likely to be stronger than *any* other relationship as far as those two individuals were concerned. At the other extreme were relationships that were simply inoperative. In traditional times this usually occurred only when the members lived in widely separated local groups (or in different societies), and when the collateral (genealogical) distance was considerable. During the recent period inoperative multi-generation relationships were in the majority, even when both members lived in the same village. Most individuals still operated in terms of at least one multi-generation relationship that was very strong, although the great strength that characterized some such relationships in earlier times was rarely realized.

Strains

Stress was usually at a minimum in multi-generation relationships. This was true partly because there were limited possibilities for strains to develop, and partly because, when they were generated, the relationships were easily deactivated.

There seem to have been only two significant sources of strain in multi-generation relationships. From the grandparental point of view, any trouble usually stemmed from disobedience on the part of the *tutik*. If continued, this led the grandparent to take a dim view of the *tutik* as a person. From the grandchild's point of view, trouble most often resulted from the strange behavior of a senile grandparent, which a young *tutik* either might not understand or simply might not wish to tolerate. Most multi-generation relationships seemed to be quite free of conflict, however, and most Eskimos thought of them in terms of harmony and pleasure.

AFFINAL RELATIONSHIPS

Membership

The affinal relationships which were carried out in other-generation terms were those between parents-in-law and children-in-law. The Eskimos distinguished four relationships in this category: (1) *aakazuak-niŋau* (mother-in-law–son-in-law), (2) *aakazuaq-ukuaq* (mother-in-law–daughter-in-law), (3) *aapazuaq-niŋau* (father-in-law–son-in-law) and (4) *aapazuaq-ukuaq* (father-in-law–daughter-in-law). These relationships were established automatically through the residential marriage of the junior members.

Like other Eskimo kin relationships, affinal ties were considered permanent. The deactivation of the marital relationship that created them did not necessarily lead to the same result at the "in-law" level (Heinrich 1972). The notion of "former parent-in-law" had little meaning to the Eskimos, many of whom maintained active relationships with the parents of a separated spouse.

Content

The content of parent-in-law and child-in-law relationships was ideally identical to that of parents and their adult children, in both the traditional and transitional periods. Informants who were asked to evaluate specific cases as "good" or "bad" *always* did so in terms of how closely they conformed to or departed from the ideal patterns of parent-child relationships. Observational data support their view; the "best" relationships in this category were indeed virtually indistinguishable from the consanguineal variety. Significantly, in these particular cases, the members often employed consanguineal labels rather than personal names as terms of address, and even as terms of reference when speaking to people familiar with the facts of the matter. Because of the virtual identity of content between the two sets of relationship there is no need to elaborate on the affinal pattern.

Sentiment

The parent-in-law–child-in-law relationships were institutionalized as involving relatively intense positive sentiment. When asked to generalize about the ideals of the *parent-child* relationships, informants first focused their remarks on content, *then* changed to sentiment. When speaking of the comparable *affinal* relationships, however, they typically reversed the sequence. Indeed, informants used the word "love" more often in connection with relationships in this category than with any other in the entire kinship system.

A large portion of the actual cases did seem to involve sentiment of considerable intensity, but the *nature* of that sentiment ranged all the way from sincere, deep devotion to what must be described as passionate hatred. Departures from the ideal seemed to follow a pattern, primarily because strains were more likely to be generated in some relationships than in others. The *aakazuaq-ukuaq* (mother-in-law–daughter-in-law) relationship was the most subject to stress and strain, hence to mutual dislike. Only rarely were members of such a membership truly fond of each other. The *aapazuaq-ukuaq* (father-in-law–daughter-in-law) relationship seemed to be much more satisfying; it was not at all uncommon to hear a man tell how pleased he was with his daughter-in-law, and vice versa. The *aakazuaq-niɲau* and the *aapazuaq-niɲau* relationships seemed to fall between the other two, apparently in that order.

The relationships in the parent-in-law–child-in-law category were supposed to be restrained. The rationale for this was that the parent-in-law was supposed to appear a somewhat awesome figure in the eyes of the child-in-law. The latter, in turn, was supposed to act afraid of his or her parent-in-law, regardless of the real feelings on either side.

The mother-in-law–son-in-law relationship came closer to out-right avoidance than any other in the entire kinship system. One man described his relations with his own mother-in-law as fol-lows:

> Just when I married that girl, I got afraid to say a word to her mother. Always I'm afraid of her. Before I got mar-ried, I could talk to her any old way, all right, but when I married her daughter I couldn't say a word to her anymore. And she never say a word to me either.

This example was constantly cited as being as close to the ideal as one could get. My informant was emphatic in claiming that he had the deepest affection for his mother-in-law. Indeed, it was precisely *because* of this affection that he would not speak to her, since he was striving to follow the ideals of the relation-ship to the maximum possible degree.

Strength

Affinal relationships in general were ideally weaker than any consanguineal ones in traditional times. The four relation-ships of concern here ranked just behind all of the marital re-lationships except that of co-spouses, and ahead of the four affinal relationships to be discussed in the next chapter. In short, they were well down the priority list as far as the in-stitutionalized pattern was concerned.

Residential arrangements complicated the picture considerably. In terms of day-to-day existence, one's obligations to resident parents-in-law often took precedence over any others, simply because they wielded so much authority in that context; the same relationships were very much weaker from the senior point of view. Sentiment confused the actual situation still further. People went to considerable lengths to support in-laws of whom they were particularly fond. In-laws whom they despised might be dealt with severely whenever a stress situation required that a choice be made.

During the intermediate period (1890–1940), but particularly after World War II, the frequency of extended family households decreased markedly. The strength of actual parent-in-law–child-in-law relationships became somewhat ambiguous in the new context, and also more difficult for the anthropologist to measure. Sentiment, and particularly the attachment that one's spouse felt toward his or her parents, seemed to be the primary determinant of strength in the 1960's.

Strains

Exemplary cases of parent-in-law–child-in-law relationships certainly existed, but in all time periods they were a distinct minority. This was so primarily because the moral obligation to live up to the ideals of these relationships was much less than it was for any consanguineal tie. In-laws were characteristically quicker to take offense than consanguines, and slower to recover. The extended family household of traditional times particularly provided a context in which strains were maximized. Greater contact led to more frequent conflict, but the residential association through the spouse made it more difficult for one to escape the resulting tension.

Traditionally, stress and strain resulted most frequently from the abuse of the junior by the senior, on the one hand, and the recalcitrance of the junior, on the other. In-marrying "in-laws" held relatively low status in a household anyway, particularly during their first few years there. Mothers-in-law tended to be particularly domineering toward resident daughters-in-law. The junior members rarely questioned the *right* of the senior to order them about, but when it was done often, and in an offensive manner, resentment followed. The feelings generated in relationships in which this occurred could be extremely intense. Even in the 1960's, I witnessed a number of cases in which the child-in-law left the house whenever the spouse was not there.

Conflict of the sort described above resulted most often under three conditions. In the first place, a lazy or selfish junior was certain to evoke indignant and over-bearing treatment from the parent-in-law, who might even go so far as to eject him or her from the household. The second situation was when the parent disapproved of the marriage in the first place, in which case even the most exemplary child-in-law was likely to be treated badly. When this happened, a co-resident child-in-law could be subjected to extraordinary mistreatment for many years after the marriage. There were also instances in which the parents themselves differed from each other in their views of the child-in-law.　As one man put it to me, "My mother sure *hate* that girl! But my father *love* her so much!"　The third and final situation that commonly contributed to the breakdown of parent-in-law–child-in-law relationships was mistreatment by the child-in-law of his or her spouse.　If a husband was cruel to his wife, he could hardly expect to get along with her parents.　If, however, it was a case of the child mistreating the spouse, the situation was sometimes reversed.　In at least one case I know of, the spouses would have separated after a very short time had the parents not intervened on behalf of their child-in-law.

SUBSTITUTION

The several relationships in the other-generation category constituted a set of distinct patterns of action which differed from one another with respect to membership, content, sentiment, or strength, and usually with respect to some combination of the four.　Nevertheless, certain features common to all made them theoretically substitutable for one another within certain limits, and under certain conditions.　The overt nature of this substitutability, its general significance in traditional life, and its peculiarly Eskimo character make it an appropriate topic with which to conclude this chapter.　Attention will be focused primarily on the traditional and early transitional periods, since substitution decreased markedly in frequency after about the 1920's.

The substitutability of Eskimo relationships in general depended primarily on similarities in content.　The other-generation relationships shared two major characteristics in this regard.　First, each was a clearly defined hierarchy, with authority being wielded by the senior member, and accountability being borne by the junior.　Secondly, each relationship was characterized by an obligation on the part of the senior member to give guidance, support, and protection to the junior during the latter's youth, and a corresponding obligation of the junior to sustain the senior in the latter's old age.　Given the fundamental Eskimo condition that *only* relatives could perform these functions, there was no way to fulfill them on any regular basis except across generation lines.[6]

Substitution was always a matter of a parent-child relationship replacing one of the others. It occurred under one of two conditions: (1) when a member of a parent-child relationship died, or (2) when the residential arrangement was such that no parents, or no children, were in the household (or, in some cases, in the vicinity). The place of a parent could be taken by a grandparent, an aunt or an uncle, or a parent-in-law; the place of a child could be filled by a grandchild, by a nephew or niece, or by a child-in-law. In most cases, substitution was automatic when the necessary conditions arose, unless there were a number of alternative relatives available.

When a choice had to be made among two or more candidates, the solution depended upon three factors. The first was the ages of the individuals involved. A healthy active grandparent would probably precede an aunt or uncle, but in the absence of such a grandparent, the chances would be reversed. The second factor involved considerations of strength. On the basis of this criterion, grandparent-grandchild or nepotic relationships would be replaced before affinal ties would be. The third factor was sentiment. On these grounds, people in highly intense positive relationships would fill vacant roles more readily than people in less intense or negative relationships. The net outcome of the interplay of these three factors could vary considerably from case to case.

The frequency of other-generation substitution in traditional times is impossible to determine. Furthermore, there was a difference between temporary and permanent substitution. The former took place for limited periods of time when the parent (or child) was alive but away somewhere, and ceased when he returned. One would suppose temporary substitution to have been common due to residential shifts during the course of the seasonal round, and between one year to the next. Permanent substitution took place theoretically only upon the death of one of the members. Wherever young children were involved, either as the deceased or as the survivor, substitution often took the

---

[6] Occasionally when the parents of siblings 15–20 years or more apart in age died, these functions could be carried out in terms of sibling relationships.

form of outright adoption. This was regarded as the total replacement of one relationship by another. When teenage or adult juniors were involved, permanent substitution occurred essentially by default, and was usually limited to a change in content, not in all aspects of the relationship.

The adaptive value of other-generation substitution in traditional times cannot be determined without more reliable data on migration and mortality than are ever likely to be available. With respect to the first half of the transitional period (1850–1910), however, with its large scale population movements, resource destruction, and recurrent epidemics, it can be stated with some assurance that other-generation substitutability was one of the few traditional social mechanisms that enabled the Northwest Alaskan Eskimos to remain a viable population. When a famine or an epidemic decimated the community, the survivors could immediately pick up the threads of life simply by recruiting new members to important relationships that had been destroyed, and they could use the traditional mechanism of substitution to do it.

5

Same – Generation Relationships

"Same-generation relationships" include sibling, cousin, and certain affinal connections. Like the category of "other-generation relationships," this one is primarily a construct designed to facilitate description rather than a class clearly distinguished in the Eskimo system. Once again, however, it is more than just a descriptive device since it consists of relationships that could be substituted for one another in a manner analogous to the process described in the previous chapter. The replacement of cousin by sibling relationships was particularly common in traditional times, and it was still practised to some extent in the recent period (1940–1970). Certain affines could also operate largely in terms of sibling patterns, under certain conditions, and they are included here for that reason.

Sibling Relationships

Membership

The Eskimo term for "sibling relationship" was *aniqqatigiik*. Within this category, the most general set of distinctions was between *aapiaq* ("older brother") or *aakiak* ("older sister"), on the one hand, and *nukatsiaq* ("younger sibling") on the other; sex was significant terminologically only with respect to older siblings. At a more specific level, the Northwest Alaskan Eskimos also divided younger siblings according to sex, hence the term *nayak* ("younger sister") and *nukatsiaq* ("younger brother"). As far as behavior is concerned, the latter version was more significant than the former. The resulting relationships were four in number: (1) older brother-younger brother (*aapiaq-nukatsiaq*), (2) older brother-younger sister (*aapiaq-nayak*), (3) older sister-younger sister (*aakiak-nayak*), and (4) older sister-younger brother (*aakiak-nukatsiaq*).

Sibling relationships obtained in the first instance among the biological offspring of a resident conjugal pair. In the recent period they were largely restricted to this sphere, but in traditional times the picture was almost always more complicated because of adoption, separation-and-remarriage, polygynous marriage, and co-marriage. There was a proliferation of same-generation relationships through these mechanisms, and every individual normally had two (and often more) *sets* of siblings.

Heinrich (1963a:177) distinguished between "nuclear family siblings," on the one hand, and what he called "para-siblings," or half- or step-siblings on the other. The former were designated by the suffix *-piaq*, the latter by the suffix *-saq*. In an analysis concerned with relationships, rather than with kinship terminology, the distinction between "real" and "para" siblings is not particularly useful, since it focuses attention on membership, and ignores content, sentiment and strength. In practise, siblings who lived together acted in "real" sibling terms whether or not they were real or fictive, "nuclear family" or "para-", half- or step-relatives. Since residential arrangements varied considerably from one household and local group to another, and for each individual through time, one was almost as likely to be living with a "para-sibling" as with a "nuclear family" sibling.

Co-marriage produced still another sort of sibling relationship: Heinrich (1963a:178) calls it the "other-family sibling" relationship, and the Eskimos called it *qatayutigiik*. In general, this relationship obtained between any and all offspring of any two people who had *ever* had sexual intercourse outside the confines of residential marriage. In practical terms, *qatayutigiik* were individuals whose parents were members of a co-marriage,

regardless of when they were born in relation to the t[...]
that the union was established. If two couples, each with one
child, became *nuliaqatigiit* (co-marriage "partners"), the children became *qataŋutigiik.* Whether or not the adults ever engaged in sexual relationships again, all subsequent children of
any of them were related to one another in terms of this relationship. Pre- and extra-marital sexual liasons also could produce these relationships for the children, as long as the adults
informed the children concerned that the link existed.

Given the fact that virtually every traditional Northwest
Alaskan Eskimo had sexual relations with at least two partners
during the course of his or her lifetime, and given the high
frequency of multiple residential marriages (either simultaneously or in succession), the dividing line between "half-,"
"step-," and "co-siblings (*qataŋutigiik*) was frequently obscure.
Heinrich (1963a:178) correctly describes them all as variations on the "para-sibling" theme. During the 1960's, they
were *all* referred to in English by Northwest Alaskan Eskimos
themselves as "half-siblings." But, I must again emphasize the
fact that technical details about recruitment mattered little.
Wherever half-, step-, or co-sibling relationships occurred within
a single residential unit, interaction was in terms of real sibling
patterns. Consequently, most of the discussion of sibling relationships will focus on the four-relationship system outlined
previously. Since the relationship of *qataŋutigiik* was distinctive in certain interesting respects when it occurred *outside* the
residential context, it will be dealt with separately afterwards.

Content

The most important aspect of sibling relationships in Eskimo
eyes was the economic one. A "good" sibling relationship was
one in which the members assisted one another at all times and
in all possible ways. Every one of the specific sibling relationships that was evaluated by my informants was judged
solely on the basis of the extent to which this ideal was approached. The rule of mutual aid was all-embracing; the substantive definition of the elements involved was so broad as to
make exhaustive treatment of the subject an impossibility.
Consequently, the following discussion focuses on only a few of
the primary considerations from the Eskimo point of view.

If an Eskimo were asked to specify the particular feature of the economic aspect of sibling relationships that was uppermost in his mind, he would probably reply that it was "sharing." This prescription referred to goods, but it included virtually every good that might exist in the Eskimo world. The rule is summed up in the saying, "if it belongs to my sibling, then it belongs to me." It would be impossible to list everything that could be included here. The range of possibilities is indicated by the following list of items actually observed by my wife and myself in the context of being shared between siblings: a can of caulking compound, a kayak, tools, money, gasoline, rifle shells, outboard motors, washing machines, buckets, food, dogs, and sleds. In traditional times, the list would have been different, but would have been similarly representative of the universe of goods available at the time.

Ideally, anything could be borrowed from a sibling without asking permission, and without incurring any disapproval on the part of the owner. Actually, items that were very difficult to replace, or items that were likely to be in everyday use, were usually requested rather than simply taken, at least when the individuals involved lived in different houses. Thus, a boat was rarely taken without the owner's permission, and the same was true of washing machines, sleds, and dogs. Expensive items frequently were owned in common by siblings, however, in which case no permission was needed. In other cases the borrowing was so common that permission was simply assumed by both borrower and lender. When such items as rifle shells were taken, it was customary for the borrower to share any game he procured with the sibling who loaned them. Returns were not required, but were indicative of the appreciation of the borrower.

The production of services was not far behind the sharing of goods in importance. Here against the prescription was all-inclusive. The following specific examples from my field notes suggest the range of services produced in terms of sibling relationships in the 1960's: (1) A younger bachelor brother helping an older married sister with her washing machine while he husband was away; (2) A young girl helping her still younger sister do up her hair; (3) An adult man taking care of all of his younger siblings after the death of their father; (4) A married older sister making boots for her unmarried younger brother; (5) A woman with an oil stove letting her sister, who had a woodburning stove, bake bread in her oven; (6) A woman babysitting for her sister's children while the former was very busy; (7) A woman helping her sister butcher an especially large number of seals that her sister's husband had killed; (8) An old man treating his not much younger sister to the plane fare from one village to another for a feast; (9) An older sister teaching a younger one how to sew; (10) A younger sister darning a pair of socks for her older brother. This list could have been enlarged considerably. For traditional times the list would have been equally extensive, although covering a number of different sorts of services.

The economic aspect of the sibling relationship was uppermost in the minds of the Eskimos themselves, but the political aspect was no less interesting from the viewpoint of the anthropologist-observer. The basic pattern of political allocation among siblings was a very simple one: older siblings had authority over younger ones, and the latter were accountable to the former. The functions involved in this prescription were again highly diffuse. An older sibling theoretically had authority over almost anything that a younger one did. A senior could also admonish and reprimand a junior, and was *expected* to do so if the latter was acting inappropriately or contrary to custom. The reverse was not permitted. Sibling relationships were institutionalized as being highly responsible (from all viewpoints), however, and the older sibling was supposed to always keep in mind the welfare of the junior in every situation in which this power was exercised.

The parents, when alive and nearby, served as a check on the capricious use of authority by an older sibling. When the parents were either dead or not there to see what was happening, the younger sibling could have a difficult time if his or her senior decided to abuse this authority. If the *nukatsiaq* was still a child, there was little he could do to stop a senior from having his way, especially if the latter was a male. If the junior sibling was an adult, on the other hand, especially if male, there was little a senior could do to force his or her authority should the junior decide to disobey. The ideal formula was that, the less the senior wielded his authority, the better.

The authority of senior over junior was established at an early age, while the senior was still a small child. At this stage, most of the situations in which authority was wielded involved the delegation of power by the parent to the older sibling for a specific purpose. For example, a child of five or six could be instructed to escort a three-year-old brother over to their aunt's house, and to do whatever was necessary to get him there safely. The pattern of obedience by the junior was internalized early. It was not long before the senior would be divesting his junior of toys and candy, making him get up so that the senior could sit down, and generally ordering him around. Usually this was done without objection on the part of the *nukatsiaq*. If the latter put up a protest, and if the parents were able to see what was happening, he or she frequently still lost out, so strong was this particular hierarchy institutionalized.

Even very young senior siblings generally wielded their authority in responsible ways, probably more often than not. In the 1960's, it was not unusual to see a five-year-old yelling at a younger sibling to get away from the water's edge, and then running down and leading the junior home if he or she did not comply. When a small child was encountered wandering around alone on the village path, even a very young senior sibling would usually take him right home. In such cases, the responsible wielding of authority by seniors over juniors was not by virtue of explicit parental delegation, but was spontaneous. These patterns, established early in childhood, were strengthened as the individuals involved grew older.

Accountability is the other side of the political coin. In the broadest sense, all Eskimos were responsible to the community at large for the misbehavior of any kinsman, with the limiting case being the blood feud in traditional times. Consequently, it was incumbent upon each person to see to it that his relatives did not step out of line. While this general rule applied to all kinsmen, it devolved most heavily on the parent-child and sibling relationships. Even in the 1960's, when feuding was no longer a factor, this old pattern of responsibility was very much in force. It was up to siblings, not to the Village Council, to restrain a drunk from wreaking havoc in the village. Significantly, if a situation exceeded their ability to control it, it was often a sibling rather than a member of the Council who made the formal complaint to the police. This particular pattern seemed to be weakening, however, and it was much less pronounced in the towns than it was in the villages.

Sentiment

Sibling relationships were ideally imbued with intense positive affect on the part of all members. They were usually quite intense in point of fact, probably as much as any relationship in the Eskimo system. The nature of this sentiment varied widely, however, between passionate hatred, at one extreme, and the institutionally prescribed affection, at the other. Although stress in many other types of relationships led more readily to violence, the most intense animosity I have ever observed or heard of among the Northwest Alaskan Eskimos was between brothers; so, too, was the greatest loyalty. In traditional times, the middle range seems to have been the exception in sibling relationships, and extremes the rule. During the intermediate (1890–1940) and particularly the recent (1940–1970) periods there appears to have been some reduction in the intensity of sibling emotions, and a concomitant lessening of variation in the nature of those sentiments.

The increase in family size in Northwest Alaska led to the development of sibling favoritism, along lines similar to those of parental favoritism. That is, an individual frequently prefered one sibling over the others, regardless of how well he might like (or dislike) the others. This pattern was not nearly as pronounced as it was in the case of parent-child relationships, however. My data indicate that, whatever factors might have been involved in the selection of a favorite sibling, sex *per se* was not one of them. There seems to have been a tendency to favor the youngest sibling, and another to favor siblings of the same sex who were very close in age, but personality factors seem to have been as much involved as anything. Otherwise, there seem to have been few changes in either sentiment or its expression between the traditional and recent periods, so the description that follows may be considered applicable to the entire period covered by this study.

The expression of *negative* sentiment between siblings was absolutely prohibited. When it occurred in fact among youngsters, parents or other relatives put an immediate stop to it.

When adult siblings conflicted openly, it was a source of shame to the principals, and of embarrassment to their relatives; accordingly, it did not occur very often.

The expression of *positive* sentiment between siblings was encouraged, but was subject to limitations according to the age and sex of the individuals involved. When one or both members of a sibling relationship were infants, the relationship was expected to be both intimate and highly demonstrative. As long as the *nukatsiaq* was a youngster, the more pronounced this pattern was. Older siblings hugged and kissed infant juniors, held them in their laps, packed them on their backs, and carried them about in their arms. Eskimo children beyond the age of six or so were often adept at handling even tiny babies as a result. Teenage sisters were especially demonstrative toward young siblings of both sexes, and teenage brothers were only slightly less so.

Sibling relationships became progressively less demonstrative and less intimate as the members got older. By the time the junior was about five, intimacy outside the house became restricted to holding hands or walking together with an arm around one another's shoulder. This was especially common when siblings were close together in age. Intimacy was perpetuated longest between sisters. However, I have seen teenage brothers and sisters walking arm in arm, and engaging in activities that involved considerable physical contact.

The last vestige of intimacy was lost from sibling relationships as the *nukatsiaq* reached his or her late teens, although the relationships continued to be open and direct. Expression was also marked by a pronounced change at this time, becoming much more restrained than it had been previously. In Northwest Alaska, restraint seems to have been *least* emphasized between sisters, and *most* emphasized between brothers, although the absolute age difference involved was also very important. When two brothers were fifteen or twenty years apart in age, for example, the relationship was extremely restrained, regardless of the state of affect which characterized the relationship. I once observed an *aapiaq* return from a lengthy stay in the hospital, which he barely survived. When he greeted his younger brother, twenty-one years his junior, neither of them said a word. They shook hands briefly, and walked right past each other, only a trace of a smile on their faces; yet they were *extremely* fond of each other, an assessment based on many sorts of evidence. I often saw brothers of disparate age pass each other on a village path, saying nothing, and not even looking at each other. Just how this would have worked in the case of sisters I cannot say, for I never had occasion to observe sisters of very unequal age. In relationships where the members were the same sex but very close in age, expression was much more demonstrative. Open conversation, smiling, and joking were more the rule than the exception in such cases. Siblings who were close in age but of opposite sex, fell somewhere between these two poles.

Strength

Sibling relationships were extremely strong in traditional Northwest Alaska, second only to parent-child relationships in the entire kinship system (Burch 1966:235ff.). More precisely, a person's relationship to his parents took precedence over those to his siblings. The strength of one's relationships to his or her children *vis-á-vis* his siblings was less clearly defined. The evidence suggests that an adult caught between conflicting obligations to a sibling, on the one hand, and to a child on the other, would be faced with a dilemma. If pressed, he or she would probably opt in favor of the child. In any case, from any point of view, the parent-child and the sibling relationships were far stronger among the traditional Northwest Alaskan Eskimos than any others.

The notion of "sibling solidarity," as a cornerstone of small-scale societies, has permeated much anthropological thought (Fortes 1969:79; Pehrson 1959:275; Radcliffe-Brown 1950:83). The concept has been applied more specifically to the Northwest Alaskan Eskimos by Heinrich (1963a:87). As I understand it, "sibling solidarity," as used by these writers, refers primarily to the strength of sibling relationships.

The Eskimo material suggests that a slight modification in the conventional notion of sibling solidarity is in order. In Northwest Alaska, sibling relationships took precedence over all others *only* when the parents were dead. In practice this meant most of the time, for adults, because of the generally short life-expectancy of individuals in this particular population. Accordingly, most local groups were built on a foundation of sibling relationships, a generalization clearly supported by the examples presented in Chapter Seven. However, when an elderly male whose own siblings were dead or absent was still active, the relationships between his adult children were subordinate to those with him. The father managed things until senility or death, and it was only then that the "unity of the sibling group" became a significant force (cf. Damas 1969a; Levy 1971:39).

One final point: "sibling solidarity" usually refers specifically to strong brother-brother relationships. The impression conveyed by the Northwest Alaskan Eskimo material is that, in cases where sibling relationships did in fact constitute the basis of local group or household composition, *any* type of sibling relationship could be involved. Thus, brother-brother, brother-sister, or sister-sister relationships, alone or in various combinations, could *all* provide the foundation of a larger kinship unit. The frequency of occurrence was probably uneven, however, the distribution ranging downward from brother-brother through brother-sister to sister-sister.

The strength of Northwest Alaskan Eskimo kin relationships in general was on the decrease in the 1960's, as was mentioned earlier. Sibling relationships participated in this decline, although their position within the kinship sphere was not materially affected. The only possible exception to this rule was the increased strength of the marital relationship of *nuliariik*. In most parts of Northwest Alaska, sibling relationships probably still ranked second in the minds of the Eskimos in 1970, but the *nuliariik* relationship had been pushed ahead in fact by virtue of the new laws on divorce. Thus sibling ties still ranked second in Eskimo theory, but probably third in actual fact.

On the concrete level, there was wide variation in strength from one relationship to another during the recent period (1940–1970). This was due primarily to the proliferation of sibling relationships resulting from increased family size. Out of the, say, five to ten or more sibling relationships of which the modern young Eskimo adult was a member, one or two tended to be very strong in fact, with the others being much weaker. Although the traditional ideals of "sibling solidarity" were very much in evidence in contemporary village life, sibling ties were becoming progressively weaker in towns, where they sometimes ranked even behind friendships.

Strains

Despite their great strength, sibling relationships were subject to considerable stress. This derived from different sources according to the ages of the individuals concerned, but seems to have changed rather little between the traditional and recent periods.

Stress between very young siblings was virtually non-existent. As they progressed into and through childhood they began to get into disputes over toys. My informants were unanimously of the opinion that much of the arguing and fighting that went on between youthful siblings in the 1960's was over playthings. In the traditional society, where there were comparatively few toys, there was little difficulty of this sort. One of my middle-aged informants recalled that he almost never fought with his siblings when he was a child—except at Christmas, when everyone received presents from school. Then they fought almost continuously until their father, in disgust, threw all their toys away. Otherwise they never had anything to fight about because they were so poor.

Abuse of authority on the part of the older sibling was a more serious source of strain. It was particularly so in traditional times. Teasing was all right as long as it did not go too far; "bossing" and scolding were all right too, as long as they did not go too far. When they *did* go beyond the bounds of acceptability, there was little a *nukatsiaq* could do anyway, simply because of the superior physical strength of the senior.

One informant, who was especially obnoxious (by his own account) to his younger siblings during his childhood, told me that he would always get his own way except when his younger brothers and sisters formed an alliance against him, in which case he sometimes got a thrashing. He also told me that after he had been particularly nasty to one of his juniors he frequently had nightmares, which suggests that he felt guilty about his behavior despite the fact that he persisted in it.

When a younger sibling was sufficiently aroused, and if he was aggressive enough, serious consequences could follow mistreatment by the senior. I know of several instances where juniors injured seniors with rocks when they had been tormented too much. In a more serious case, a boy stuck an ice pick into his older brother's leg after the latter had been pestering him unmercifully for some time. The Eskimos, however, were generally opposed to retaliation by juniors, except in the most extreme circumstances.

By the time siblings reached adulthood, overt disputes were rare. When they did occur, they were frequently severe and long-lasting in their consequences. Conflicts between adult siblings were apparently most frequent and most serious between brothers, far more so in both respects than between two sisters, or between brother and sister.

Stinginess was the most common source of conflict between adult siblings. In view of the strong value attached to sharing, it may be readily understood that a refusal might produce a strong negative reaction on the part of a sibling who wished to borrow something. If the situation of the refusal was significant enough, or if it followed upon a number of other irritations, it could produce a serious rift.

The most extreme case of this sort that I actually observed involved two brothers. The older one had a skin boat but no wooden one; the *nukatsiaq* was an excellent carpenter. So, the *aapiaq* asked his junior to make him a wooden boat, and promised to give him the skin boat in return. The *nukatsiaq* complied with the wishes of the senior, made a very good wooden boat, and gave it to him. The older brother gave him the skin boat in return, as agreed, but the next year took it back. Then he refused to let his younger brother use either of the boats. Previously the two men had been very close. After that time they went through superficial motions of cooperation, but generally remained quite hostile toward each other. The public recriminations that the two indulged in from time to time were a disgrace to the entire village.

The refusal of assistance was a second common source of stress between adult siblings. The pattern of mutual assistance was so strongly institutionalized in these relationships that, when one requested help from a sibling, he definitely expected to get it. In one case that I observed, a man was building a house, but because of the lateness of the season he had to build it fast.   His older brother, however, refused his request for help.   A few years later it became apparent that the latter's house was no longer fit to live in because of the advanced state of decay of the supporting timbers.   He thought he could blithely move into the house that he had refused to help build a few years previously. The younger brother's reaction to this idea is unprintable, but he refused to even consider it.   The case was cited by informants as an example of how brothers should *not* behave.

"In-law" trouble was another common source of conflict between adult siblings.   In the majority of such cases, it was the wife or husband that caused trouble between the spouse and his or her siblings.   Although the specific circumstances varied widely, the problem usually resulted from the wife or husband preventing the spouse from fulfilling certain of his or her obligations as a sibling, usually where sharing or assistance was concerned.

Physical violence between adult siblings was rare.   Every case that is known to me involved brothers.   In traditional times, the limiting case was the murder of one brother by another, always in a dispute over a woman; although rare, it happened often enough to establish a pattern.   Murder was superseded as the extreme form of sibling violence by severe beating during the transitional period.   Usually this occurred when one or both individuals were intoxicated.   The case described below is typical.

> A man had been mistreating his younger brother in very serious ways for years (usually when under the influence of alcohol), but he had never been taken to task for his actions. One day, when drunk, he started annoying his brother's wife and children.   The junior sibling lost his temper and attacked him.   He would have killed him with his bare hands if their mother had not appeared in time to stop him; as it was, a severe beating was administered.   Interestingly, the junior sibling suffered severe guilt feelings as a consequence of his actions.   From what he told me it is apparent that he experienced recurrent hallucinations for almost eighteen hours afterwards, and for weeks was ashamed to look any of his fellow villagers in the eye.   Even several years later, he still got extremely agitated when talking about the incident.   All this despite the fact that everyone agreed that he did what he had to under the circumstances.

As Wrong (1963:72) once pointed out, "to say that a norm has been internalized, or introjected . . . , is to say no more than that a person will suffer guilt feelings if he fails to live up to it in his behavior;" it says nothing about whether he will live up to it or not in fact. It might also be assumed that, the greater the guilt feelings resulting from failure to live up to a norm, the greater the degree to which that norm has been internalized. Consequently, I suggest that the above case, while noteworthy for its extreme departure from the ideal, is most significant in the respects in which it exemplifies the ideal. I know of no incident of any kind that could produce such extreme feelings of guilt in a Northwest Alaskan Eskimo as physical violence against a sibling, unless it be violence toward a parent or child.

Before concluding the discussion of strains, it is appropriate to mention two types of conflict that might be anticipated by the reader, but which did not occur in fact. The first is sibling rivalry for the affection of the parents. During the 1960's, competition of this sort was extremely rare, and every observed case involved young children of highly acculturated parents. The questioning of elderly informants revealed complete ignorance of any behavior that might be subsumed under the heading of "sibling rivalry", so presumably it did not exist at all before the recent period. The second type of conflict that might be expected is that of resentment of the special treatment shown by parents to their favorite children. Interestingly, it too was extremely uncommon. Even in families where the discrepancy in the treatment of favorites and non-favorites was pronounced, any hostility that was engendered as a result was directed toward the parent rather than toward the favored sibling. In fact, a parent's favorite child was not uncommonly an unfavored child's favorite sibling, especially when it was the last born.

Qataŋutigiik

The *qataŋutigiik* relationship, or that of "co-siblings," was basically a regular sibling relationship of the type discussed so far, with the appropriate variations with respect to the sex and absolute and relative ages of the members. It has been claimed by Spencer (1959:85), however, that "under most circumstances *qataŋutigiit* could marry." Heinrich (1955b:116), on the other states not only that they could *not* marry, but that their descendants were also subject to the incest taboo. My own data agree with Heinrich on this point. My informants did not know of any *qataŋutigiik* who married, and the notion struck them as being at least as reprehensible as any other sibling marriage. These considerations of course apply to the ideal pattern. Co-siblings no doubt did marry in fact from time to time; Milan (1964:63) cites one such case.

When two co-siblings lived in the same settlement, they normally interacted in terms of a regular sibling relationship of the type discussed above. Under such conditions, the relationship of *qataŋutigiik* simply merged with the others. This was true not only with respect to content, sentiment, and strength, but also with respect to the use of kinship terms. Every example of the *qataŋutigiik* relationship that I personally observed operating in the context of a single village featured the use of real sibling terminology.

What, then was the difference between *qataŋutigiik* and the other sibling relationships? Primarily, it was in the circumstances in which it normally operated. The relationship was operative in a distinctive form *only* when the parties to it resided in different villages most of the time. It might be labelled the relationship of "other-village siblings" rather than "other-family siblings."

The *qataŋutigiik* relationship, as such, was one in terms of which action was primarily oriented to matters of mutual protection and support in a strange village context. A *qataŋun* was a sibling who lived in another village, and who, if you happened to go there, would take you in, protect and succor you until you left, and for whom you would do likewise. The following story, in the words of an informant, is indicative of how it worked.

> Two men were putting out a seal net in the springtime down at Wales. And those two men was drifting out from the shore on the sea ice, and they stayed out on the ocean all summer until the ice was almost gone. When they wanted to eat, they ate a little piece of seal-skin rope. They got real skinny. When the piece of ice they were on got close to

Cape Thompson, they wanted to swim to the beach, but they were too weak, and the current took them right down to Point Hope. And when they got down there, the Point Hopers was getting them with a boat. They sure wanted to kill them right there! But the oldest one, by name of Arnaaluq, he remembered that his father told him that he had a *qataŋun* in Point Hope. Only one—one man; and he told him that if he ever got down there just to say his name.

And when they got to the beach, the Point Hopers were going to kill them right there. Arnaaluq told the people that he didn't figure to die on the ocean, but he was willing to die on the land. But he had a *qataŋun*, he said, and he mentioned the name of the *qataŋun*.

That *qataŋun* had never done anything against the peoples before, all right; but just when he hear that word, just when he hear his name, he start to walk down, pushing the people away with his elbows. And when the people see him, they stand back. Just when he got to those strangers, he grabbed them by their arms, and started to walk back to his house. And the people were scared of him, and they made a path for him through the middle.

And when they got to his house, he put the two strangers inside, and turned around and talked to the people: "Now any of you fellas, be sure and don't come to my house! If you come to my house, that's the end of your life! Don't try to do anything to my house or my family or you will die *right away*!"

He was always quiet before, but now he talks like that! And he keep the strangers right there inside the house, and never let them go out. And they stay there all winter, and he take them back to their home the next summer. That's the kind of *qataŋun* they had long ago—he always help them.

This is a classic case. Arnaaluq's father once had had sexual relations with the *qataŋun's* mother, probably at the summer fair, and he had told Arnaaluq his *qataŋun's* name. Arnaaluq had kept this information to himself. Finally, finding himself in a strange place and confronted with the certain death of a man without kin, he remembered that name and said it aloud. The *qataŋun* heard his name being called. Without ever having seen Arnaaluq before, and possibly not even knowing his name, he took immediate charge of the situation; he rescued the strangers, fed and sheltered them for a whole year in hostile territory, and eventually returned them safely to their homes.

My informants were unanimous in declaring the virtues of the *qatayutigiik* relationship. Typically the relationship was described not as one between *mere* brothers (or sisters), but as one between *good* brothers (or sisters). The following excerpt from an interview is indicative of this feeling:

> *Anthropologist:* Tell me about *qatayutigiik*. How are they supposed to be to each other?
>
> *Informant:* Well, they are just like good brothers. That's the *best* one! When I hear my *qatayun* is coming here, I have to go and invite him to stay with me. They love each other, the *qatayuns*. Just like *real good brothers!*
>
> *Anthropologist:* Just like brothers, or different?
>
> *Informant:* More better, I think.

My informants were equally certain that the *qatayutigiik* relationship was a very strong one. They even claimed that, if one had to choose between supporting a *qatayun* and any other kind of relative except parents and other siblings, one should stand by the *qatayun*.

Following the extinction of the institution of co-marriage, the relationship of *qatayutigiik* began to disappear. Fortunately for the Eskimos, the need for protection on the inter-village level was no longer so great, although shelter was still sought from a *qatayun* in a strange village. Incidentally, it is worth noting that, while the above examples involved males, *qatayutigiik* could be persons of either sex, and the general obligations involved were identical. It was simply in the nature of the case that, in the traditional society, a man could offer more support than a woman could. A woman would take in *qatayun* who appeared as a stranger in her village, however, and her husband was bound to support both her *and* the *qatayun* under such conditions, or suffer the consequences of a blood feud. During the recent period, I personally saw *qatayun* relationships of all sexual combinations in operation, including one in which a widow put up a male *qatayun* for several months.

Cousin Relationships

Membership

Depending on the district and on the context, the *traditional* Northwest Alaskan Eskimos operated in terms of either a "two-cousin" or a "three-cousin" pattern, a distinction that was outlined in Chapter Two. To recapitulate briefly, the difference between the two involved differences in membership criteria. In the three-cousin system, membership was determined on the basis of the sexes of the connecting links in the *parental* generation. The resulting relationships were: (1) *aɣutiqan-aɣutiqan*, in which both connecting parents were male; (2) *arnaqan-arnaqan*, in which both connecting parents were female; and (3) *illuq-illuq*, in which the connecting parents were of opposite sex. The conventional terms "patrilateral parallel," "matrilateral parallel," and "cross cousins," respectively, can be employed to refer to these relationships—as long as it is understood that the degree of collaterality between them was irrelevant. In the two-cousin system, on the other hand, the memberships were (1) *arnaqan-arnaqan*, in which both members were male; (2) *anyak-anyak*, in which both were female; and (3) *arnaqan-anyak*, or male-female cousins. Collateral distance was again irrelevant.

Traditionally, the three-cousin system operated primarily in the societies whose home districts were on the coast, along the Lower Noatak, Kobuk, and Selawik Rivers, and on the Seward Peninsula (Heinrich 1960:112–113). The two-cousin system was operative primarily in the societies of the northern interior. During the population movements of the last quarter of the 19th century, this reasonably even distribution was disturbed, particularly in the north, where many "two-cousin people" came to reside in "three-cousin areas." Subsequently, in the northern districts, the two-cousin system gradually became the predominant one. The three-cousin system was still found in the Kobuk and Selawik Valleys, and on the Seward Peninsula in the 1960's, although in many areas the general American cousin system was replacing both forms of Eskimo arrangement.

The reasonably clear-cut traditional distribution of the two systems between comparatively rich (three-cousin) and poor (two-cousin) environmental zones invites analysis in ecological terms, and Heinrich (1960:112) has provided just such an account. To one concerned with terminology *per se*, the ecological contrast is convincing. If one shifts attention to behavior, however, the distinction becomes less significant. Many individuals living in "two-cousin districts" had cousins in "three-cousin districts," and *vice versa*. Depending on whom they were talking to and about, such individuals could and did employ two- or three-cousin terms with equal facility. Furthermore, the major *behavioral* distinction in cousin relationships was between cross-cousins (*illuriik*), on the one hand, and parallel cousins on the other. While the contrast between the two was usually greater in three-cousin areas, it was by no means limited to them. Finally both kinds of parallel cousin interacted primarily in sibling terms. Consequently, sex and relative age were much more significant bases of role differentiation in these two relationships than was sex of the "connecting link"—a generalization that holds equally for both two- and three-cousin areas. It appears to me that the two-cousin/three-cousin distinction appears to have reflected a dialect difference more than anything else.

Only two types of cousin relationships will be distinguished for purposes of the following analysis. One of these is *illuriik* (cross-cousins), or the "joking cousin" relationship. The other is a residual category, which I will refer to as the relationship of *arnaqatigiik* (parallel cousins). These two patterns account adequately for all available data on behavior from all areas of Northwest Alaska for all time periods, regardless of the kinship terms used in any given district. Viewed from this perspective, cousin relationships were very similar throughout the Northwest Alaskan area, and they changed little between traditional and recent times.

Content

The content of both types of cousin relationships was very similar to that of the various sibling relationships. That is to say, the cousin relationships were functionally diffuse, responsible, and hierarchical. Cousins were expected to share with and assist one another in any and all circumstances, a prescription that could cover practically anything one could do. Following the sibling pattern, older cousins had authority over younger ones, although the extent of this authority was more restricted in most contexts than was that of siblings.

Sibling and cousin relationships, although *similar* in content, were not identical. The difference lay not in what was done, but in the degree to which the appropriate behavior was institutionalized. The moral compulsion to live up to the ideals of a sibling relationship was *much* greater than it was with respect to a cousin relationship, even though the types of activity involved were the same.

The major evidence regarding the degree of institutionalization consists of the relative quantity and quality of the departures from the ideal. Most revealing is the matter of incest. My informants and the literature are in agreement that both cousin and sibling relationships were covered by the incest taboo. However, as was noted previously, cousins frequently became involved in a residential marriage, and even more frequently had casual sexual relations with one another. I recorded eight cases of sexual relations between first cousins, and five between second cousins (in our sense of those terms) in one restricted region. These were noted more or less in passing rather than after a detailed examination of genealogical connections, so there may well have been more. By contrast, only one case of sibling incest was recorded in the same population.

The degree of moral outrage with which the two kinds of incest were viewed by the Eskimos is more significant than the frequency of departures from the ideal. It was easy for an anthropologist to learn about the residential marriage of cousins, and it did not require very sophisticated techniques to learn about casual sexual relations between cousins; they simply were not serious enough to be kept secret. Sibling incest was quite another matter, and only luck and persistent searching provided me with any information at all. It is significant that this unwillingness to divulge information characterized the whole population of the village where it occurred, and was not restricted to the principals in the case. It was simply too shameful to talk about.

Less striking, but nonetheless important, was the number of cousin relationships that were marked by petty bickering. Again, the most interesting feature is not the frequency of the disputes, but the fact that the participants took no special pains to hide them. In the case cited earlier in which two brothers parted ways over disagreement about boat ownership, the principals used to lie in the most blatant fashion to keep a stranger from learning about it. Indeed, the village as a whole tried to cover up the incident. But where cousins were concerned, even when the matter was serious enough for the principals to be ashamed to talk about it, almost anyone else might be willing to volunteer information.

Sentiment

Cousin relationships were institutionalized as being imbued with positive affect, which was expected to be of relatively high intensity. In both respects, they were closer to the mid-point of the emotional continuum than were their sibling counterparts. My basic evidence on this point was in the nature of the reaction with which infractions of the ideal patterns were greeted. The assumption is that the degree of emotional reaction to improper behavior is an indicator of the intensity of the relationship. If someone gets extremely angry or upset when his opposite number behaves improperly, then the relationship is probably imbued with sentiments of high intensity. If one reacts with back-biting, petty insults, and the like then the relationship involved is probably of relatively low intensity.

A regular pattern of differences in reaction emerged from my data. It was noted above that departures from the ideals of sibling behavior were sometimes greeted with violent reactions. Killing and severe beatings were cited as extreme examples. But, while many cases of improper behavior on the part of cousins were recorded, I did not learn of a single instance of physical violence occurring. Cousins certainly got angry with one another, but instead of getting altogether distraught, they merely called each other names, usually behind each other's back. There was very little of this "behind the back" activity on the part of siblings. If they were at serious odds with one another, siblings generally hashed things out face to face, preferably in private.

The most distinctive features of the cousin relationships emerge in the realm of expression, and here the relationships of *arnaqatigiik* and *illuriik* differed notably from one another. The former was similar to the sibling pattern, in that childhood intimacy gradually shifted to non-intimate directness among adults, although the change proceeded more slowly among cousins, and it did not go quite as far. Adult *arnaqan* of both sexes seemed to be much more demonstrative in each other's presence than adult siblings were. Male cousins several years apart in age talked and laughed together in a manner that would have been considered quite improper between male siblings of the same ages.

The *illuriik* bond was a radical departure from all other Eskimo kin relationships as far as expression was concerned. This was the Northwest Alaskan Eskimo version of the "joking relationship" reported from various societies around the world. As a joking relationship, it was one characterized by extreme lack of restraint. In contrast to most other Eskimo kin relationships, it became progressively less restrained with the passage of time.

The Eskimos used to say that *illuriik* could "talk to each other any old way." By this they meant that joking cousins could tease and insult each other as much as they wanted to without evoking ill feelings. In most cases, the distinctive feature of the relationship was a general lack of restraint, with much laughter, and loud talk. Public derrogation and teasing characterized only a few cases. The members of such relationships were always mature adults who had gradually developed their association from a solid foundation, and who were *very* fond of one another. They would address one another as *illuq*, openly and loudly question each other's sexual prowess, intelligence, industry, physical appearance, and prospects of going to heaven. The insults were often so close to the mark as to produce considerable uneasiness in observers, who sometimes got so embarrassed that they would leave. Among the Northwest Alaskan Eskimos, *no one* but an *illuq* of long and close association could do this without evoking a violently hostile reaction.

A member of a well-developed joking relationship would often go to considerable lengths to contrive a situation that would provide him with an opportunity to make fun of his *illuq*. Competitions were an especially common device, since the winner could always ridicule the loser. Practical jokes were less common, but where particularly close cousins were involved, they were sometimes indulged in with a vengeance. The following story illustrates just how far this sort of thing could go.

> One time two *illuqs* were sitting together in the house talking, and one of them was smoking his pipe. After a while, the man who was smoking got up and went outside to pee, leaving his pipe behind. After he went through the door, his *illuq* took the pipe, stuck it up his ass, pulled it out, and put it back where he got it. When the smoker returned, the pipe was just where he left it. He picked it up and put it in his mouth before he noticed the smell. Right away he started to vomit, laughing same time. His *illuq* beat him right there!

My informant went on to tell how the smoker proceeded to tear off and destroy his *illuq's* clothes. The latter was laughing so hard he could not defend himself. My informant admitted that he probably would have lost his temper if his own *illuq* had done that to him, but he also maintained that the story was illustrative of the highest standards of joking cousin behavior.

Strength

Cousin relationships were ideally much weaker than sibling relationships. Three sorts of evidence point to this conclusion. In the first place, although older cousins had authority over younger ones, older siblings could always override the dictates of a cousin. This being the case, the sibling relationship inevitably took precedence over the cousin relationship simply by virtue of differential allocation of authority.

The deactivation pattern also points to the same conclusion. If a particular cousin relationship became unsatisfactory to the members, regardless of the reason, there was practically no problem in their deactivating it, i. e., in ignoring its existence. In effect, this amounted to a person saying "the heck with *that* cousin," and proceeding to pretend that that person simply was not related to him. On the whole, it was easier for second (or more distant cousins) to do this than it was for first cousins since, in the latter case, the parents involved would be siblings. Frequent contact between cousins as a result of the close ties of the parents could actually preclude the deactivation of a relationship, or at least make it very difficult to effect. If the cousins were not residing in the same village, however, there was relatively little problem in this respect. Theoretically, sibling relationships could *never* be deactivated in this fashion.

The third possibility was that, when a relationship between cousins actually became very strong, the members could begin to operate in terms of sibling rather than cousin ties. Such cases were indicated to the world at large when the principals began to use sibling terms when speaking to or about one another. In other words, when a cousin relationship became as strong in fact as a sibling relationship was in theory, the latter simply replaced it. Cousin relationships thus tended to sow the seeds of their own destruction, both when they were much weaker *and* when they were much stronger in fact than they were in theory.

Affinal Relationships

Since people tended to marry individuals of approximately the same age, hence of comparable generations, certain of the Eskimo affinal relationships are appropriately considered in the "same-generation" category. These relationships, four in number, are usefully divided into two groups according to whether they involved individuals in the same or different generation as the individuals whose marriage led to their establishment. The former category consists of three relationships, the latter of just one. The two groups will be discussed separately.

The relationship of co-parents-in-law, or *nulliriik*, involved individuals whose children were *ui* and *nuliaq*, i. e., husband and wife in a residential marriage. In marked contrast to the comparable relationship among many Eskimo groups in Canada, this one was very poorly defined in terms of both content and sentiment. It was also the weakest relationship in the entire kinship system. As an institutionalized pattern, the relationship traditionally seems to have corresponded closely to that of a friendship in the United States. It was thus functionly diffuse, responsible, and egalitarian. In the recent period (1940–1970), the *nulliriik* tie became more like what we might call an "acquaintanceship," that is, a very casual, insignificant form of association. Many adults in the 1960's had never even heard the term *nulliq*, and some went so far as to suggest that I must be mispronouncing the word *nulik* ("copulate") when I asked about it. The institutionalized insignificance of *nulliriik* in both traditional and recent time obviates the need for further discussion of it.

The remaining affinal relationships were those of (1) *sakiraq-niɣau*, (2) *sakiraq-ukuaq*, and (3) *aɣayunruq-nukaunruq*. A *niɣau* was an "in-marrying" male, i. e., a male who married any of a person's (female) consanguineal kin; *ukuaq* was the corresponding position for a female. A *sakiraq* was basically any consanguineal relative of one's spouse, usually excluding his or her parents. The relationship of *nukaunruriik*, or "co-affines," obtained between the spouses of siblings or cousins, regardless of the sex of either the members or of the connecting relatives. The *aɣayunruq* was the spouse of the older sibling (or cousin), and the *nukaunruq* was the spouse of the younger one. Although the criteria for membership in these three relationships did not include generation, they all were normally operative primarily at the "same-generation level" as that level is defined here.

The three relationships listed in the preceding paragraph were often active associations having a high "functional yield." In traditional times, when extended family households and local groups were nearly universal in Northwest Alaska, virtually every residential unit included a number of individuals related to one another in these ways. In the 1960's they were becoming less frequent within households, but were still found in virtually every neighborhood.

The content of each of these three relationships was very similar to that of sibling ties. My informants were in unanimous agreement that, when these relationships were operating properly, *all* of them were characterized by the content of sibling relationships. My own observations confirmed this view, for the "best" examples from the Eskimo's own point of view did approach the ideals of (adult) siblingship to a marked degree; however, the ideal was approached more often by co-affines than by in-laws.

Like most Eskimo kin relationships, the affinal ties under consideration here were hierarchical. Ideally, and often actually, a *niŋau* or *ukuaq* was subordinate to a *sakiraq*, regardless of the sex or age of the individuals concerned. In the co-affinal relationship (connecting individuals married siblings or cousins), the spouse of the older sibling or cousin (the *aŋayunruq*) theoretically had authority over the spouse of the junior sibling or cousin (*nukaunruq*), regardless of their own ages relative to one another. In practice, it sometimes happened that the relative ages of individuals involved, rather than the relationship of the connecting links, determined the flow of authority. Thus, an older *niŋau* might wield authority over a younger *sakiraq*, just the reverse of the ideal situation. The most frequent and most extreme departure from the rule was in the co-affine relationship many of which were non-hierarchical.

The affinal relationships under consideration were ideally imbued with positive sentiment of moderate intensity, while expression was supposed to be relatively restrained. In fact, the variation was considerable. My observations during the 1960's indicated that practically every adult was a member of at least one relationship in this category which was characterized by a great deal of mutual affection, as much as a very intense sibling tie. Where the strains were considerable, on the other hand, the relationships could be marked by considerable hostility. Where the relationship was inactive, it could be nearly devoid of any sentiment at all.

In terms of strength, these three relationships were ideally near the bottom of the entire kinship system, ranking below all consanguineal and marital relationships, and above only the *nulliriik* bond. The relationship of co-affines ideally ranked slightly below the other two being discussed here. Actually, there was the usual variation, and co-affines particularly seemed to develop very strong ties with one another. Affinal relationships involving individuals of the same sex were likely to be stronger in practice than those involving members of opposite sex, especially if the members were relatively close together in age.

Substitution

Substitution was particularly common with respect to same-generation relationships in traditional times. It was much more commonplace in this sphere than in that of other-generation relationships. Heinrich (1963a:100) was quite correct in focussing his attention on substitution in this domain, although his failure to mention the phenomenon in connection with other-generation ties constituted a serious omission. Similarly, his emphasis on the replacement of cousin by sibling relationships was correctly placed; his failure to mention any affinal relationships in this context was an oversight.

The substitution of cousin by sibling relationships normally occurred under one of two conditions. By far the most common situation was when cousins relatively close together in age were raised in the same household. If co-residence began early and lasted for a number of years, even if only on a seasonal basis, cousins often interacted exactly as siblings would under the same conditions, and they used sibling terminology for one another in both vocative and reference contexts.

The second situation in which cousin relationships were commonly replaced by sibling ties was when adult cousins who got along especially well spent a number of years living in the same local group, particularly if one or both of them lacked siblings there. Under the latter conditions, cousins would be virtually forced to interact as siblings simply because the limitations of the social system required that siblings, or their functional equivalents, be present if life was to proceed normally. When cousins acted as siblings to one another's satisfaction, replacement usually occurred; again, the shift was typically symbolized by a switch to sibling from cousin terminology.

Substitution always began with a modification of the content of the relationship, at least when the members were adults (v. Heinrich 1963a:100ff.). Although it was sometimes almost mandatory that a change in content occur, substitution beyond that point was always completely voluntary. Often it proceeded no further. However, when the content of such a relationship was especially satisfactory to the members for an extended period of time, a gradual shift in sentiment might ensue. When both the content and the sentiment had followed the sibling pattern for a time, a gradual shift in strength might begin. When the content, sentiment, *and* strength of a cousin or affinal relationship all became identical in fact to the ideals of siblingship, complete replacement had occurred.

From the Eskimos' point of view, the change in sentiment seems to have been the critical matter, because, when it had transpired, the principals typically began to use sibling terminology for one another. Except when cousins were raised as siblings, this transition usually took several years to complete. In the case of the in-law relationships, the appropriate shift in sentiment apparently occurred only occasionally, but it seems to have been fairly common among same-sexed co-affines (v. Heinrich and Anderson 1968). I was unable to collect information concerning actual shifts in strength from affinal to sibling levels for any time period, but it must have been very rare indeed during traditional times, and probably was uncommon subsequently.

6

Strategies of Affiliation

Relationships of the kind described in the preceding chapters represent the simplest type of social system, since each defines the actions that interrelate just two individuals in any given case. Such relationships of course do not operate in isolation, but in a more complex social network of which they are just the basic structural entities. In accordance with the procedure of "building the Eskimo system from the bottom up," as prescribed in Chapter Two, it is now necessary to place the separate relationships into the broader social context in which they actually occurred.

The material on the larger organizations that were constructed of the different relationships is presented in two sections. First, in the present chapter, I describe the considerations, or strategies, that affected an individual's decisions regarding whom he would relate to in terms of the various relationships that made up the system. Then, in the following chapter, I describe the situations that resulted when these strategies were put into practice.

Flexibility

In Chapter Two I pointed out that traditional Eskimo social organization is often said to have been "flexible," or even "formless." Specifically, this flexibility is said (e. g., by Guemple 1972b:2) to have inhered in two specific characteristics of that

195

organization. The first is that people were allocated to membership in an ambiguous way. The second is that there were very few prescriptions stating how people were supposed to treat each other once they were allocated.

In the three preceding chapters I have attempted to demonstrate that the second of the above assertions is untenable: Eskimo social organization *did* specify how people were supposed to interact. In the kinship system alone, there were at least twenty-seven different patterns in terms of which people were supposed to interact, at least at the level of generalization of concern here. Furthermore, the values associated with conformity to those patterns were strongly institutionalized; they were *not* vague guidelines that one could follow or ignore simply according to one's personal whims. In short, the view that the Eskimos did not know and/or did not care how to interact with their fellows is nonsense.

The flexibility that characterized Eskimo social organization lay, instead, in the first of the two reported sources, i. e., that of membership, or the allocation of individuals among the various positions distinguished in the system.[1] At the most general level, the sources of this flexibility lay in the various factors of augmentation and limitation discussed in Chapter Two. At lower levels, it resulted from the interplay of those general factors, the specific criteria for membership in each relationship, and the more or less accidental circumstances of life in which people found themselves at any given time. But once in a position, an individual knew precisely how he was supposed to behave, and everyone else knew just what they could expect of him.

Strategies of affiliation were possible in the Eskimo kinship system precisely because of the flexibility it offered with respect to filling the various roles distinguished in terms of it. Guemple (1972c:56) has argued in this context that social relations were "to a large degree negotiable" (cf. Guemple 1972a, 1972b). The term "negotiate" is a reasonable one in that it implies that (1) individuals could choose among alternatives, and that (2) the choice was not simply an individual decision, but one worked out by two or more people. However, the term is misleading in that

---

[1] This type of flexibility seems to have been quite common in hunting-gathering societies, and was by no means unique to the Eskimos (cf. Leacock 1969:14–16; Lee and DeVore, eds., 1968a; 1968d:7, 9; Woodburn 1968:103).

it implies discussion explicitly directed to the specific topic of who should interact with whom in what specific ways. Actually, negotiation in this sense occurred only with respect to involvement in marital relationships, and it was often limited even there. In other contexts, the word "develop" would be more appropriate. It suggests that the details were not worked out quickly, but emerged gradually over a long period during which the individuals involved may not have been very aware of the changes that were taking place. For most of the people most of the time, strategies of affiliation were formulated and implemented in an essentially developmental context which extended quite literally over the course of a lifetime for each individual.

Types of Strategy

It is useful for present purposes to distinguish between "basic" and "intermediate" strategies of affiliation. The former are those concerned with sheer survival. The latter are those that lead to a standard of living over and above the minimum. Under the heading of "intermediate" strategies would fall decisions relating to the accumulation of wealth or power, just to list two possibilities.

In theory, it would be possible to carry the analysis one step further and talk about "immediate" strategies. These would be considerations involved in decisions affecting day-to-day existence, i. e., those affecting immediate goals. However, concern with questions at this level would involve so much detail—on individual personalities, weather, food supply, etc., etc.—that it is simply not feasible in a study of this kind.

Basic Strategies of Affiliation

The Traditional Period

Among the traditional Northwest Alaskan Eskimos there were two strategies of affiliation that fall under the heading of "basic." The first was that one had to be actively affiliated with kinsmen of some kind if one was to survive. The second consideration, a more specific version of the first, was that, in order to survive, one had to belong to an organization in which at least one of each of the following kinds of relationships was represented: a marital relationship, an other-generation relationship, and a same-generation relationship. These two principles will be discussed separately in some detail.

The most fundamental consideration in traditional Northwest Alaskan Eskimo strategies of affiliation was that not a single goal in life, including the basic one of sheer survival, could be achieved without the help of kinsmen. An individual could relate peacefully to non-kin, for example, in terms of a partnership (*niuviriik*) (v. Burch 1970a), but one could never depend on a partner who did not have the support of several relatives himself. Since this was a reciprocal consideration, it follows that people had to be actively affiliated with kin in order to participate successfully even in this non-kin relationship. But even the strongest non-kin tie was considered weaker than the weakest kin relationship. In times of crisis, such as famine or war, one always had to opt for a kinsman in favor of a partner, and one knew that one's partner would have to do likewise. There was practical as well as moral compulsion in this, because, *if* an individual *failed* to support a relative over someone else, he would be ostracized summarily by all the kin who knew about his behavior.

Ostracism could take a number of forms, varying from the "silent treatment" at one extreme, to loud and continuous haranguing, and perhaps even to physical expulsion at the other, although this was rare. In any case, once word got around that a person's relatives would no longer support him, he would become a target for the hostility of everyone else. The sequence would begin with the ridiculing and shoving of the (socially) isolated individual. If he did not quickly restore the good will of his kin they would not come to his aid, and the pushing and ridicule would gradually escalate to robbery and torture. If the relatives still refrained from rescuing the afflicted kinsman, he would eventually be killed, and his death would not be avenged. Since the pattern was part of the basic knowledge of every Northwest Alaskan Eskimo, each person knew that he had to maintain good relations with at least some of his kinsmen at all times.

The Northwest Alaskan Eskimo emphasis on kinship ties, and their corresponding devaluation of all others, was basically an ethical matter. It was not a constraint imposed on human activity by the extreme environment, for ecological requirements could have been satisfied through any one of several other social mechanisms. Nonetheless, the Northwest Alaskan Eskimo on kinship ties seems to have been nearly as great as that of the traditional Chinese, probably exceeding in intensity that of the majority of hunting peoples (cf. Lee and DeVore 1968a, 1968c). The ethical nature of this emphasis on kinship in no way reduced its importance, however, for it seems to have been the most pervasive and deeply ingrained moral standard that existed in Northwest Alaska until well into the intermediate period (1890–1940).

The second basic strategy of affiliation in traditional Northwest Alaska focused on the specific types of kin relationship that had to be represented in kinship units if they (and their members) were to be viable over any extended period of time. The three types, as mentioned previously, were at least one marital relationship, at least one other-generation relationship, and at least one same-generation relationship. I must emphasize the fact that, when I say that these "had to" be represented, I mean that they "had to" in terms of the Northwest Alaskan Eskimo set of *values*, not because the environment or Eskimo heredity made them necessary in some strictly physical or biological sense. To belong to a unit minimally comprised of these relationships was a basic strategy of affiliation because, given the general conditions of life in Northwest Alaska *and* the structure of the Northwest Alaskan Eskimo type of society, an individual could not do otherwise and survive for very long.

The first of what might be called "requisite kin relationships" in traditional Northwest Alaska was a marital one. More specifically, it was a relationship between residential spouses (*uinuliaq*). The significance of this relationship rested on two factors. First, although it was not the only relationship in Northwest Alaska involving sexual intercourse, it was the only relationship in which sexual intercourse had the specific objective of producing children, and children were important for several reasons which are listed below. Children could be (and were) produced also in terms of co-marital (*uiŋuzaq-nulizaq*) relationships. However, since sexual intercourse was infrequent between co-spouses, it was a very risky way to go about it. Furthermore, since offspring typically lived with the biological mother rather than with the presumed biological father in such cases, co-marriage provided for the old age of only one of the two co-spouses, and not for both of them.

The second factor that made a residential marriage essential in traditional Eskimo eyes was the division of labor along sex lines. Since men's work and women's work were so different, it was necessary for adult members of both sexes to be represented in every household. Theoretically this requirement could have been resolved through non-marital relationships, such as the brother-sister relationship, and sometimes it was for short periods of time. However, the only way that both the "division of labor problem" and the "production of children problem" could be resolved reliably for most individuals over extended periods of time was in terms of the residential spouse relationship. For these reasons, each Eskimo tried to acquire a spouse as soon as possible, and, except for brief intervals of separation or widowhood, attempted to remain married continuously throughout his or her adult life.

The second type of requisite relationship was at least one in the other-generation category. More specifically this was a parent-child relationship. This type of relationship was necessary in Eskimo eyes for various reasons, which applied more or less sequentially during the course of the domestic cycle. In the first place, and most obviously, the presence of this type of tie in a family unit was essentially a "given" while the children were infants or still very young; the only alternative was not to have any children at all. As the children grew older the emphasis changed to general education and training for adult life, most of which was conducted in terms of parent-child ties.

As the members of the younger generation reached adulthood, there was sometimes a period of what might be called "balance" —if the senior members were still young enough to look out for themselves. In such cases, there was a period of a few years in which the individuals involved conceivably could have gotten along all right without the representatives of the other generation, and thus the element of sheer survival indicated by the label "basic strategy" would not apply. However, it was at precisely this point in the domestic cycle that intermediate goals, such as the accumulation of wealth or power, could be pursued most effectively in terms of parent-child relationships, since still active parents and their mature offspring could make a very productive team.

Once the members of the senior generation began to pass beyond their most active years, the dependent role began to devolve upon them. At this point, other-generation relationships began to be necessary from the senior, not from the junior point of view, since old people could no longer survive without the help of younger adults. The dependence was rarely completely one-sided, however, because old people, although less able to hunt or scrape skins, were usually capable of performing a number of important chores around the house, such as making thread or twine, scraping skins, or repairing equipment. At least as significant was the fact that old people typically had the greatest knowledge of the all-important taboos everyone had to conform to plus a number of amulets and charms whose effectiveness in coping with both the empirical and nonempirical environments had been clearly demonstrated. Thus, while it was absolutely *necessary* for every old person to live with a representative of the younger generation, it was usually to the advantage of the latter to have an old person around as well.

The third type of relationship that was considered necessary for the survival of a traditional Northwest Alaskan Eskimo was one in the same-generation category. Specifically, it had to be a relationship between adult males. It could involve individuals who were brothers, (male) cousins, or (male) in-laws, as long as the content of the relationship conformed in practice to the sibling pattern.

The requisite basis of a relationship having the content of the ties between adult brothers rested on three considerations. First, it was nearly impossible for a single adult male to carry out effectively the hunting activities of an entire yearly cycle; at least during peak hunting seasons (summer and/or fall), he would require the aid of one (or more) other active hunter(s). Second, at least two adult males were required for purposes of defense. If an attack came from a war party from another society, even two men would not be enough; but two could often discourage the efforts of an adversary from their own society who was pursuing a blood feud since people bent on vengeance normally acted alone. The third reason for the requisite basis of this relationship was the belief that individual hunters were wide open to attack from supernatural entities of all kinds, whereas two men traveling together were not.

The combination of the above factors made it very risky for anyone to belong to a unit that did not include at least two active adult males among its members. Every family member stood to suffer because of the increased likelihood of famine or death which would result from the absence of such a team. Of course it does not follow automatically that these two adult males had to be brothers (or cousins interacting as brothers). The requirements could also be met by a man and his adult son, a man and his adult son-in-law, and by two brothers-in-law. All three types of arrangement did occur, but both were subject to limitations that made them unsatisfactory over the long term. The first two relationships involved people in different generations, which meant that there were relatively strict time limits on how long both individuals would be capable of filling the adult roles to the necessary degree. The second pair of relationships involved affines, and, given the Eskimo set of values, affines were always to be mistrusted to some extent during times of crisis, particularly when a blood feud was at issue.[2] On the basis of these considerations, therefore, it followed that the most satisfactory long-term associations between adult male kinsmen involved brothers.

The Transitional Period

The basic *strategies* of affiliation changed very little during the first decades of the transitional period. However, they became much more difficult to pursue successfully as disease and famine began to take their toll of the Eskimo population.

Several times in this volume it was pointed out that, although the number of *relationships* in the Eskimo kinship system was limited, the number of *individuals* who could interact in terms of those relationships was theoretically infinite, and actually rather large for most of the population. The fact that the Eskimo system placed no limits on relationships by descent, combined with multiple marriages, adoption, and the theoretical permanence of all connections between individuals, meant that

---

[2] It is important in this connection to note that, in traditional times, one could never be sure when a feud was *not* at issue because feuds were sometimes latent for decades. They were normally pursued *only* when an avenger felt that the situation was overwhelmingly in his favor. The opportunity to strike might not come until even a generation or two had passed since the precipitating incident.

practically everyone could choose to affiliate with one of two or more *sets* of parents, siblings, and spouses. In traditional times, systematic use and manipulation of the various alternative sets of kin relationships was normally a factor in intermediate strategies of affiliation, but not in the basic ones; one could live with almost any set of individuals filling the requisite roles and survive.

When the negative effects of disease and famine began to reduce the Eskimo population of Northwest Alaska in the early phase of the transitional period (1850–1890) mere survival became more difficult than it had been previously. In terms of affiliation, people were increasingly (and recurrently) faced with the problem of finding new spouses, or new children (or parents), or new siblings to replace those who had died. Thus it became increasingly necessary in the early transitional period to utilize alternative sets of kinship ties, not to *improve* one's standard of living, but simply in order to *survive*.

Substitution apparently increased steadily in significance as a *basic* strategy of affiliation from the very onset of the transitional period (1850) until well into the intermediate phase (1890–1940) of that period. During particularly severe famines or epidemics people apparently associated themselves with practically anyone who was available, at least for a time. If the individuals involved were already kin, they would substitute the "peripheral" relationships for the "requisite" ones, as necessary, and carry on. If accident brought together individuals who were not kin, but who felt that they had to join forces or die, they would make each other kin via some combination of sexual intercourse and adoption.

Sometime during the intermediate phase of the transitional period, this downward population trend was reversed, but at this point in my research on demographic changes I cannot state precisely when it occurred. Perhaps the turning point was the flu epidemic of 1918–19 on the Seward Peninsula, perhaps it came somewhat earlier. In any case, by 1920, at least, mere survival began to become less of a problem than it had been for three or four generations. Once again the *basic* strategies of affiliation became less difficult to pursue successfully and people could begin to focus their attention on some of the intermediate ones.

The basic strategies themselves began to undergo a number of changes during the intermediate phase of the transitional period (1890–1940). Particularly affected was the requisite status of the relationship between (real *or* fictive) adult male siblings. Less and less was this relationship necessary for survival; more and more it began to be significant in the achievement of intermediate goals alone.

At least three factors were involved in this reduced significance of the adult brother relationship. Probably the first in time was the rapid acquisition and use of rifles during the last three decades of the 19th century. Rifles greatly reduced the need for team hunting in most areas, particularly since the caribou had all but vanished from Northwest Alaska. The second factor, also in point of time, was the gradual institution of United States Government authority in Northwest Alaska, and the elimination of assassination as a means of obtaining vengeance. Feuding continued, but it was limited to verbal exchanges; people were correspondingly less afraid to live in families involving only one adult male. The final factor in the removal of the brother-brother relationship from its traditional requisite status was Christianity. As I have noted elsewhere (Burch 1971), Christianity, with its powerful spirit, its Bible, prayers, and hymns, gave the Eskimos a means of combating successfully the various supernatural entities that inhabited Northwest Alaska. Armed with Bible or prayer, a hunter was no longer afraid to venture alone away from camp, for he could now defend himself quite adequately against any attack from the nonempirical world.

By the beginning of the recent phase of the transitional period, affiliation with a unit containing adult brothers had become entirely an intermediate, not a basic consideration. Indeed, from 1940 (at the latest) on, it can be questioned whether *any* kin relationships held requisite status in the sense that everyone *had* to belong to units including them simply in order to survive. The aged were increasingly being looked after by the U. S. Public Health Service, and there were institutions available to look after even the tiniest orphan. Accordingly, it seems reasonable to suggest that, probably by the beginning of the recent period, and certainly by its end, affiliation with kinsmen had become primarily an intermediate rather than a basic consideration.

Intermediate Strategies of Affiliation:
General Considerations

Skill, strength, intelligence, physical attractiveness—these and other personal qualities, though important, are never sufficient in any society to guarantee either survival or success. One must also have the right "contacts," be they with friends, relatives, customers, or any other category of persons which may be crucial in the structure of a given system. In terms of the structures of the several traditional societies in Northwest Alaska, the "right contacts" were kinsmen first and foremost; this rule applied just as strictly in the pursuit of "success" as it did in the maintenance of life itself.

A point that needs to be made at the outset, and emphasized, is that in traditional times, both individuals and groups of Northwest Alaskan Eskimos could and did achieve a standard of living far above that of their fellows. In terms of Fried's (1967) classification, the traditional Northwest Alaskan Eskimos operated in terms of "rank," not "egalitarian" societies (v. Ray 1967:377; Smith 1966:5–7).[3] Anyone who suggests otherwise is probably confusing the 1890–1910 situation with the traditional one, or else is applying the (reasonably accurate) stereotype of Canadian Eskimos to the Northwest Alaskan population; either procedure would be in error.

The general fact of ranking in Northwest Alaska can be inferred from the accounts of early writers (e. g., Aldrich 1889:31; Brower n. d.:141,294; Hooper 1881:62; Seeman 1853:59–60, 135; Simpson 1875:273). It was also brought to my attention repeatedly by informants, the best of whom were concerned that I might present an artificial picture in which the actual variation in the behavior of their ancestors would be obscured.[4] They insisted that, in traditional, as well as transitional times,

[3] According to Fried's (1968:109) scheme, a "rank society is one in which positions of valued status are somehow limited so that not all of sufficient talent to occupy such statuses actually achieve them."

[4] Their insistence on variation is a good indicator of the high quality of my informants. In contrast to the usual problem of reconstructive ethnography (Lee and DeVore 1968c:1946–1949; 1968e:5–6), in this case it was the anthropologist, and not the informants, who had a tendency to focus on the ideal situation.

some individuals were shiftless, unhappy, stupid, luckless, weak, poor, and/or ineffective, just as some were in 1970; *some* other individuals were, during the same period, energetic, happy, intelligent, fortunate, strong, rich, and/or powerful. *Most* people were distributed between those two extremes, again, just as they were in 1970.

The majority of Northwest Alaskan Eskimos aspired to a standard of living well above that of mere persistence. The stereotype of Eskimos being content with the condition of abject poverty did not apply to most of the Northwest Alaskan Eskimo population at any time during the century and a quarter covered by this study. That they were able to *cope* with poverty and adapt to it when nothing better was possible does not mean that they *accepted* it. Furthermore, at all time periods for which I have information, a large percentage of the Eskimo population in Northwest Alaska apparently desired *much* more than the minimum, and some people were willing to work hard to get it.

The conventional stereotype about Eskimos not being competitive or ambitious is another one that did not apply in Northwest Alaska. The Northwest Alaskan Eskimos are one of the most competitive groups of people I have ever been associated with, and according to my informants, were at least as much so during the traditional period. One of the things they competed at—in addition to (hunting, singing, dancing, sewing, shooting, story-telling, etc.) ability, agility, strength, trading, knowledge— was hiding the fact that they were competing. The more wealth or power a person acquired, the more modest he had to act, at least if he wanted to receive help from his relatives in getting more. As the modern politician desperately seeking power must sometimes hide his ambition by denying that he is even a candidate for office, so an Eskimo with similar aspirations had to manifest indifference and humility, *especially* if he wanted to succeed. The minutes of village meetings all over Northwest Alaska are full of speeches made by nominees for office about how they were unqualified to serve, etc., etc.,—just before they got elected.

Power, then, was one of the major intermediate goals of the Northwest Alaskan Eskimos. Wealth was another. To some extent these goals could be achieved through extraordinary personal qualities alone. But if one really wanted to reach the top, one had to associate oneself in the right way with the right people. Intermediate strategies of affiliation were thus a major concern of ambitious people.

Wealth and power, which usually went together, were not the only intermediate goals that Northwest Alaskan Eskimos sought. There was also a third, rather vague, intermediate objective which, for lack of a better word, I am going to call "happiness." "Happiness" was a situation in which an individual was far enough above the bare subsistence level to be comfortable, yet was not so high up that he had to work very hard to get or stay there, and where he had relatively little in the way of responsibility; "contentment" might be just as appropriate a term.

Options

The Northwest Alaskan Eskimo emphasis on kin relationships as the most important means of affiliation has been noted repeatedly during the course of this volume. The fact that a number of alternative, but structurally and functionally equivalent avenues of affiliation were available within the kinship system has also been pointed out in several places. It is necessary to return briefly to this latter point in order to set the stage for the analysis that follows.

Four characteristics of the Northwest Alaskan Eskimo kinship system served to increase the number of one's kinsmen beyond the bare minimum, namely, consanguineal, marital, and fictive augmentation, and permanence. Through these mechanisms any given individual might acquire two or more "duplicate" sets of relatives. An individual could be involved with all of these sets, or he could "deactivate" (i. e., ignore) one set and participate actively with another. Furthermore, because many individuals were theoretically related to one another in terms of two or more relationships simultaneously, say those of cousins and siblings-in-law, there was often some choice as to which of the existing avenues of affiliation people could utilize. And, if the need was extreme and no other possibilities were available, individuals could "create" new kinsmen for themselves via sexual intercourse. All of those factors combined to provide the Northwest Alaskan Eskimos with a wide range of alternative avenues of affiliation with people who were already kinsmen. Individuals could pick and choose among them to some extent in order to pursue personal goals.

Choosing among the various alternatives was not always as simple in practise as the above account makes it appear (v. Hennigh 1972). In the first place, every relationship is a two-way affair; a single individual cannot have his own way without the concurrence of his "alter." Thus, the wishes of at least one other person always had to be taken into account. Secondly, there was the "third-party" problem. If one especially admired a particular cousin, for example, and wished to move in with him (or her), there was the necessity of having to get along with the *other* people who might also share that residence, such as the cousin's spouse, parents, or children. The greater the number of people involved, the more complex this problem. Finally, there was the matter of moral obligation. It will be recalled from earlier chapters that the several relationships in the Northwest Alaskan system were by no means equally strong. There was a relatively clear-cut order of precedence, as follows: (1) parent-child, (2) sibling, (3) nepotic/multigeneration, (4) cousin, (5) marital, (6) affinal. What this means is that one had much stronger obligations to some relatives, e. g., to parents, than to others, e. g., to spouses. Virtue and expediency did not always coincide, and people often had to make difficult choices between the two.

The reciprocity requirement, the third-party question, and moral obligation were structural problems that made any given person's decisions regarding affiliation relatively complex. All the factors had to be considered, weighed against one another in the light of current conditions, and a course of action decided on and pursued. One final complicating factor that should be mentioned here is that of individual personality. Even when all the structural considerations pointed toward an association between two particular individuals, and even if that association would have been quite feasible to create and maintain on general grounds, personality clashes sometimes precluded it. The reverse problem also occurred when people who, for various reasons, ought *not* to have affiliated with one another got along so well that they wanted to anyway. The latter was usually the easier of the two variations of the "personality problem" to deal with, because it was generally easier and more acceptable in the Eskimo system to create a brand new kinship tie than it was to deactivate one already in existence.

Intermediate Strategies of Affiliation:
The Accumulation of Wealth

The accumulation of wealth was a major intermediate goal of many traditional Northwest Alaskan Eskimos. Wealth, in traditional times, was reckoned primarily in terms of inventories of food, clothing, and skins. Houses, boats, and other items of equipment or property were also important, both as a means for obtaining food (etc.), and for their intrinsic value. The *minimum* requirement for being considered wealthy was, in addition to a full stock of clothing and equipment for oneself and one's family, enough food in any given October to last all winter. A really wealthy man (*umialik*) would have much more than that, however. He would have available every fall not only enough food for himself and the entire local group that he headed for the next twelve months, but he would also have enough to provide for a big feast for at least several dozen guests during the holiday season of early winter. He would have not just adequate clothing, he would have several changes of the very finest clothing, made of matched skins, and elegantly designed and constructed; and so would all the members of at least his own household. His storehouses, cold cellars, and caches would be full of furs, and caribou and seal skins and Russian tobacco as well. As Brower (n. d.:160) said of the *umialik* of Kotzebue in 1884, "he had his choice of all that was good."

Wealth was thus one of the realities of traditional Northwest Alaskan Eskimo life, but so was extreme poverty. At the opposite end of the economic ladder was the person who had *nothing* of his own. Such a person, usually referred to as *tigutaaluq*, had to depend on others for literally everything—his food, his clothes, and his shelter—and he would have to operate essentially as a slave for the *umialik* and his family in order to acquire even that (cf. Seeman 1853:59).

The accumulation of wealth was inextricably bound up with intermediate strategies of affiliation with kinsmen (v. Simpson

1875:273). So closely were kin relationships and wealth associated in people's thinking that, even in 1970, if one asked an
old-timer to state the Eskimo word for "a person with many
kinsmen," he would reply *"umialik"* as likely as not. Similarly,
the notions of "orphan" (*iliapak*) and "slave" (*tigutaaluq*) were
practically synonymous to people knowledgeable about the old
ways.

The accumulation of new wealth in traditional times had to
begin with certain personal qualities. Minimally, one had to be
a good hunter, which meant that one also had to be male. Secondly, one had to be intelligent enough to maximize one's
strengths and minimize one's weaknesses. And thirdly, one
had to be an effective trader. Usually one also had to be generous and modest in order to acquire and retain the support of
one's relatives, although those requirements could occasionally
be offset, at least temporarily, if one was strong enough physically or a powerful enough shaman to intimidate them. But the
help of relatives was normally essential, and to this important
issue I now turn.

A Hypothetical Case

Let us begin with a hypothetical young man who started out
relatively poor, but who wished to become wealthy, and follow
him as he sets about achieving his goal. First, we will assume
that he is the ideal candidate: tall, strong, handsome, intelligent,
a good hunter, a good craftsman, and, most important of all,
the oldest of several siblings and cousins residing in the same
local group. This would give him a set of key personal attributes, as well as a power base (through his institutionalized authority over younger siblings and cousins) from which to proceed. Then he would have to marry a young woman who was
also diligent, intelligent, capable, and, in the ideal case, the oldest
of several siblings and cousins in *her* local group.

This young couple would then embark on a normal marital
career, except that they would approximate more closely than
most the ideals of the various relationships to which they belonged. They would probably live in his parents' household. She
would obey her mother-in-law at all times without objection, she
would work hard to do more than her share of the household
work, and she would make particularly fancy boots or other

clothing for her father-in-law from time to time. Her husband, in turn, would work hard at hunting, and would increasingly take the lead in keeping full the larder of the entire local group. The couple would visit her parents two or three times every year and take them presents whenever possible. They might lose one child in an accident, and another might be adopted by the husband's parents or grandparents, but they would keep and raise successfully perhaps two sons, and a daughter, a bit more than the average.

Assuming that no mishap befell them, our hypothetical couple would likely be in very good circumstances by the time they reached their late thirties. The grandparents would probably all be dead, as would perhaps two or three of their own parents. All of their children would be living with them again, and the oldest would be approaching maturity. The husband, being senior to the other siblings and cousins in the same local group, would be head of the unit, which might thus consist minimally of his wife and children, his siblings and some cousins, their spouses, and children.

The period of succession, during which the husband's parents (and their siblings) in the local group concerned were passing away, would be a critical one. Once the members of the senior generation were gone, the obligation for all of the siblings and cousins to stay together would be substantially reduced. If our couple had not treated their same-generation kin well during previous years the unit might well split up, each conjugal family going its own way. If, on the other hand, our couple, especially the husband, had gained the respect and support of his siblings and cousins, they might decide to stay together under his leadership for their own well-being. Faced with much the same sorts of problems, some of the wife's siblings and cousins (with their spouses and children) might decide to join the unit as well (cf. Lee and DeVore, eds., 1968a).

If stability characterized the period of succession, the local group would change rapidly in structure, if not in size, for a few years thereafter. Acceptance by the others of the leadership of the man in our example would mean that they had attached their star to his, much as the success or failure of a junior executive follows that of his superior in a large modern corporation. Given this state of affairs, it was to the advantage of each member of the local family concerned to try to augment the wealth and influence of their leader. Increasingly they would give his senior wife—he would probably have two or more by this time—all the game, skins, etc., that were taken; she would manage the stores for the entire local group, issuing supplies when needed. The *umialik* would cease active hunting, and devote most of his attention to problems of administration.[5] He would decide who would hunt, what would be hunted, and where and when the hunting would be done. He would also determine who would stay home and make any utensils, weapons, and other equipment which might be needed, either for local use or for trading purposes. Items actually in use would remain in the various households. Everything else would be stored in a central location and issued as needed according to the wishes of the *umialik* and/or his senior wife. The *umialik* would decide if, when, and where the group should move during the course of their annual cycle.

Under the direction of an effective leader, the material resources of a given local group could increase well beyond the average. Internal friction would be minimal, partly because an *umialik* could manage things so as to keep difficulties at a reduced level, and also because he would have enough authority to adjudicate any serious conflicts that did arise. Under these circumstances, such a local group would become an attraction to other members of the society. Instead of having to recruit actively for new members to the unit, the *umialik* would find himself receiving what amounted to applications for membership in it. Anyone with ·kin ties to any member would be eligible to join, and admission could be refused only to known troublemakers.

As the size of such a local family increased, so would the wealth of its leader. With so many individuals contributing

---

[5] Pospisil (1964:420) claims that it was unusual for an *umialik* to delegate to others the leadership in hunting operations; my data indicate that the *really* wealthy men in traditional times typically did so. I suspect that part of the difficulty relates to the meaning of the word "*umialik*." Unfortunately, this single Eskimo term means several different things in English, according to the context in which it is used. Appropriate glosses include the following English terms: "boss," "rich man," "underwriter," "creditor," "employer," and "boat captain." In the sense of "boss" or "boat captain," an *umialik* would probably be the man leading the hunt, in the sense of "wealthy man" or "underwriter," he often would not be.

both raw materials and manufactured goods to the central supply, the *umialik* would have a large pool of resources from which to select what he wanted. It was assumed that the *umialik* would *always* choose the best for himself; few would object as long as the membership as a whole was adequately looked after. Those individuals particularly close to the *umialik*, either by descent or by marriage, would expect to receive special treatment. Since such individuals were usually delegated a certain amount of authority by him, they could usually take care of themselves fairly easily.

Complications

The above account was hypothetical in two important respects. First, it described an imaginary individual, one who existed only in the mind of the anthropologist. Given the fact that case history data from traditional times were inaccessible to field investigators during the recent period, there is no satisfactory solution to this problem. Informants during the 1960's were able to provide *general* information on the relevant processes, however, and a fictional account is a convenient way of presenting this material. The second, and perhaps more significant hypothetical feature of the above account was that it dealt with an ideal case. In other words, it presented success in its purest form. Judging from my informants' accounts, however, at least some real people must have approximated fairly closely this idealized version, so the account is not as misleading as it might appear. But it is also true that many an ambitious young man failed to achieve his goal of becoming a wealthy man. Often this was due to personal deficiencies, but it could also be the result of affiliation problems. It is the latter that concern us here.

There appear to have been three major complicating factors in utilizing interpersonal relationships as a means of accumulating wealth in traditional Northwest Alaska. The first was the problem of acquiring an adequate number of the right kinds of same-generation kinsmen. The second was the recruitment of the "right" spouse. The third complicating factor was having an adequate number of other-generation relatives. Each of these problems is discussed separately below.

The acquisition of an adequate number of the right kinds of
same-generation relatives was the first affiliation problem that
one had to solve if he wished to become wealthy. Same-generation kin had to have three characteristics if they were to be of
"the right kind" in this sense. First, they had to be younger.
Only thus would a man have enough authority to be able to
manipulate others for his own ends rather than vice versa.
Secondly, they had to be male. Males, as the hunters, acquired
most of the raw materials (i. e., game) that constituted the ultimate source of wealth in traditional times. Also, by virtue of
their superior physical strength, males held more intrinsic power than women. Thirdly, the same-generation kin had to be
sufficiently skilled to be able to contribute to the productivity of
the local family as a unit. To have many younger siblings and
cousins who were lazy, stupid, or otherwise personally ineffective would be a disaster to an ambitious young man; he would
be obliged to support *them*, and they would be a constant drain
on his resources.

What constituted the right *number* of same-generation kin is
impossible to specify because so much depended on their personal
qualities. Two or three highly energetic and able younger siblings and cousins might provide enough support to launch their
senior (and thus themselves) on a very successful career. Ten
or fifteen shiftless or fractious younger siblings or cousins could
reduce the entire unit to the bare subsistence level, no matter
how extraordinary their senior sibling/cousin might be.

The problem of getting an adequate number of the right kinds
of same-generation kin was, in the first instance, completely
beyond one's control. No one can determine one's position in
the birth order, one's sex, or the personal qualities of others.
Our hypothetical individual was extremely fortunate because
the problem was essentially solved for him; all he had to do is
keep in order the several same-generation relationships to which
he belonged essentially by accident. Others less favorably provided for, could often take active steps to improve their situation, however. For example, the younger brother (or cousin)
of an extremely able man would probably find that the quickest
road to riches lay through the whole-hearted support of the
older sibling (cousin). His circumstances would improve at only
a slightly slower rate than those of his senior, and if *anything*

happened to the brother, he would be in a good position to succeed him in the *umialik* role.   If, on the other hand, a man had
ineffective older male siblings or cousins, he might be able to
take active leadership of the group himself, and in effect act as
the oldest person of his generation.   This was a more difficult
task, though, and success would depend largely on the extent to
which the other siblings and cousins were willing to step voluntarily into subordinate roles.

The matter of sex could also be compensated for to some extent by individual action.   A female's only means of acquiring
wealth was by affiliating herself with the right man.   In terms
of same-generation relationships, which is the concern here, she
would have to do this by maintaining residence in the family of
a wealthy male sibling or cousin, supporting him, and by having
a husband who would do likewise.   A different kind of situation
would be the one in which a male had only (or mostly) female
siblings or cousins.   This was a very difficult problem to solve
indeed.   According to my informants, about the only recourse a
person in this situation would have would be to work hard to
retain the affection and support of his female kin, and take an
active part in influencing their choice of spouses so as to en-
sure their marriage to capable men from several different local
groups.[6]   Then he would have to keep all of them within his own
local group subsequently.

The question of ability was also a difficult one to deal with.
If one's male siblings and cousins were incompetent or lazy,
there was really little one could do except abandon them, and
attempt to exploit marital, co-sibling, or step-sibling ties as a
means for acquiring wealth.   Unfortunately, however, to abandon one's siblings or cousins was diametrically opposed to the
ethical standards of the relationships concerned.   Anyone who
did so was likely to be regarded as unworthy of trust, and was
thus not likely to receive support from any other kin as a consequence.

The second major problem of affiliation as a means of accumulating wealth in traditional Northwest Alaska was recruit-

6 The advantage to be gained by having them come from several different
local groups was of the "divide and conquer" genre.   If many of them came
from one such unit, there would always be the question of who was joining
whom, hence the question of leadership would be a difficult one to resolve.

ment of the "right" spouse. The ideal spouse, for this particular purpose, was one who met four criteria. First, he or she
should have the personal qualities of skill and industry, and the
physical attributes considered ideal for one of that sex. For a
man these qualities included hunting, trading, and magical skills,
in descending order of importance. For a woman they included
sewing and other technological skills primarily, but trading ability and magical expertise were valuable to women as well as
to men. Both spouses would have to be hard working, physically
strong and active, modest, tactful, and, particularly after a
period of early success, effective managers. This last quality
should not be overlooked, since the truly wealthy people in traditional Northwest Alaska Eskimo societies were ones who were
able to influence and coordinate the activities of others.

A good spouse was also one who had numerous kinsmen whose
active and productive support could be counted on. One without such kin could bring little more than personal qualities to
the enterprise of accumulating wealth. Although personal qualities were obviously important, the lack of kin would make the
accumulation of material resources much more difficult. A
spouse with shiftless or incompetent kin would be even worse
than one with no kin, however, since the relatives might make
use of their ties to drain an ambitious couple of all the fruits of
their labors.

The third important characteristic of a spouse was fertility,
since the active support of adult children during the mature
years of an Eskimo couple provided the most reliable source of
income they could have. More will be said about the need for
children below.

The fourth and final characteristic of the ideal spouse, insofar as accumulating wealth was concerned, was what might be
called an "achievement orientation." On the one hand, I mean
by this that, if they were poor at the outset of their marital
career, both spouses had to be interested in becoming well-to-do,
enough so to be willing to work hard toward that end. On the
other hand, I mean by "achievement orientation" that, if the
spouses were relatively well-off at the start, they would be interested enough in having the material comforts to do what was
necessary to maintain and/or improve their position.

The significance of having the right spouse in traditional Northwest Alaska should not be underrated. Any woman obviously had to have an effective husband, because so much depended on hunting skills and sex-based authority. But, it was also important that a man have the right wife. The wife was the one who had to retrieve, process, and store all the game that her husband killed. A man whose wife could not deal effectively with the output of his hunting labors was a serious liability since, because of her inadequacy, much of the family's income would be dissipated rather than put to profit.

Often a man who was a very good hunter had to have two wives to keep up with his production. The common view is that the second was usually the favorite. Actually, although a young second wife (*nukaraq*) may have been sexually more stimulating than the first, it was usually the effectiveness of the first in other areas that led to both the need for and the ability to support a second. A man who reversed priorities in this regard, would find himself in difficult circumstances after a time because the senior wife would leave him.

The third and final major problem of affiliation as a means of accumulating wealth was belonging to an adequate number of the right kinds of other-generation relationships. It was particularly important to have children, especially sons (v. McElwaine 1901:12; Mikkelsen 1909:295). In the hypothetical example discussed earlier, the couple had a total of four children, at least two of which were sons. More children, and especially more sons, would have been better, but given the average family size of only two in traditional times, the chances of any couple having more were remote. A sterile couple could adopt children, of course, but having one's own was a more reliable method.

A couple that had only daughters was faced with a problem familiar to people in many societies, namely, the need for sons, or, more specifically, the need for capable hunters in the next generation. The Eskimos used two procedures to solve the problem. The first was to try to adopt one or more sons. The second was to try to recruit first-rate husbands for their daughters, and then get the couple to remain with them subsequently. Fathers who were already well-off were usually in a good position to do this successfully, since they could tempt a potential son-in-law with promises of material wealth, and then live up to their promises afterward. The advantage of the first procedure was that even an adoptive-child relationship was stronger than any affinal tie, and the support of a son was generally much more reliable than that of a son-in-law. On the other hand, any infant is an unknown quantity. Infant adoption could never guarantee an effective son, and the Eskimos rarely adopted people after they had reached adolescence. When one was looking for an outstanding son-in-law, however, one could usually get a good idea in advance of the kind of person he was trying to recruit. A couple with only daughters might employ both procedures in order to increase their chances of success.

The importance of other-generation relationships in any strategy of affiliation lay most obviously in the members of one generation acquiring numerous and effective kin in the next. But it was also important for people to have good parents, for, as in almost all societies, a Northwest Alaskan Eskimo's circumstances of birth affected his chances later on in life. There were three major things that the "right" set of parents could do for their offspring as far as wealth was concerned. First, they could teach them the skills required to make them superior hunters, seamstresses, and managers, etc., plus the various social graces and mannerisms necessary for success in a Northwest Alaskan Eskimo society. Secondly, and nearly as important, the "right" parents could work to keep residentially intact the full set of siblings that constituted their offspring. Although they could never guarantee it, parents could thus greatly increase the chances that their oldest offspring would have an adequate power base from which to proceed once they had passed away. The third benefit that the "right" set of parents could pass on to their children was their own substantial resources as a basis for further aggrandizement. In addition to material things, such as boats, tools, weapons, etc., these resources could also include a network of alliances (trading partnerships and co-siblings) with individuals in other societies (v. Burch and Correll 1972). The "right" parents, therefore, could do a great deal to give their offspring both the material and the social bases of economic success.

The preceding paragraph dealt less with *strategies* of affiliation than with *facts* of affiliation, since children have little or no control over who their higher generation relatives are. However, in the Northwest Alaskan Eskimo system there was some room for strategy here as well. In the first place, as noted in Chapter Four, children could establish such a close relationship with certain adults that they could in effect adopt themselves out to them. Much more important and much more frequent, however, was selective affiliation with kinsmen that one had automatically as a function of one's birth. For example, practically everyone had several sets of grandparents in the Eskimo scheme of things. If some of these were wiser and more skillful than others, an ambitious young man might undertake to recruit these people to his own local group, or he might go to live with them. In return for food, shelter, and protection, they could provide instruction and advice of a kind few of his same-generation kin could offer. Furthermore, such individuals would likely have a supply of amulets and charms that they would use for the benefit of this local group, and they might well pass these on to a grandchild who had attached himself to them. Finally, such people were the repository of the songs and stories that made up the traditional history of their people. Just to have them around made life in a local group more interesting than it would have been in their absence, and thus they would serve to stimulate others to join the unit. Similar possibilities could be exploited from among the kin of the parental generation. In either case, the consanguineal kin of either husband or wife, or both, could be drawn upon for this purpose.

Summary of the Traditional Situation

In the foregoing analysis I have attempted to outline some of the strategies that traditional Northwest Alaskan Eskimos could use in order to improve their material circumstances to a level well above the minimum. Because individual case data from the traditional period do not exist, the analysis was phrased in general terms; it was essentially a composite picture based on diverse kinds of information contained primarily in my field notes, but partly also in the literature.[7] I have attempted

---

[7] Of particular importance here were the contributions of Brower (n. d.:160, 161, 244 *et passim.*; Pospisil 1964:419–422; Ray 1967:377; Smith 1966:6–7; Spencer 1959:151–158 *et passim.*).

to make three basic points in this presentation, and it is appropriate to restate these more succinctly before proceeding to the topic of change.

The first basic point is that, in the early and middle 19th century, it was possible for some Eskimos in Northwest Alaska to achieve a level of affluence which greatly exceeded that of their fellows. Social stratification based on wealth was greatest in the coastal areas. Each large coastal settlement contained a number of affluent local groups, and each large constituent local group contained at least one or more families whose members were relatively better off than the rest. Affluence was not limited to coastal areas, however, because rich people were also found in societies whose territories were far inland. Interestingly, the wealthy inlanders all seem to have lived near the upper reaches of large rivers, and they all seem to have come from families whose members specialized as traders.[8] Among the inland peoples there seems to have been only one wealthy local group in an entire society, rather than one or two rich local groups in each settlement, as there appear to have been on the coast.

The second major point is that wealth could be obtained only through a combination of luck, exceptional personal qualities, and relationships with the "right" people, the great majority of whom had to be kinsmen. Luck and exceptional personal qualities alone might lead to a brief "boom" period for an individual or family from time to time, but relationships with the "right" people were absolutely necessary for the kind of sustained accumulation and management of resources that characterized the very richest of Eskimo families. Of the three requirements, the last was the most important.

The third and final concluding point is that the accumulation of wealth through affiliation with the "right" people was a very complex matter. Kinsmen could be liabilities as well as sources of support, and there was no guarantee that the relatives a person was most obliged to help would be the same

8 Geographic location seems to have been critical. They were far enough inland to give them ready access to people in the next drainage during the winter, yet they could also traverse the entire river system along which they lived, and participate in the hunting, fishing, and trading that took place on the coast in the summer.

ones most capable of reciprocating effectively. Thus, an individual would have to weigh the obligations and commitments inherent in the various relationships to which he belonged against a predominately rational assessment of his relatives' abilities. The fact that affiliation for this purpose had to involve kinsmen almost exclusively seriously limited one's freedom of action. On the other hand, the factors of augmentation, extension, and multiple connections offered a range of alternatives in this sphere that relatively few kinship systems provide.

The Transitional Period

The early phase of the transitional period (1850–1890) brought a number of developments that greatly altered traditional patterns of wealth accumulation. The earliest of these was the tremendous reduction in the primary sources of wealth: the bowhead whale, walrus, and caribou. The sharp drop in the numbers of these three species led to a great reduction in the gross national products of all of the societies in Northwest Alaska, and to a general lowering of per capita income as well. As mentioned previously, throughout all of the early and much of the intermediate phases of the transitional period, the attention of most people turned increasingly to efforts toward sheer survival. The accumulation of wealth was simply out of the question in most regions.

Changes in the human population during the early phase of the transitional period also affected the accumulation of wealth. The same *strategies* of affiliation were still in force, but they became more difficult to pursue effectively. Just when an ambitious and effective leader had organized a local group of the size and composition needed for the accumulation of substantial reserves, a famine or epidemic could strike and eliminate a substantial portion of the membership. Even if the *umialik* himself survived such an incident, it would undo all of his work. He would have to begin all over again, but without the "social capital" of kinsmen that he had had previously. The possibility of disaster had always existed in Northwest Alaska, of course, but sudden reverses increased in both number and severity during the second half of the 19th century. By 1890, affluence had become such a transitory state in most districts that it was hardly worth seeking anymore.

The third major change that occurred during the early phase of the transitional period was a shift from the accumulation of food reserves to *trade*—in skins, furs, and whale bone (baleen)—as the primary source of wealth. In terms of affiliation, this meant that relationships with partners and Whites became progressively more important, and those with kinsmen progressively less so. This general trend is illustrated by developments in the Kotzebue Sound area. In this huge tract of country, extending from Cape Espenberg to Point Hope, and including the entire Selawik, Kobuk, and Noatak drainages, there were apparently only four men who qualified for the designation "wealthy" by 1885. These men were Surluq, on the Upper Kobuk River, Kapurina in the Selawik district, Kilagzaq at Kotzebue, and Aataŋauzaq at Point Hope. All of these men were traders first, hunters second.[9] In the South Kotzebue Sound, Kobuk Delta, Upper Noatak, Lower Noatak, and Kivalina districts, there was literally no one who qualified as *umialik*, in the sense of "rich man," by this time.

During the intermediate phase of the transitional period (1890–1940) truly affluent Eskimos seem to have been all but non-existent in Northwest Alaska. A good year of trapping or a lucky whale kill would provide riches for awhile, but such wealth took the form of a windfall, and was soon gone. A few men were in the process of accumulating considerable capital in the form of domesticated reindeer herds during the 1920's, and some of them might have become extremely well-to-do in time. However, for a set of reasons too complex to go into here, this possibility was eventually denied them.[10]

Goods *per se* remained the physical evidence of wealth in the recent period (1940–1970), but the means of acquiring those goods had become restricted to money almost exclusively. To get money one had to have a job. Getting a job, by this time,

[9] Aataŋauzaq was apparently also a powerful shaman and a strong man physically, one who was quite willing to use these qualities to serve his own ambitions (v. Brower n. d.:153–154). He was widely regarded by my informants as the *least* typical of all *umialiks* known to them.

[10] The complexities relate largely to U. S. Government policy, which was opposed to the expansion of individually owned herds.

meant affiliation with non-kin certainly, and with non-Eskimos probably (v. Harrison and Morehouse 1970). In fact, by the recent period, close affiliation with large numbers of kin was sometimes disastrous for people with ambition. No matter how hard one worked, and no matter how much money he earned, his kin would be sure to spend it, either directly, or indirectly by consuming the goods one acquired with it. Reserves could rarely be accumulated for the kinds of investments needed to create wealth in a modernized society. Here we have the final irony: the accumulation of wealth for most Northwest Alaskan Eskimos in the recent period meant either the absence or the rejection of the very sort of relationships that had been so essential to its attainment in the traditional era.

Intermediate Strategies of Affiliation:
The Acquisition of Power

The Traditional Period

"Power" is defined for present purposes as the ability to influence and to exercise control over the actions of others (Levy 1952:333). In the political sphere, as in the economic one, the traditional Northwest Alaskan Eskimos were ranked, and some individuals had much more power than others (v. Aldrich 1889:31; Simpson 1875:273; Smith 1968:5; Ray 1967:377). Practically all of the early explorers in Northwest Alaska found that, if they wanted to maintain good relations with, or get reliable assistance from, the native population, they had to work through men whom they called "chiefs" (Kotzebue 1821 vol. 1:208ff.; Seeman 1853:135; Simpson 1875:273). These "chiefs," variously referred to in Eskimo by the terms *umialik* or *ataniq* (or their derivatives) [11] were men with power, the ones who led where others had to follow. The sources of this power were numerous, but since many of them were discussed

[11] "*Ataniq*" refers specifically to a person's power rather than to his wealth. The term may be glossed as "boss," "leader," "director," etc., according to the context. So closely was power associated with wealth, however, that "*umialik*" was used to refer to the leader of a local group most of the time, and *ataniq* was typically reserved for situations when an *umialik* (or someone else) was directing some particular project, such as the preparations for a messenger feast, or perhaps some organized hunting operation.

already under the heading of "wealth," the presentation here can be comparatively brief.

Several sources of power in traditional Northwest Alaska involved personal characteristics which individuals could do little or nothing to modify. They included sex (male over female), generation (parents over children), absolute age (age over youth), and seniority (older over younger). Each of these characteristics, as a source of power, was manifested in terms of the various kin relationships that were analyzed earlier in this volume, and they conveyed power (or accountability) to an individual only in terms of kinship ties.

A second set of characteristics that conveyed power to an individual consisted of personal qualities that one *could* modify through systematic effort. This category consists of physical strength, general knowledge, and skill. In aboriginal Northwest Alaska, physical fitness was considered important, and men trained and exercised to increase their strength and endurance in much the same way a modern athlete does. Physical strength seems generally to have been greatest in men who were well into their thirties, so the strongest people were likely also to be males, parents, and mature adults. Knowledge was assumed to increase with age, and obedience to older people was generally rationalized as deference to wisdom. The third basis of power in this category, namely skill, covered a wide range of applications, extending from hunting and sewing skill to trading and magical abilities, and skill, like strength, could be increased through constant practice. All other things being equal, the greater the amount of skill a person had in several different areas, the more power he was likely to acquire.

Wealth was another source of power in traditional Northwest Alaska. To the extent that wealth was relevant, all of the factors discussed in the previous section of this chapter apply. As was pointed out there, however, it was generally necessary to have some power over others in order to acquire wealth, so there was a feedback relationship in which each contributed to the other. But it is important to keep in mind that the extension of power over people who were not immediate kin absolutely required the accumulation and use of material wealth. In addition to being able to pay people to work for him, a wealthy man could also afford to make loans and gifts to others, and thus keep a large number of people beholden to him. That wealth was the only effective and stable source of power in traditional Northwest Alaska was very clearly recognized by the Eskimos; few tried to increase the one without systematically attempting to augment the other.

The final major source of power in traditional Northwest Alaska was sheer numbers of people. In societies that were so similar to one another in their general structure, there was little to choose between one and any other in terms of organizational superiority. However, if two war parties (or factions, or local groups, or families) used essentially the same procedures to pursue identical ends in competition with one another, but one had twice as many members as the other, the larger unit was very likely to come out on top.

The advantage of numbers as a source of power was clearly understood by the Eskimos, so much so that the aggressiveness and belligerence of *individuals* increased or decreased markedly according to the extent to which the *group* they were with was numerically superior or inferior to another. Maguire (1854:-171) observed this tendency at the very beginning of the transitional period, and his remarks on the subject are worth quoting at length.

> When the natives were collected in any numbers the difference of character displayed by them when so, and the reverse, is worthy of remark. In the former case they are bold and overbearing, and when meeting the parties from the ship, gather around them, and, apparently in a half playful way commence shoving them about and feeling their clothes. When, if they fail in getting what they want given to them, they help themselves, and with their knives soon remove any buttons that happen to be bright . . . on the contrary when they are in small numbers, they are not like the same people, but seem quiet, harmless, inoffensive, and obliging; even while displaying these good qualities, should their numbers become increased, they lose no time throwing off their assumed humility to join in any plunder going on.

John Simpson (1875:250) made similar observations about Eskimo behavior as he saw it during the same time period; Thomas Simpson (1843:183) had noted the same thing somewhat earlier.

Maguire was speaking of the relationships between Eskimos and Whites, but the natives followed exactly the same practice in their dealings amongst themselves. They would also subject smaller parties of Eskimos to much harsher treatment than they are known to have subjected parties of Whites to, frequently increasing their aggressiveness to the point of massacring the inferior group.[12] In a settlement or even in a society where one or a few local groups were very large, hence very powerful, it was necessary for everyone else to try to form units of comparable size if they wanted to live unmolested. Individuals or families who, for some reason or other, could not exploit kinship ties for the purpose of forming a separate local group of sufficient size for this purpose were forced to place themselves under the protection of the leader of one of these large local groups in order to survive; they often had to submit to a life of virtual slavery in order to effect even this arrangement. In this context, as in others, wealth and power tended to accrue to those who already had an abundance.

Certain elements in any individual's position in the "power structure" were more or less given. These were the unalterable factors included in the first category of power sources, namely, sex, generation, absolute age, and seniority. These four factors alone, expressed in terms of kin relationships, provided for a differential allocation of power, since practically every relationship in the system was hierarchical. The senior male in at least a small household or local group automatically had more power than any other member, and everyone else had progressively less according to their sex, age, and precise consanguineal and affinal (including marital) connections to the leader. In an important sense, therefore, a differential allocation of power was built into the structure of every household and local group, expressed in terms of the various kin relationships.

The differential allocation of power in terms of each of the several relationships that comprised the Eskimo kinship system was usually quite clear to their members. In families, and in local groups comprised of just two or three domestic units, the problem was scarcely more complicated, because so few people were likely to be involved. If there were only six adult males in

---

[12] It was only after the Eskimos acquired firearms that the effectiveness of numbers *per se* began to be neutralized.

the unit concerned, and if two of them were siblings of one generation and the balance were siblings and cousins in the next, there would be no confusion at all as to who the leader of the organization as a whole ought to be. But as the size of a local group increased beyond, say, four or five domestic units, the respective generations, absolute ages, and relative ages *vis à vis* one another of *all* of the adult males were likely to become increasingly more difficult to ascertain. Furthermore, as a unit grew in size, the number and diversity of relationships represented in it would multiply, and increasingly overlap and/or conflict, thus complicating the question as to who ought to have the most authority in the organization as a whole.

The larger a local group happened to be, the greater the extent to which factors over and above the four basic ones of sex, generation, absolute age, and seniority came into play as sources of power. The factors which were significant at this level were the already mentioned ones of physical strength, skill, knowledge, and wealth. Each, or any combination, of these four, could be used by an individual to either increase his power over a number of individuals with whom he was already affiliated, or else to tempt or (rarely) coerce others into associating themselves with him in subordinate positions. Because of the Eskimos' awareness of numbers as a source of power, one's actual influence seems to have increased or decreased exponentially, not arithmetically, in relation to the number of one's subordinates.

The general strategy for acquiring power via affiliation thus becomes clear: one had to associate oneself with as many people as possible who were inferior in terms of age or generation, and preferably in other respects as well. The more respects in terms of which one was superior to the others in the same local family, and the larger the local family happened to be, the more power one had. With respect to age alone it was primarily a waiting game, since the older a person got, the more younger kinsmen he was going to have. With respect to generation, it was of course necessary to have children. Apparently individuals who coveted positions of wealth and power would not only have and keep as many children of their own as they could, they would also try to adopt as many as possible, particularly sons. Beyond this, an individual seeking power via affiliation had to do one of two things. The more reliable procedure was to demonstrate that one was clearly a more successful hunter, a better trader, and a more generous person than anyone else, thus leading others voluntarily to attach themselves to him for the sake of their own interests. The other procedure involved more active recruitment. This usually required frequent outlays of gifts to make it worthwhile for others to join the organization in the first place. Success in those endeavors obviously depended on wealth, and all that it required and implied.

The Transitional Period

The transitional period saw pretty much the same changes in strategies of affiliation for the purpose of gaining power that occurred in the economic sphere. In the first place, as the influence of Whites increased in Northwest Alaska, the power of the Eskimos, both individually and in the aggregate, generally decreased. It declined still further as a result of the drop in population, which meant both smaller and less permanent households and local groups. The deliberate search for power became an increasingly fruitless exercise, and by 1890 most of the local group leaders in Northwest Alaska held their positions by virtue of their age, sex, and generation, and not for any other reason. The only exceptions to this rule seem to have been in the very largest of the coastal villages.

The kin-based exercise of power in terms of rather small local groups apparently lasted throughout most of the intermediate and on into the recent phase of the transitional period. The men who got elected to positions of leadership in the mission-school villages during these years were usually the same ones who just happened to have the most kinsmen in the settlements concerned. Thus, such influence as could be obtained by Eskimos during this period tended to be acquired by traditional procedures, despite the efforts of school teachers to introduce more universalistic criteria into the leadership process, and to set up village "republics" for the purpose of educating the natives on U. S. ideals of democracy.[13] Open elections were held in most villages every year, but the votes followed kinship, not party, lines. Still, having an election at all made the native leaders vul-

---

[13] Some school teachers also interfered with the democratic process they were supposedly introducing by attempting to rig village elections for their own purposes.

nerable in a way that they had never been before, and gradually things began to change.

The acquisition and retention of power through family connections remained a significant factor in the native politics of most villages and towns throughout the recent period. New skills, such as ability to read and write English, or to keep financial records or knowledge of land-claims laws, had also become important by the 1960's. Since such skills and knowledge were most widely held among young high school graduates, the ancient criteria of age and generation were being eliminated. The remarkable advances made by many individual Northwest Alaskan Eskimos in regional and state politics during the 1960's were achieved not by traditional means, but through mastery of the techniques of "politiking" as practised in the United States generally. By 1970, affiliation with kinsmen for the purpose of acquiring power, the heart and soul of traditional political endeavor, was becoming viewed more and more as an evil at the regional level, but nepotism was still commonplace locally in the towns and villages.

Intermediate Strategies of Affiliation: The Pursuit of Happiness

The third and final intermediate goal of the Northwest Alaskan Eskimos that I am going to discuss is the one that I have labeled "happiness." This goal was rather vaguely defined by the Eskimos, but it seems to have influenced strategies of affiliation often enough to justify separate treatment.

Happiness, it will be recalled, meant certain things. Minimally, it meant a standard of living far enough above the mere survival level to make it possible to pursue intermediate goals with some chances of success. On the other hand, happiness meant freedom from the many responsibilities associated with wealth and power, as well as from the considerable effort involved in acquiring and maintaining them. But most importantly, happiness meant general satisfaction with one's life situation, a feeling that there really was not a better way to live than the way one was already going about it. Obviously, the requirements of satisfaction varied from one individual to another, but there seems to have been a tendency for most people to find it some-where in the middle stratum of their society.

There were really two general considerations involved in the pursuit of happiness by the traditional Northwest Alaskan Eski-mos. These might be labeled the "material" and the "solidarity" aspects of happiness. The first had to do with the provision of food, clothing, shelter, and the like. The second concerned in-volvement in relationships which were regarded as intrinsically rewarding. The two aspects of the more general phenomenon will be discussed separately below.

Strategies of affiliation for the purpose of satisfying the ma-terial aspects of happiness were very simple and obvious in theory, if not always easy to achieve in practice. All one had to do was associate oneself with a local group whose members were numerous and productive enough to be fairly well off in the material sphere. This association would not be parasitical, for one would have to contribute goods and services to the common fund, and also support actively the aspirations and goals of the *umialik*. But association is a subordinate capacity with an or-ganization that was characterized by general affluence would greatly relieve the pressures on the individual, because the re-sources controlled by the *umialik* were always being employed for the benefit of all the members—at least in the properly man-aged organization.

In practice it was not always so easy. In the first place, the resources available to the members of the society as a whole varied widely from one region to another. In the central Brooks Range, affluence was rarely come by, and always transitory, so that happiness in a material sense was usually out of the ques-tion for all of the people much of the time. At Barrow, Wales, or Point Hope, on the other hand, a wealth of resources made affluence possible for both individuals and groups on a more or less continuous basis.

A second practical problem was the particular connections one could exploit in order to gain membership in an affluent local group. If one, or one's spouse, was closely related through con-sanguineal ties to the *umialik*, there was little problem. On the other hand, if one (or one's spouse) was only distantly related to the *umialik*, one would either have to put up with a comparatively modest standard of living, or else contribute more than most to the activities of the organization—and that required more work.

A third practical difficulty in pursuing the material aspect of happiness was that the solution to the material problem sometimes conflicted with the solution to the solidarity problem. In other words, it could happen that one's richest relatives were also people that one did not get along with—for one reason or another. One could thus find material satisfaction in associating with them, but only frustration and unhappiness from other points of view. In such cases the former consideration would have to be weighed against the latter, and some compromise course of action taken.

The second major aspect of the goal of happiness was satisfaction through solidarity itself. By this I mean affiliation with individuals with whom an association was so intrinsically satisfying that mere participation in it became a major goal in its own right. In the three preceding chapters I frequently mentioned that individual examples of almost every relationship very closely approximated the societal ideals, and that the individuals involved in them gained great personal satisfaction from their membership. As a general strategy of acquiring happiness through solidarity, the objective for the individual was to increase the number and variety of such relationships in which he was personally involved.

Variety of relationships was perhaps even more important than sheer number. For example, if one belonged to a local group in which one had ten cousins, and even if one got along well with *all* of them, the goal of happiness through solidarity would not be achieved if one also had cruel and overbearing parents, and shiftless and irresponsible siblings living in the same place. On the other hand, if one had ideal relations with one's parents, one's siblings, and perhaps also one's spouse, one might be fairly satisfied with his situation no matter how bad relations with his cousins were. Happiness through solidarity thus had to begin at home, particularly in terms of parent-child and sibling ties.[14]

[14] A satisfactory spouse was also important, but it was much easier to get a new spouse than it was to get new parents or siblings when things did not work out well. Since many people had two or more sets of parents and siblings, however, there was sometimes room for maneuver even there.

But harmony at home was only the beginning. Each relationship in the Northwest Alaskan Eskimo system had some characteristic that all the others lacked: a grandparent could tell fascinating stories, a brother probably could not; a brother could provide strong support in hunting or warfare, a grandparent probably could not; a same-aged cousin could be joked with, a brother probably could not. In order to enjoy the full potential of human relationships that the traditional society provided, an Eskimo had to be actively involved in at least one example of every kind of relationship in the kinship system.

It is difficult to convey to the non-Eskimo reader of the late twentieth century an understanding of just how important kinship solidarity was to the Northwest Alaskans. In our society, many individuals thoroughly enjoy the company of others for the intrinsic value of the relationship, but most relationships of this kind are with friends, not with kinsmen. Furthermore, a great many individuals derive their greatest satisfaction from some other facet of life. By contrast, the overwhelming majority of Northwest Alaskan Eskimos found their greatest personal satisfaction in associating with their fellows, and, to an extent that it is difficult for most of us to conceive, these relations were with kinsmen.

Solidarity *per se* seems to have remained an important intermediate goal of the Northwest Alaskan Eskimos from traditional times right down to the end of the recent period. During the decades when survival itself seemed to be at stake, rather less attention was paid to it than was formerly the case. But as the general material circumstances of the Northwest Alaskan Eskimos improved during the recent period, particularly during the 1960's, there was a marked resurgence of interest and effort in this sphere. As I mentioned previously, transistor tape recorders, airplanes, and, more recently, snowmobiles, greatly facilitated this development. But the technological advances simply provided new means through which ancient goals could be achieved. Relatives who would have belonged to a single local group in traditional times, but who were distributed in villages all over Northwest Alaska in 1970, not only re-established contact with one another, they positively thrived on their renewed association.

Once the new means of transportation became available, increasingly large gatherings of people began to take place. Traditional Eskimo holidays, such as Thanksgiving [15] and the whaling feast, and new ones, such as Easter and the Quarterly Meeting of the Friends Church, were the focal points for these occasions. In either case, the general procedures followed were very similar to traditional ones. The guests would arrive in town, and would be quickly ushered to the houses of their kin, where they would stay throughout their visit. Sleep would be forgotten as people visited and talked and ate together. Then there would be a major gathering in the church, just as there used to be in the *qazgi*. Hours and hours of singing, speeches, and storytelling would follow, duly recorded on dozens of tape recorders and captured on film, all to be repeated and remarked on for months afterward.[16] And then there would be a feast, usually in the church, the school, or the armory, just as there used to be in the *qazgi*. Then it would be back to the houses to listen to the tapes and to talk and to visit some more.

The 1960's witnessed the beginnings of a dramatic renewal of Eskimo wealth and Eskimo power in Northwest Alaska. But of all of the changes that occurred in the area during the decade of my field research, none seems to have affected the morale of the people as significantly as the reactivation of a wide network of kinship ties. Just when the extensive network of Eskimo kin relationships seemed reduced to insignificance in Northwest Alaska, the pursuit of happiness through kin solidarity suddenly became a major goal of the people once again.

[15] Thanksgiving as such was not a traditional Eskimo holiday. But American Thanksgiving and Christmas fall within the traditional Eskimo holiday season, and they merged neatly with the traditional annual cycle.

[16] Relatives who were in hospital or otherwise unable to attend these affairs would be able to participate in them vicariously because someone would be sure to make a recording for them, usually accompanied by a tape or two of commentary.

*

7

Patterns of Affiliation

The various strategies of affiliation, combined with the material circumstances of life in Northwest Alaska, made it necessary for people to become involved in kinship organizations more comprehensive in scope than dyadic relationships. These larger organizations have been referred to rather vaguely as "families" and "local groups," but it is now both appropriate and necessary to be more precise. In order that analytic rigor be achieved, however, it is necessary to digress a bit on the concepts involved.

The term "family" is defined for present purposes as an organization in which membership, and the nature of the relationships among the members, are importantly oriented to real or assumed facts of biological relatedness *and* sexual intercourse (Levy 1965:30). This definition is not a radically new one, but it is different in certain respects from many others common in the field. In the first place, it does not say anything about the economic or political attributes that an organization must have in order to be a family. Secondly, it does not equate, either directly or by implication, a family unit with a household—or any other type of residential unit, for that matter. And finally, this definition does not specify either directly or by implication, any specific relationships that must be included if an organization is to be a family. All of these consid-

235

erations are matters of analysis, not of definition (cf. Buchler
and Selby 1968:21ff.; Mair 1965:85ff.; Murdock 1949:1ff.).

It is useful to illustrate the implications of the above definition of "family" with reference to a hypothetical example.
Figure 10 shows an imaginary organization in which eleven

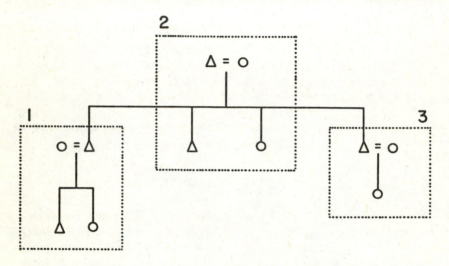

FIGURE 10   Diagram of a hypothetical family unit.

positions are distinguished. The diagram represents a mature
couple, their non-adult children, their two adult sons, the wives
of those two sons, and the children of those two sons.

Disregard the dotted lines for a moment, and assume that all
of the positions in the system are filled by people who live in a
single dwelling, stay together throughout most of the yearly
cycle, and generally operate under the supervision of the senior
couple. Under those conditions, the organization concerned
would be a family, as defined above. More specifically, it would
be a patrilocal extended family in the conventional anthropological sense. Included in it are marital, parent-child, sibling,
grandparent-grandchild, neopotic, cousin, and various affinal
relationships.

Now change the first assumption. Instead of having all of
the individuals involved living in the *same* house, assume that

they are distributed among *three* houses, as indicated by the dotted lines. However, retain the assumption that these people stay together throughout most of the year, if not in the same house, then as close neighbors. Also retain the assumption that everyone involved generally operates under the direction of the senior couple. Under these assumptions, how many families would there be, one or three?

Given the above definition of "family," the answer to the question is that there are probably both one *and* three families represented in the diagram. On the one hand, there continues to be the patrilocal extended family that was there under the first set of assumptions. On the other hand, there are probably also three families, namely, the three conjugal families whose members live in different houses. I use the word "probably" because it is likely that the relationships among the individuals involved would be differentiated to some extent by virtue of their residence in different houses, but it would be impossible to know that for certain without more information.

Given the above analysis, it is useful to distinguish *two levels* of family unit. Using terminology suggested by Carrasco (1963) for somewhat different purposes, I call these two levels "domestic" and "local" families. A *domestic family* is defined as a family organization whose members occupy a single dwelling. It is distinguished from a household by virtue of the fact that *any set* of individuals living in one house would qualify as a household, whereas only the members of a family (as defined above) could qualify as a domestic family. A *local family*, by contrast, would be a family whose members occupy different dwellings (but whose members still operate in terms of a single overriding family organization). In terms of these distinctions, Figure 10 illustrates one local family with three domestic family subsystems.

Most anthropologists concerned with hunting-gathering societies have written about "families," on the one hand, and "bands" or "local groups" on the other, usually without providing an explicit definition of any of those terms (cf. Damas, ed. 1969; Lee and DeVore, eds., 1968b). June Helm (1965:375ff.; 1968:118) has been a bit more precise, however, and has distinguished two levels of "socioterritorial organization" above that of the family among the Arctic Drainage Dene, these being the "local band" and the "regional band." The former is a unit comprised of several families linked together by a variety of bilaterally radiating kinship ties; the individual families occupy separate, but adjacent dwellings, and tend to remain together throughout the annual cycle. This unit appears to be identical to what I call a "local family," whereas Helm's "family," without modification, is probably equivalent to my "domestic family." The regional band, in her classification, is a unit constituted along the lines of a local band, but it is made up of several such units whose members occupy an entire region rather than a specific point within one. In my terminology this might be called a "regional family." In traditional Northwest Alaska, the boundaries of a regional family were isomorphic with the boundaries of a society, as I am using the latter term. This identity is a function of the nature of the phenomena at hand, rather than a direct consequence of the definitions, and there is no reason why the two units must always coincide in societies of this type.

Given my definition of family, it would be inconsistent to refer to the organization represented in Figure 10 as a "patrilocal extended family" under the first set of assumptions, and as a "patrilocal band" or "local group" under the second set. The two situations are not identical, but the difference falls *within* the area covered by the definition of family; it does not set family-type units apart from band-type units. Accordingly, different modifiers, rather than distinct basic terms, should be used to indicate the difference. I suggest that most writers on the topic have been inconsistent and unnecessarily vague in their use of these concepts, and those are problems I wish to reduce, if not eliminate, here. For the same reasons, I will be more precise in the analysis that follows than I have been in previous chapters, referring specifically to domestic or local families, and not to "families" and "local groups"; the term "band" will be avoided.

THE TRADITIONAL PERIOD

Families

Virtually every individual operated primarily in terms of family units throughout his lifetime in traditional Northwest Alaska. The only exceptions, according to informants, were the few individuals who, lacking *any* recognized kin, maintained themselves at a marginal level in the role of slave. Everyone else was actively involved in family units. For most of the people most of the time, these units included *both* domestic and local families.

A traditional domestic family, according to informants, consisted of a single conjugal family, as a minimum. In terms of relationships, this meant that the *minimum* Eskimo family was comprised of husband-wife and parent-child ties. The great majority of domestic families were more complex, however, being either extended or polygamous (usually polygynous), or both. According to my informants, practically every conceivable kind of domestic family was to be found. Emphasis was on two basic types. The first was a unit comprised of aged parents, one (or more) adult offspring and spouse(s), and grandchildren. The second major type involved two or more married siblings, their spouses, and their children. Most exceptions were either polygynous units, or conjugal units whose members were living apart from their kin for only short periods of time. But the basic points made by informants were: (1) that the great majority of domestic families included relationships over and above the minimum, and (2) that there was no institutionalized emphasis on either male or female lines in domestic family composition.

Direct observational data on family composition from the traditional period do not exist. However, there is some information on *household* composition. Since individuals apparently never lived alone in traditional times, and since unrelated families reportedly never shared a single dwelling, it may be assumed that household membership and domestic family membership coincided. The available data, which derive from 325 households (observed at various points in time), were analyzed by

Foote (1965:214–320).   His conclusions regarding the *average* traditional household were as follows:

(1) It contained seven persons.

(2) It was comprised of 65% of adults and 35% of children.

(3) It consisted of 52% males and 48% females.

(4) It contained as many adult males as adult females.

(5) It contained between one and two adult males.

These "hard" data, derived from the traditional period proper, confirm the view presented by my informants over a century later.

Local families were virtually identical in structure and composition to domestic families, but they were usually larger, and their members were distributed among two or more households instead of being concentrated in just one.   They were, in short, large extended families composed of nearly the full range of relationships that the system provided.[1]   Local families were not necessarily exogamous, although they usually were in practice, and they were never named.

The separate dwellings occupied by members of a single local family were occasionally located some distance apart, but most of the time they were situated very close together, sometimes almost touching one another.[2]   Indeed, the boundary between domestic and local families was often obscure.   Whenever it was physically possible, people belonging to the constituent domestic units of a single local family would connect their dwellings by passageways, with the result that the residents could move from one to another without going outside.   If there were more than three or four domestic units, and if the members expected to stay in one place for more than a few weeks, they would usually also build a *qazgi*.   In most areas, a *qazgi* was simply a regu-

---

[1] The only relationships that were *not* normally included in local family structure were those of co-spouses, co-husbands, and the *qataŋutigiik* version of the sibling relationship (which was carried out in regular sibling terms in this context).

[2] There was a certain amount of variation in dwelling construction, both from region to region and from season to season.   A good idea of this variation can be found in the following sources: Giddings (1956:29ff.), Murdoch (1892:72–86), Nelson (1899:242–263), and Spencer (1959:43–61).

lar dwelling-like building which lacked a sleeping area, and which had instead a relatively substantial floor on which people could work or dance.

Local families were the major organizational components of a traditional Northwest Alaskan Eskimo society. In other words, for all of the people most of the time, the local family formed *the* social unit in terms of which daily activities were carried out. Children would move back and forth between the houses, eating and sleeping wherever the mood struck them, and the men usually would be found clustered together in one house (or in the *qazgi* or else hunting), and the women would often work together in another. The one cooked meal of the day, consumed in late afternoon or early evening, would typically find the entire membership concentrated in two of the constituent houses, the men and adolescent boys in one, and the women, girls, and young children in another. In this type of situation the so-called "nuclear family" all but vanished, and the domestic family was scarcely more significant. A local family was a single, coherent organization, one in which the constituent relationships were articulated with one another in terms of a definite pattern. The Eskimos did not have a name for this type of organization, as such, but they referred to the members of one simply as *ilagiit*, i. e., as people interacting in terms of kin relationships.

Variations

The question of variation is always germane in a study having the geographic scope of the present one: was the pattern described above found in all parts of Northwest Alaska, or only in restricted regions? In order to answer that question, it is necessary to distinguish between variations in *structure*, on the one hand, and variations in *membership*, on the other. The former concerns variations in the number and type of relationships that comprised the organization concerned. The latter concerns the individuals who interacted in terms of those relationships. Finally, in both spheres, one must distinguish between variation in space, and variation in time.

All available evidence suggests that the *structure* of both domestic and local family units was highly uniform throughout traditional Northwest Alaska, and it varied little from one season to the next. In other words, most family units throughout the entire area were comprised of essentially the same set of relationships throughout the annual cycle. However, there was considerable variation in the *membership* of family units, both in space and through time. Accordingly, the discussion that follows is concerned primarily with variations in membership rather than with variations in structure.

The *size* of local family units varied considerably from one place to another, primarily according to the wealth or poverty of local resources. For most of the people most of the time, in all districts, the basic organization was a local family comprised of just two or three domestic units, involving perhaps 14 to 21 people. Wherever or whenever game was more abundant, the size was usually larger, sometimes quite a bit larger. Along the Kobuk River, for example, local families were often comprised of as many at ten or more domestic units in early fall, and sometimes involved over a hundred people. Local families of at least this size were also common at many coastal points, such as Barrow, Point Hope, Kotzebue, Wales, the Diomede Islands, and King Island. Elsewhere, families of this size were rare, and usually only temporary, coming into existence upon a particularly successful game harvest, and dividing again once supplies had been exhausted. (Further details on seasonal variations in scale are presented below in the section on societies).

The ultimate development of the local family was an organization involving as many as two or three hundred kinsmen whose houses were built adjacent to one another. The members of such a unit were known as *amilraqtuyaat*, or, in some dialects, *inugialiŋmiut*. In its ideal form, such a unit was characterized by centralized leadership and a complex division of labor. These large local families were sometimes so distinct from one another that, even within a single settlement, such as Point Hope, a person risked assault and possibly even murder just by walking unannounced into the area occupied by the members of one to which he did not belong.

The existence of large local families of the sort described above has been documented for Point Hope, where the remnants of at least one of them persisted into the present century (v. Rainey 1947:241). There was also one on the middle Kobuk in the late 1890's; it was so impressive to the Eskimos of the time that the term for the members of such a unit (*amilraq-tuyaat*), and the geographical designation for the inhabitants of the whole district were virtual synonyms. The two (Ray 1964b:79) or three (Greist n. d.: Chapter II) "villages" located at Wales in the early 1800's look suspiciously like units of this type, although the information required to determine this definitively does not exist.

To judge from the fragments available to me in the 1960's, the *amilraqtuyaat* of the traditional Northwest Alaskan Eskimos must have been the most complex and sophisticated organization found anywhere among any Eskimo-speaking people. The almost total lack of data on the precise composition of these units, as well as the absence of contemporary observations on how they actually worked, are great losses to Eskimo ethnography that will probably never be recovered.

A final matter to be discussed under the heading of "variation" is *continuity* of membership in particular local family organizations from one year to the next. As Barth (1964:-25–26) has pointed out, this question is always particularly important in the analysis of nomadic societies because the members of such societies are uniquely capable of fissioning at almost any time. In Northwest Alaska there were at least two regular moves built into the yearly cycle of every society during which the potential for changes in family membership was particularly great.

According to my informants, most local families contained at least a core of members which remained relatively constant, not only from season to season, but from year to year (cf. Damas 1968a:113). They indicated further that continuity was much greater at the local than at the domestic family level. In other words, people moved more readily between domestic family units within the same local family than they did from one local family to another. Informants emphasized this point just as strongly when referring to the highly nomadic people of the Upper Noatak as they did when speaking about the semi-nomadic people of Point Hope. Here again, the evidence points to local, and not to domestic family units, as being the primary focus of solidarity in traditional times. Unfortunately, specific case data from the relevant period do not exist. It is therefore impossible to determine quantitatively just what the turnover rate was, and it is also impossible to either refute or corroborate informant accounts in any definitive way.

Communities

Chang (1962) pointed out some years ago that there is an important analytic difference between the physical arrangement of a set of individuals, on the one hand, and the social organization of those individuals, on the other. In order to indicate which one he was talking about, he distinguished terminologically between "settlement" and "community."

> A definition of the community may be superfluous, but it might be emphasized that, in contrast to the concept of "settlement" which stresses the locale rather than its occupants, the concept of "community," as social group, centers around the occupants of a locale rather than the locale *per se*. This point may be made clear by stating that conceptually a community does not refer to the community site but to the whole group of inhabitants of that site, whether at a certain point of time they are inhabiting the community site or happen to be scattered around in small camp sites fishing and hunting. With reference to a community, we aim at investigating its demographic constitution, the recruitment of community members, the relations among the occupants at a particular locale, and the regulations governing the relations between a local group and its locale of settlement. (Chang 1962:33).

In differentiating between a locale and its occupants, Chang was on the right track, but he did not go far enough; he failed completely to recognize the distinction between people, on the one hand, and the organization(s) they are involved in, on the other.

It is useful to separate conceptually three orders of phenomena—the spatial, the demographic, and the social.[3] The spatial order, as the label implies, concerns the distribution of phenomena in space. In traditional Northwest Alaska, the minimum spatial unit was the dwelling, and the most comprehensive unit was the region, i. e., the home district of the members

---

[3] At the (domestic) family-household-dwelling level, the three-fold distinction between organization, personnel, and locale has been pointed out by Bender (1967).

of a particular society. The *demographic order*, by contrast, consists of the people themselves. In any demographic analysis, the minimum unit is the individual; any set of individuals is a "population." In traditional Northwest Alaska, the maximum population unit was the "regional group," which consisted of the entire membership of a society. Finally, the *social order* consists of the system(s) of action in terms of which a set of individuals operates. In this context the minimal unit is the role; any system of roles is an organization. The minimal organization, in turn, is a dyadic relationship, while the most comprehensive organization is a society.

In traditional Northwest Alaska there were four patterns of affiliation above that of the dyadic relationship. These patterns, which were simply organizations of increasing degrees of inclusiveness, were the domestic family, the local family, the community, and the society. Three of these terms have been defined and discussed already. The fourth, which I call "community" (cf. Chang *Ibid.*), is defined for present purposes as an organization in terms of which the members of two (or more) different local families interact when occupying the same settlement. A "settlement," in turn, is any cluster of two or more dwellings that is quite distinct from every other such cluster.

Before commenting on community structure, it might clarify matters to indicate more precisely the relationship between the different levels of social phenomena, on the one hand, and the different levels of demographic and spatial phenomena, on the other hand. This is done in Table 8, in which the different *orders* of phenomena are presented in columns, and the corre-

TABLE 8   Levels of Affiliation in Traditional Northwest Alaska

Social Unit	Demographic Unit	Spatial Unit
Society	Regional group	Region
Community	Villagers	Village
Local family	Local group	Hamlet (or neighborhood)
Domestic family	Household (or domestic group)	Dwelling

sponding *levels* in each order are on the same line. A "settlement," as defined above, could consist of a single isolated dwelling, a small cluster of dwellings ("hamlet"), or a large cluster of dwellings ("village"); the village/town distinction did not become relevant until Nome was established around the beginning of the 20th century. Given these distinctions, the dwellings of the members of a single local family constituted a "hamlet" when they comprised an entire settlement, and they constituted a "neighborhood" when they were incorporated into a larger spatial unit of the type I call a "village."

The existence of the local family level of organization within the community context has not been recognized by most anthropologists who have worked in Northwest Alaska.[4] The common view, expressed in the terminology outlined above, is that each community was a relatively well integrated organization composed of *domestic* families whose dwellings were scattered rather haphazardly over a village site (Murdoch 1892:-242; Spencer 1959:51). Actually, a community was composed of *local* family units each of which, in turn, was made up of two or more domestic families; most activities were carried out in local family rather than in domestic family or community terms. Dwellings were *not* scattered haphazardly about in a village site, but built in clusters (or neighborhoods), each of which housed the members of a single local family. Each social center (*qazgi*), a supposedly non-kin, village-wide type of organization, was in fact built by the members of a single local family in the vicinity of their dwellings, and maintained and used primarily by the members of that family. Similarly, a hunting crew, another ostensibly non-kin organization (Spencer 1972), was organized and staffed primarily by individuals from a single local family.

A traditional Northwest Alaskan Eskimo village (in the technical sense used here) may be thought of as being occupied

---

[4] For the most part the oversight seems to have been the result of failure to push the investigation far enough back in time. For example, Spencer's (1959:50–51) description of *Utqiarvik* as of about 1895 represents a situation substantially different from the one existing half a century earlier. Earlier observers, such as Nelson (1899) and Murdoch (1892) apparently thought that they were close enough to the aboriginal situation to obviate the need for reconstructing an earlier state of affairs. According to my information, their assumption was incorrect.

by the members of two or more autonomous local families whose members happened to live very close together more or less by accident. The two (or more) local families concerned constituted factions (v. Pospisil 1964:415ff.) between (or among) which rivalry and hostility could be fairly intense if residential proximity was maintained over any length of time. Usually expressed in terms of peaceful dancing, athletic, and feast-giving competitions, inter-local family conflict sometimes resulted in bloodshed, particularly in the large whaling villages that were found at various places along the coast (v. Larsen and Rainey 1948:27).

Some solidarity at the community level did exist, just enough to give the term some meaning. This solidarity was achieved primarily through intermarriage between the local families concerned. However, the rate of marriage between the two (or more) local families occupying a single settlement was not much greater than it was when the people concerned lived in different settlements scattered about an entire region. In addition to intermarriage, it was possible for a member of one local family to participate in the *qazgi* organization operated primarily by the members of another. But, according to my informants, one would involve himself thus in the affairs of another local family *only* by invitation, and an invitation would come only from a close relative except in very rare instances. Consequently, much of the integration that existed at the community level was a function of the operation of kin relationships. Social integration at this level was only slightly greater than it was among the entire set of local family units that comprised a society as a whole.

Societies

The most general pattern of affiliation in traditional Northwest Alaska was the society. This type of organization was defined and briefly described in Chapter One, but it is appropriate to re-examine it now in the light of the analysis contained in the intervening chapters.

A society is an organization (1) whose members are recruited at least in part by the sexual reproduction of members, (2) that is capable of existing long enough for the production of stable adult members from the infants of members, and (3) that constitutes a set of structures such that action in terms of them is at least in theory capable of self-sufficiency for the maintenance of the members (Levy 1966:20–21). In traditional Northwest Alaska, the first two criteria were met by many local families, so interest here is on the third criterion, namely, social self-sufficiency.

Local families were self-sufficient to a considerable degree in traditional Northwest Alaska. They were relatively self-sufficient both economically and politically; as a rule, the members were capable of educating the children, observing religious and magical practices, and generally operating for extended periods of time without reference to the members of any other unit. In all respects, self-sufficiency tended to increase or decrease with scale.

But self-sufficiency was never quite complete at the local family level. In the first place, very few local families were large enough to remain totally endogamous for any extended period of time because of incest restrictions. Sooner or later, some members of each such unit would have to look elsewhere for spouses. The second limitation on self-sufficiency was in part a consequence of environmental factors. In most regions, the resource base was too precarious for the members of each local family to persist indefinitely without help from the members of other such units. But even where this limitation was uncommon, the need for defence in time of war (Burch n. d.) led to mutual interdependence among the local families in a region. Since marriages and crises (famine, war) occurred fairly frequently, the survival of a local family over any extended period of time required that its members establish relations with the members of other such units. Since, in the Northwest Alaskan scheme of things, one could not associate peacefully with strangers at all, not to mention rely on strangers for help, these relations had to be kept in operation more or less continuously if they were to be there when they were really needed.

The general pattern of affiliation in a society as a whole can be better understood with reference to a specific case. Figure 11 shows the location of the various settlements occupied annually by the members of traditional Kotzebue society at the time

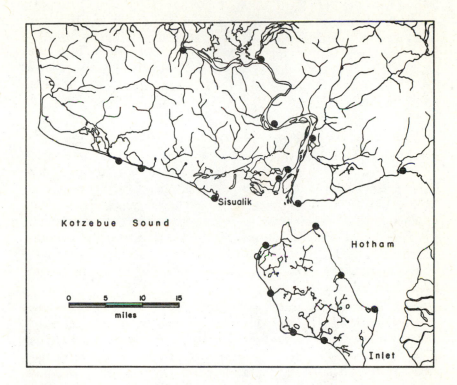

FIGURE 11 Map showing major fall settlement locations, traditional Kotzebue Society.

of freshwater freeze-up.[5]   Each dot on the map indicates the location of a hamlet, i. e., a settlement occupied by the members of a single local family.   Most of these units were very small in scale at this time of year, numbering fifteen to twenty members each.   The one circle on the map indicates the location of a village, whose 100 or more occupants were normally organized in terms of two or more local families.   This settlement was located at the best hunting and fishing area in the entire Kotzebue region.

The important point for the present discussion is that people belonging to each local family were related on a kinship basis

5 Kotzebue society is one of those described in some detail in Chapter One.

to people in each of the others. Thus, the society was a network in which the nodes (i. e., local families) were subsystems of active kin relationships. Lines between the nodes would represent kin ties which were temporarily inactive, but which could be activated immediately should the need arise. The outer boundary of the system was defined by a sharp (although not complete) break in the network of kin relationships connecting individuals in different local families.

Subsistence strategy dictated that the members of a society should spread out over a large tract of country each fall in order to maximize the chances of at least some people being in the right place at the right time to have a successful hunting and fishing season. Since some locations were consistently more productive than others, they were usually tried first; it is these sites that are indicated in Figure 11. The strategies of affiliation described in Chapter Six dictated further that the population so distributed should be organized in terms of domestic and local families.

As the fall season progressed, some groups would be less fortunate than others. Except in unusually bad years, at least some of the sites would be productive enough for the people living there to set aside a surplus. As winter approached, the people who had had a bad fall would move in with relatives who had been more successful. In a normal year there would be a considerable realignment of the population during the course of the fall months. By the onset of the holiday season in early December, the members of the society would be clustered in fewer, but larger aggregations than they had been involved in at the time of freeze-up. These aggregations would be located precisely where food surpluses had been established. The locations could vary considerably from one year to the next. Only the one site indicated on Figure 11 by the circle was productive enough year in and year out to support a large population, but it was rarely so productive that the entire societal membership of 400-odd people could congregate there at any one time between October and May.

In organizational terms, the early winter units were of two basic types. The first was a single local family with a fairly large membership, say, of thirty or forty people, or perhaps more. Such an organization usually resulted from the union of two smaller local families whose members were both closely related and on particularly good terms. In such cases the two smaller units simply merged to form another, one which was obviously larger than either of them, but which was virtually identical in structure. The second type of early winter organization was a community which, by definition, was comprised of two or more local families. The members of one of these communities might be located at the site indicated by the circle in Figure 11, in which case the organization was more or less continuous in duration. In all other cases, the involvement of the members of two or more local families in a community organization would be merely temporary. Such amalgamations occurred for one of two reasons: first, so that the members could enjoy the early winter holiday season in style; or, second, because the members of one unit had done poorly, the other well, during the fall hunting and fishing.

The relatively large concentrations of people which occurred in early winter, combined with the reckless consumption of foodstuffs during the holiday season, typically exhausted the supplies of all but a few unusually affluent families. Accordingly, beginning in January, the members of most communities and large local families began to disperse. Food supply seems to have been the critical limiting factor at this time of year. Wherever and whenever a large kill was made, related domestic and local family units would congregate, separating again once supplies became depleted. In times of famine, the entire societal population would fragment into isolated single-dwelling settlements.

When life became easier once again in the spring, the members of the family units who had separated earlier began to come together once again, usually at spring hunting locations on the outer coast. In June and July substantial concentrations of people occurred at Sisualik, as noted in Chapter One. During the fair, members of several societies would come together for a period of two or three weeks or more.

Despite the large numbers of people involved, the primary operating unit at the fair was the local family. The tents of the members of each local family would be situated next to one another, and slightly apart from the rest; the tents of the members of each society would be separated from one another by a somewhat larger interval. Food would be distributed freely within, but not between local family units, and athletic and dancing competitions, as well as feasts and ceremonies, would be organized by the members of one local family for the members of another. In some respects these inter-local family activities were similar to those that occurred during the holiday season of early winter; the big difference was that, at the fairs, relations between local family units were structured along *partnership* lines, whereas in winter they were structured along *kinship* lines.

After the people began to spread out again after the fair, the representatives of each society would return to their home district. The members of the Kotzebue society would normally return to the locations indicated in Figure 11. As indicated earlier in this chapter, there seems to have been a high level of continuity from one fall to the next, not only in the gross distribution of the population of the society, but also in the location of specific individuals. In other words, the same people tended to return to the same site each fall with considerable regularity.

The above account focused on only a single society, but the same general pattern occurred throughout traditional Northwest Alaska. The major differences occurred in settlements on the islands in Bering Strait, and in the larger villages on the mainland coast. On the islands people returned to the same villages and dwellings every fall, but they were normally isolated there until break-up the following summer permitted boat travel. In the coastal villages, such as those at Wales, Point Hope, and Barrow, large concentrations of people occurred during the holiday season of early winter, but even greater ones took place during the whaling season in the spring. In both cases, the major dispersal of population occurred in summer, most of the settlements concerned being virtually abandoned between the end of the spring seal hunting season and the onset of freshwater freeze-up.[6]

---

[6] This pattern is another one that changed quickly after whaling and trading vessels began to frequent Northwest Alaska, at least as far as the mainland villages were concerned. Once the ships began to touch at these villages at various times during the summer, many people found it more advantageous to remain home and trade with the Whites than to go to a fair and trade with other Eskimos.

THE EARLY TRANSITIONAL PERIOD

The early transitional period, it will be recalled, began with the influx of whaling and exploring ships into Northwest Alaska around the middle of the 19th century, and ended with the establishment of missions and schools there in the 1890's. Although much remains to be learned about the period, it is possible to state with assurance that it was a disastrous time for the Eskimos. Newly imported diseases and whisky combined to decimate the population and, the precipitous decline in the major food resources—the bowhead whale, walrus, and caribou—contributed to widespread famine. These developments began at different times and proceeded at different rates from one region to another, but the overall trend increased in speed and scope with each passing year. By 1890 it had reached and significantly affected affiliation patterns in all districts of Northwest Alaska.

Families

Traditional *strategies* of affiliation continued to guide people's actions during the early transitional period. Accordingly, people continued to be involved in both domestic and local family units which were quite traditional in structure. However, as noted in Chapter Six, it became increasingly difficult during this period to establish and maintain the kind of large local family unit required for the effective pursuit of intermediate goals. This was the case partly because the greatly depleted resource base throughout Northwest Alaska placed progressively narrower limits on the number of people who could live at any one place, and partly because famines and epidemics simply annihilated the members of one family after another. Survival, not the pursuit of wealth, power, or happiness, became the primary goal of most of the people in most areas of Northwest Alaska during this period.

During the early transitional period continuity of local family membership also began to decline, again, primarily because of famine and disease. An epidemic would often wipe out a substantial proportion of the membership of a local family, affecting each domestic unit in the process. The survivors would consolidate their forces and flee the scene of the disaster—if they could; but often the sickness had such a debilitating effect on the survivors that they were unable to hunt or fish, and they died anyway from starvation.

People who lived through such a disaster were faced with the problem of creating a viable existence out of the ruins of the old one. In most cases they were able to do so fairly quickly by employing the traditional procedures of adoption, substitution, and *ilaliuqtuq* ("making" kin via sexual intercourse). For example, if a child survived an epidemic but its parents did not, it might be adopted by an uncle. The uncle, in turn, might have lost his wife from the same sickness, and he might marry a widow. The trio would then join forces with other relatives, and life would proceed more or less as before. Obviously, when domestic and local families are fragmenting and reforming under such conditions, continuity is very difficult to maintain.

By the end of the early transitional period, experiences with famine and disease, occasionally exacerbated by alcoholic binges, had become familiar to the people of Northwest Alaska, and greatly feared by them. By 1890, when someone was thought to be ill, particularly if the person exhibited symptoms of the "red sickness" (apparently measles), the settlement would be abandoned *immediately*, along with much of its contents of food and equipment; the sick would be left behind to make out as best they could. I have interviewed several people who, as youngsters, lived through epidemics and famines of this kind. In a few cases I tried to get them to trace in detail the membership loss in the initial organization and the new arrangements that were created subsequently. Without exception, they refused to do so, the recollection being simply too painful for them.

Some Examples

Observational data on family structure and composition from the early transitional period are very limited. However, I was able, through informant recall, to acquire fairly detailed information on two examples of local families from the very end of this period. The information is summarized here in order to illustrate several of the points that have been made so far.

The first example is a local family whose members wintered in the Upper Noatak District; it is presented as it existed about 1885. At this particular time, Upper Noatak Society was still a viable organization. During the previous decade or two the region had received migrants from several other districts, and the population of the area had apparently increased in size as a result. Most of these immigrants had come from regions farther south, which the caribou had abandoned. A few had come from coastal areas in an effort to escape the sickness and drunkenness that were becoming increasingly prevalent there.

The local family in the example consisted of thirty individuals who belonged to four domestic units. The genealogical connections and household affiliation of these individuals are indicated in Figure 12.[7] As can be seen, membership was based on a variety of sibling and cousin ties, but many others, including marital and in-law relationships, were also employed for this purpose.

The Upper Noatak people were highly nomadic, traveling the whole way down to Kotzebue Sound early every summer, then returning to the Upper Noatak early in the fall.[8] The members of this local family normally stayed together throughout the entire annual cycle. Although they could winter anywhere they wanted to in the Upper Noatak basin, the members of this particular unit preferred the lower reaches of Makpik Creek as a base of operations, and they returned there regularly every fall when they ascended the river from Kotzebue. Only when a lean winter season made such a large aggregation impossible would the constituent domestic families separate and spread out in search of food. On the other hand, in a time of local abundance, their numbers would be increased through the addition of relatives from other local families who had not fared so well.

The household distribution of the individuals represented in Figure 12 changed somewhat from one year to the next, although

[7] All of the relationships represented by diagrams in this chapter are presented as though they were real rather than fictive; in fact, many fictive ties are included. My information regarding fictive elements in the cases in the early and intermediate periods is a bit spotty, and possibly unreliable, and is not included for those reasons. For the recent period the information is reliable, but is omitted to protect the individuals involved.

[8] The traditional annual cycle of this society was described in greater detail in Chapter One.

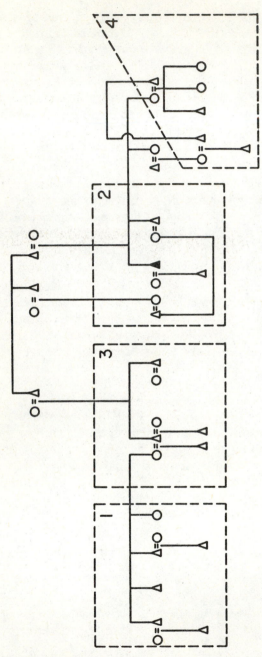

FIGURE 12   Diagram showing the composition of an Upper Noatak local family, circa 1885.

the arrangement indicated was the most common one. In most winters the houses were connected by tunnels anyway, in which case the domestic/local family distinction became substantially reduced in significance. More important was stability and the composition of the unit as a whole, membership changing little except through birth, death, or the marriage of one of the members. This stability was attributed by my informant primarily to the effective leadership of the oldest male in the unit (indicated by the blackened triangle in the diagram), although all of the members were said to have been remarkably compatible with one another.

By 1888 the caribou population of the Upper Noatak had declined to such an extent that the people too were forced to leave the region. Most moved north across the Brooks Range and scattered along the Arctic coast. The people represented in the diagram however, along with the members of a few other local families, preferred to stay in familiar country. For another ten years or so, they continued to stay together, following a modified version of their traditional annual cycle. Instead of wintering in the Upper Noatak basin, they located their fall settlement in the upper reaches of the forested portion of the Lower Noatak basin where they barely managed to eke out a living. Each spring they went to Point Hope to work for the White whalers there. Only after they got paid would they move to Sisualik, usually too late to participate in the major beluga hunting season. By 1910, most of the individuals represented in the diagram were still alive, but the domestic families had separated, and their members were scattered among the new mission/school villages of Kotzebue, Noatak, Kivalina, and Point Hope.

Another example of a local family from the end of the early transitional period is illustrated in Figure 13. This unit involved fewer people than the previous example, and the size and composition of its domestic families were less representative of the traditional pattern. Both households number two and number three had an unusually small number of occupants; household number one was within the traditional range. In addition, the membership was based on a very simple core of three brothers, whereas many traditional local families, even of this small size, were built of a more complex combination of consanguineal and affinal ties.

Burch—Eskimo Kinsmen—17

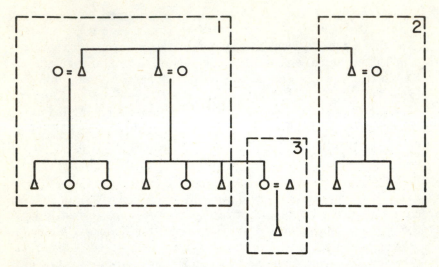

FIGURE 13 Diagram showing the composition of a Kobuk River local family, circa 1890.

The particular local family in question here is represented at a peculiar point in its history. Not long before this, the unit had had many more members. By 1890 its membership had been reduced through a combination of (1) sickness, which had wiped out many members of the generation above the oldest one represented in the diagram, and (2) the emigration to the North Slope of most of the people who had survived the sickness. Immediately after the period represented in the diagram, the unit grew very large once again when a number of relatives moved down from the upper river. My informant was a "big boy" during the second growth period, but the unit was too large for him to remember its precise composition; he refused to speculate. He did say, however, that, during the second period, the unit had been large enough to qualify for the label *amilraqtuyaat*, and it had been the largest local family in the entire Kobuk valley at the time. There had been several domestic families in it, all large, and the unit had had a very large social center (*qazgi*). After the establishment of the Friends Mission at Kotzebue, in 1897, and particularly after the disruptive period of the Kobuk gold rush in 1898–99, the unit again went into decline. By 1905 or so, the entire membership had either died, or else had emigrated to the coast of Kotzebue Sound or to the Barrow region.

Other Developments

Community organization retained its traditionally vague structure during the early transitional period, but viable examples of this type of organization became increasingly scarce. Indeed, by the end of the period, it is meaningful to talk about communities only with reference to the organizations whose members lived in the old coastal villages on King Island, the Diomede Islands, Wales, Point Hope, and Barrow. In these settlements there was a high level of *organizational* continuity during this period, although there was a considerable reduction and turnover in *membership*. In 1890 these villages were inhabited by individuals operating in terms of exactly the same *type* of family and community organizations that people there had been involved in forty years earlier, but each community was made up of fewer local family units than previously had been the case. In other districts, communities had ceased to operate, even on a temporary basis, by 1890. The reason for this was very simple: there were never enough people in any one settlement to make them possible any more.

The traditional societies had ceased to operate in Northwest Alaska by 1890, primarily because of the biological extinction and dispersion of the members (cf. Levy 1952:137). In some cases, e. g., Kivalina, Lower Noatak, and Kobuk Delta, the population was all but wiped out by starvation. In other regions, the people had observed the decline in their food resources, anticipated what would happen, and abandoned their territory *before* disaster struck; Upper Noatak and Kauwerak societies are examples. In still other cases—primarily the societies whose territories were on the coast—the descendants of the traditional population had been greatly reduced by disease and emigration, but total population size had been maintained to some extent by immigration from other regions. In these cases, new societies would probably have developed eventually, under aboriginal conditions, but it never occurred in the late 19th century because the population of Northwest Alaska as a whole began to be absorbed by United States society before the trend could develop very far.

THE INTERMEDIATE TRANSITIONAL PERIOD

The early part of the intermediate transitional period saw a continuation of the trends just described, but witnessed the addition of a few others as well. The most important innovation was the establishment by Whites of permanently occupied settlements having missions, schools, and stores throughout much of Northwest Alaska, beginning about 1890. These villages began to serve as focal points for the native population, increasingly so as time passed. Typically, the early mission/school village was surrounded in winter by a series of satellite native hamlets. These would be located either at good trapping places, or else on or near the territory of a particular reindeer herd. These general developments will be discussed in greater detail with reference to three specific examples.

Tikiraq, 1908

During the first half of the 19th century, Tikiraq, at the tip of Point Hope, had been the largest settlement in Northwest Alaska; as many as 800 (Foote 1965:245) to 1000 (Rainey 1941:10) people may have occupied winter dwellings there. During that period the village had been inhabited by the members of a community made up of several large, highly organized, and largely autonomous local families. If the number of social centers (*qazgit*, pl.) is any indication, there had been at least seven large local family units in the settlement (Larsen and Rainey 1948:26). In addition, there had been several small, impoverished, genealogically isolated domestic family units attached to them, their members filling the role of slave or servant for the member of the larger units.

By 1880 the population of Tikiraq had been reduced by starvation and disease to about a third of its former size. The community still consisted of a number of local family units, but only one of them approximated in size the type of organization which had existed previously. The entire settlement was under the control of a single individual, the infamous Aataŋauzaq, a man generally felt by the Eskimos to have been the most powerful and despotic individual who ever lived in Northwest Alaska. Significantly, Aataŋauzaq's power was based *not* on kinship ties, but on physical strength, magical ability, and on effectiveness in dealing with Whites.

In 1887 a shore whaling station was established just east of Tikiraq, and several more were established soon after. Managed by Whites, these stations were manned by Eskimos, most of whom had been brought in by the Whites from the Seward Peninsula. They were not permitted (by the local Eskimos) to live at Tikiraq, so they established their own settlements near the whaling stations. In 1889 Aataŋauzaq was assassinated, and in 1890 a mission was established by the Episcopal Church between Tikiraq and the whaling stations.

The period 1890–1905 was a period of tremendous flux in the Point Hope area. Most of the Seward Peninsula people left, and their places at the whaling stations were taken by migrants from the Kobuk, Upper and Lower Noatak, Kivalina, Kotzebue, and several other regions. Many of the native Tikiraq people left for the north, and famine, disease, and alcohol continued to take their toll. Besides all that, the north side of the point at Tikiraq had become so badly eroded that it became necessary to abandon the old site entirely, and to construct a new one just to the east of it (v. Klengenberg 1932:64, 67, 70). This new settlement is the subject of the following account.

In October, 1908, a detailed census of the Point Hope area was made, apparently by the missionary.[9] At the time, the population was distributed among four settlements, Tikiraq, Coopertown, Jabbertown, and a reindeer camp. The respective populations and the general ethnic composition of these settlements are indicated in Table 9. As the Table indicates, Tikiraq was entirely Eskimo, and most of its population was of local ancestry. Coopertown and Jabbertown were made up largely of outsiders—White whalers who had married Eskimo women, and Eskimo migrants from other regions. The ethnic composition of the population of the reindeer camp is not certain.

Tikiraq consisted of 23 occupied dwellings and a few abandoned ones when the census was taken. The dwellings were built

[9] The census is contained in the files of the Episcopal Church in Point Hope. I am grateful to Reverend Donald Oktalik for giving me access to this material.

TABLE 9   Point Hope Population, October, 1908

Settlement	Population	Ethnic Composition
Tikiraq	179	Almost entirely Eskimos of Point Hope ancestry.
Coopertown	44	A few white men, and several Eskimos from other regions of Northwest Alaska.
Jabbertown	48	A few white men, and several Eskimos from other regions of Northwest Alaska.
Reindeer Camp	16	Native Point Hopers (?)
TOTAL POPULATION:	287	

in parallel rows along two beach ridges. The southern ridge was occupied primarily by the survivors of a single traditional local family, while the ridge to the north held most of the balance of the population.

With the aid of informants in Point Hope and Kotzebue, it was possible to reconstruct many of the connections that existed among the people living at Tikiraq at the time the 1908 census was taken. The genealogical data, combined with information on the spatial distribution of the houses and other information, indicate that Tikiraq at this time was occupied by five local family units, plus three isolated (and marginal) domestic families. For convenience of description, the local families are identified by letters A through E. The composition of their respective memberships is indicated in Figures 14 through 18.

Local Family A was a conservative type of organization comprised of eight domestic units linked together by a variety of sibling, cousin, and marital ties. My informants were not sure of the details of two of the links, which are indicated by unconventional symbols on the diagram. The dotted line connecting the individuals in House 4 to those in House 7 symbolizes the fact that they were cousins of "some kind," but my informants did not know the connecting links. The double arrow linking Unit

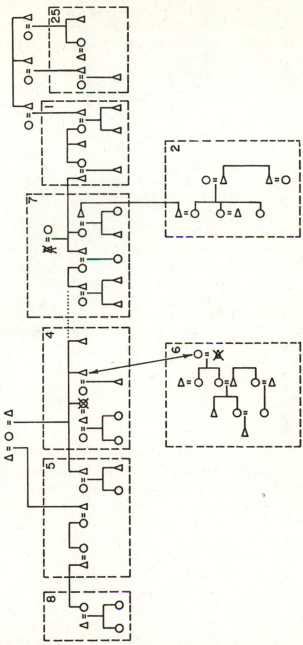

FIGURE 14 Diagram showing the composition of Tikiraq local family A, 1908.

4 to Unit 6 indicates that the two individuals concerned were related "somehow," but my informants did not know how. Each domestic unit except one consisted of an extended family in which adults outnumbered children, usually by a considerable margin. The one exception is Household 8, which was occupied by the members of a monogamous conjugal family.

Local Family B previously had been linked with Family A in a much larger unit known as "*inugialiɣmiut.*" The members of this unit had been the first ones forced to leave the traditional habitation site because of flooding, and the organization had fragmented to some extent in the process; indeed, members of some of the constituent domestic family units apparently left Point Hope area altogether. Of the five domestic families that remained, three were extended families of traditional size and composition. Two of these three contained striking anomalies, however. In Household 10 there was a single individual not con-- nected in the diagram to any of the others; in Household 12 there is an entire conjugal family occupying this status. According to my informants, these people were not related to any other members of the unit, but were there just as "visitors" on a more or less permanent basis. Every time I have been able to get additional information on people who were "just visitors," I have discovered that they were, in fact, related to household members through co-marital or co-sibling ties. Such information was not forthcoming in either of these cases, however, so "visitors" these people must remain—the only examples of this kind I have ever recorded for Northwest Alaska prior to the recent period.

The remaining three local families were both small in size and simple in structure compared to the first two. The simplest of all, local family C, is represented in Figure 16. It was a very simple extended family whose members were distributed in two houses. It is not clear why they built two houses, however, since the total membership of eight could have fit easily into one typical Point Hope dwelling. Local family D, represented in Figure 17, is a bit more complicated, membership being based on a variety of marital, parent-child, sibling and cousin ties. Unfortunately, my informants did not know the precise details of some of these connections, a fact symbolized by the double arrow between houses 20 and 21. Finally, local family E is represented

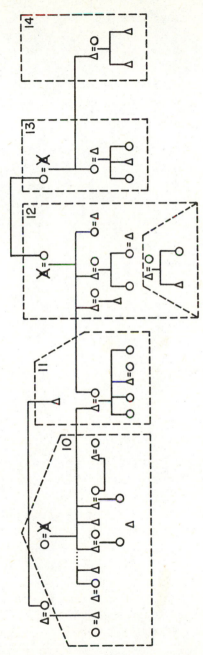

FIGURE 15 Diagram showing the composition of Tikiraq local family B, 1908.

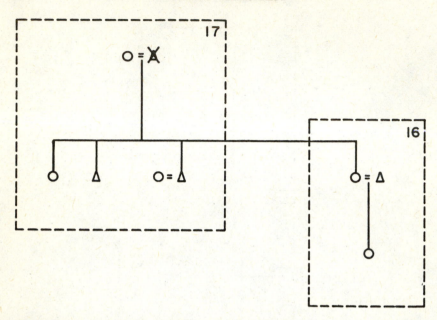

FIGURE 16 Diagram showing the composition of Tikiraq local family C, 1908.

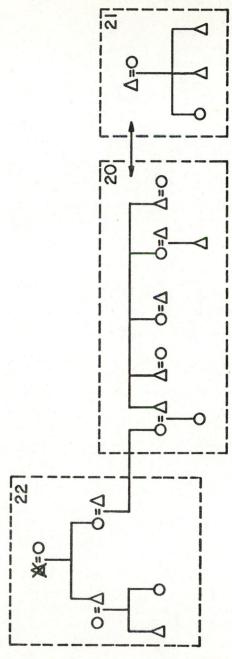

FIGURE 17 Diagram showing the composition of Tikiraq local family D, 1908.

in Figure 18. This unit was composed of one large extended family, and one small conjugal unit. The members of the former were related in a variety of ways, the details of which remain uncertain. The members of this organization were all closely related to people in local families A and B.

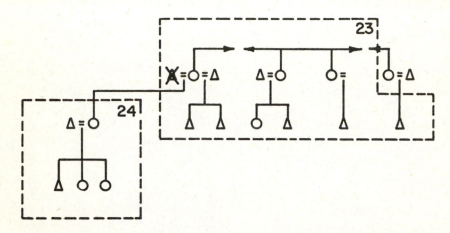

FIGURE 18 Diagram showing the composition of Tikiraq local family E, 1908.

Tikiraq was inhabited in 1908 by the members of a relatively conservative community. The organization was composed of relatively autonomous local family units, plus a few marginal, genealogically isolated domestic families not represented in the diagrams. Two of the local families, A and B, were dominant. As indicated in Table 10, each of these two units is more than twice as large as any of the others; together they comprised 54% of the population. According to my informants, the over-all picture is representative of the structure of a traditional community except that *each* of the major local families would have been at least as large as units A and B combined then, and there would have been perhaps three, four, or more units of that size.

The 1908 situation in Tikiraq represented the relatively recent fragmentation of the single large traditional local family mentioned previously. Units A, B, and D, involving 78% of the 1908 population, had all been part of it. The tensions that

TABLE 10   Family Units at Tikiraq, 1908

Local Family	Number of Constituent Domestic Families	Members Number	% of Total
A	8	66	37.0
B	5	49	27.0
C	2	8	4.5
D	3	24	13.5
E	2	16	9.0
—	3	16	9.0
TOTALS:	23	179	100.0

had been building up during Aataŋauzaq's reign and the influx of outsiders to the vicinity finally erupted during the 1890's. The initial result was a considerable shift in social center (*qazgi*) affiliation, so that by 1908 *qazgi* membership crosscut local family ties to a large extent. When it became necessary to build a whole new village because the old one was being washed away, the conflicts became manifest in the new residential arrangements. These arrangements persisted in the same general form represented in the diagram until these dwellings too had to be abandoned because of the encroaching sea.

Napaqtuqtuq, Circa 1900

Large settlements, such as Tikiraq, were not representative of the general situation in the early years of the 20th century just as they had been atypical of the traditional one, fifty-odd years before. Much more representative of the prevailing pattern was the settlement at Napaqtuqtuq about the turn of the century. Most of the very large traditional settlements on the coast had had populations sufficient to maintain some organizational continuity despite their tremendous changes in personnel after 1850. The same could not be said about settlements in most regions, however, where population reduction eventually made it necessary for people from different regions to join forces in order to survive. Napaqtuqtuq was such a settlement.

Napaqtuqtuq, founded just before the turn of the century, was not situated at a traditional habitation site. Instead, it was located with specific reference to the new Friends Mission, where Kotzebue now stands, which was established in 1897. The people wanted to be within easy reach of the mission because it was an interesting place to visit. On the other hand, they did not want to be too close to the hunting and trapping area of the people who already had houses at the mission. Napaqtuqtuq, just across the bay from the mission and near the mouth of the Noatak River, was a useful compromise.

The local family whose members built winter houses at Napaqtuqtuq consisted of survivors of two different traditional societies, Lower Noatak and Kotzebue. Both societies had been particularly hard hit by famine, especially during the 1880's, and there were very few survivors of either one by 1900. One group of survivors belonged to a local family of three domestic units, and the other group to a local family of two such units. It is not clear whether an agreement was made to join forces before they moved to Napaqtuqtuq, or whether they arrived there independently and then amalagmated into a single organization.

By about 1900, Napaqtuqtuq was inhabited by individuals involved in a single local family comprised of five domestic units. The composition of the unit is indicated in Figure 19. The survivors of one of the traditional societies lived in Houses 1, 2, and 5; survivors of the other traditional society were in Houses 3 and 4. Integration between the two was made via a co-marriage. Unfortunately, my informants would not tell me specifically who was connected to whom in terms of that relationship, so I was unable to indicate the connection on the diagram. My informants did state that such a tie existed, however, and that it had been the link that had made such an organization possible.

The local family whose members had their winter houses at Napaqtuqtuq apparently remained a viable entity for nearly a generation. Part of the reason for its success was that also resident in the settlement was a white trader, who helped keep

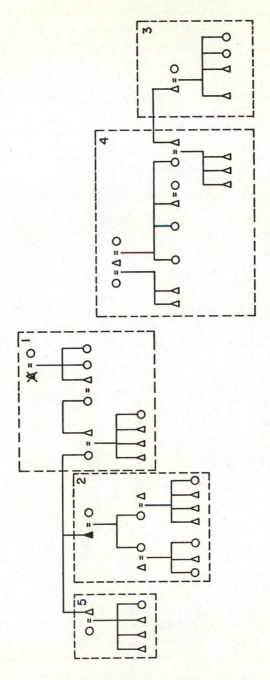

FIGURE 19   Diagram showing the composition of the local family
at Napaqtuqtuq, Kotzebue district, circa 1900.

the natives supplied with ammunition and white man's food-stuffs in return for furs. The other reason for the compara-tive stability of the organization, and by far the more important one in the view of my informants, was the vigorous leadership provided by the man in House 2 indicated by the blackened symbol. Eventually, the drawing power of the growing settle-ment of Kotzebue became too great, and the group moved *en masse* across the bay and settled there.

Nilik, Circa 1915

In the Selawik region, in traditional times, the typical settle-ment had been a hamlet occupied by the members of a local fam-ily consisting of just two domestic family components. That pattern continued to predominate in the region through the early transitional period and on into the intermediate one. The only change was in the reduction in the total number of such units in the region as a whole. In 1908, a mission and school were established in the Selawik region (on the site where the village of Selawik stood in 1970). Due to the demands of trapping and reindeer herding, however, many local families continued to live "on the land" in settlements of traditional size and composi-tion. Nilik, as it was in 1915, illustrates the general pattern.

The local family that occupied Nilik about this time consisted of four households of close relatives. The composition of the unit is indicated in Figure 20. Certain differences between this unit and all of those illustrated previously are readily apparent. One striking difference is the very large number of offspring belonging to the couples in Houses 1 and 2. One couple had seven children, the other eleven. Not all of them lived to ma-turity, but there were so many living at this one period that my informant, one of the children in Household 2, could not recall the names or sexes of some of his cousins, who lived in House-hold 1. The only reason that he could tell me the total number was that he recalled that the children in his aunt's house out-numbered by four those in his own.

The second trend illustrated in the diagram is the developing habit of elderly people to live in houses by themselves. Both the widower in Household 4, and the divorcé in Household 3 were quite a bit older than the other adults in the settlement.

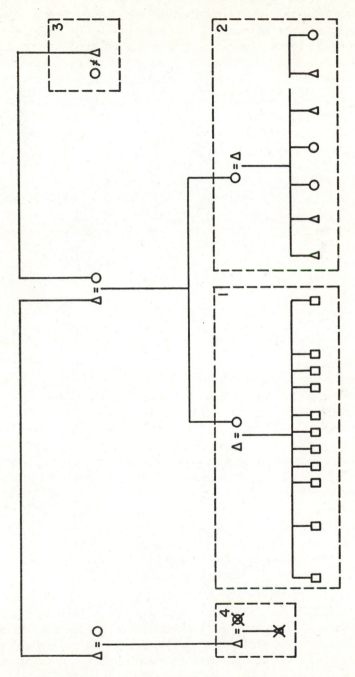

FIGURE 20   Diagram showing the composition of the local family at Nilik, Selawik District, 1915.

They lived by themselves partly because there was little room for them in the other two houses, but primarily because they wished to escape the noise created by so many children. Both of these trends continued into the recent period; what we observe in Figure 20 is simply their beginning.

Not indicated in Figure 20 are two other dwellings which were part of this settlement. One of them was occupied by a white man (a bachelor) who apparently just liked to live there. The other house was occupied by an Eskimo couple with their two children. They were not Selawik people, but migrants from another area. Significantly, both of these houses were located across the river from those indicated in the diagram. Although everyone involved got along well enough, both the white man and the other Eskimo family were outsiders who had *not* been incorporated into the social unit represented in the diagram. Even at this late date, the social distance inherent in the absence of kinship ties led to the physical separation of the individuals involved.

Discussion

The local family remained a fundamental social unit among the Northwest Alaskan Eskimos as long as the requirements of trapping and herding kept most of the population spread out in relatively small, isolated settlements for much of the year. The domestic units of which they were composed underwent two important changes, however. The first was the elimination of polygynous families. Still present in the early period, as illustrated in some of the diagrams just presented, they had been virtually eliminated from Northwest Alaska by the onset of World War II.

The second important change in domestic family structure that occurred during this period was the gradual but persistent reduction in the percentage of extended family domestic units (cf. Rainey 1947:240). In traditional times, when few couples had more than two children, there was plenty of room left in the house for other kinds of kin. As the number of children per couple began to increase, while *household size* remained relatively constant, the structure of domestic family units became progressively simpler. A ten-member domestic family unit in 1890 invariably would have represented in it marital, parent-child, sibling, nepotic, grandparent-grandchild, cousin, and in-law relationships. The same sized domestic unit in 1939 just as typically contained only a single marital couple and their children. In short, the extended domestic family of traditional times had changed to the conjugal domestic family of the recent period.

The progressive simplification in the demographic and social structures of domestic family units, combined with the general trend toward the reduction in size of local families, led inevitably to simplification in structure at that level as well. Instead of being connected by a wide variety of parent-child, sibling, cousin, marital and other kinship ties, the domestic family components of local family units were bound together by parent-child and sibling ties alone. By the end of the intermediate period many local family units were similar in composition to the domestic families of a century before. Local families as complex as units A and B in Tikiraq in 1908 (Figures 14 and 15) had all but vanished from the Northwest Alaskan scene.

The situation with respect to community organizations changed considerably during the intermediate period. The few communities which had remained viable during the early period continued to operate, but a number of new ones were established as well, all of them at mission/school villages. Some missions (which were often combined with schools in the early years) were located at traditional settlements—including all of those where community organizations continued to function—but many were not. Most were situated instead at places where it was convenient for the Whites to build them. At first Eskimos were attracted to these locations primarily out of curiosity, although this factor was rapidly replaced by more serious concerns as the people became dependent on churches, schools, stores, government sponsored reindeer herds, etc., for the satisfaction of their material and spiritual wants.

The original native populations of these new villages often consisted of a conglomeration of people from many districts. Some would be native to the region, but many would not. In fact, many of the original inhabitants of these newly created villages were individuals who just happened to be passing *through* the district when the school or mission was being built; they stopped for awhile to see what was happening, and ended up staying at the site permanently. Under such conditions it took some years for a community organization to evolve out of the set of local family units whose members were living at the site. With the decrease in nomadism and migration, and the White-stimulated establishment of village-wide organizations, such as village councils and reindeer companies, the change was usually effected within two generations. By the time the recent period began, the development was already completed, or else in the advanced stages, in most villages.

THE RECENT PERIOD

The Great Depression of the 1930's had a significant impact on Eskimo affiliation patterns in Northwest Alaska. In the first place, the price of furs dropped dramatically early in the Depression, thus removing one of the reasons for people to spread out in small, isolated settlements (most of which were occupied by the members of small local family units). The drop in fur prices, along with the poor financial situation generally, wiped out the many small independent White traders who had been scattered throughout many regions, thus eliminating a second stimulus for people to live in small communities. Finally, the Depression contributed materially to the loss of practically all of the reindeer herds in Northwest Alaska, because none of the reindeer companies could afford to pay the herders a decent wage. The loss of the herds had the same effect on the distribution of the Eskimo population as the other two developments. The three together combined to eliminate practically all of the reasons the Eskimos had had to spread out in isolated local family settlements instead of congregating in mission/school villages.

The Depression did more than just remove the stimuli for population dispersal; it also provided a number of positive reasons for concentration in the mission/school villages. In the first place, because of government support of the schools and many village stores, these centers were about the only ones in Northwest Alaska that remained economically viable during this period. Secondly, welfare funds were distributed either by the teacher or by other government agents located at the schools.

Toward the middle of the decade of the 1930's, the Civilian Conservation Corps make-work projects were begun, and these too were administered through agents located at the mission/ school centers.

The final decade of the intermediate period thus saw the termination of most of the reasons the Eskimos had had for living in isolated hamlets, and an increase in the number of reasons for which they might want to settle permanently in villages built around missions and schools. During the 30-year span (1940– 1970) defined for present purposes as the "recent period," these forces intensified. In addition, the widespread use of outboard motors and large teams of small but fast dogs (and later snowmobiles) made it possible for large numbers of people to concentrate residentially in a single settlement and still hunt and fish over a wide area. By 1960, isolated local family settlements were rare, and most of those that did exist were actually temporary camps of people who had houses in a village. By 1970, the type of settlement that had been by far the most common in traditional times, namely, the isolated local family hamlet, had vanished from the Northwest Alaskan scene.

By 1970 there were just two kinds of settlement in Northwest Alaska. One was the village,[10] consisting of a state or federally operated school (pre-school through eighth grade), one or more churches, one or more stores, a National Guard armory, an airstrip, and perhaps 15 to 60 dwellings. Village population ranged between 90 and 500 people. The other type of settlement was the "town," of which there were three examples: Nome, Kotzebue, and Barrow. Each of these towns had a hospital, many stores, at least one hotel, jet landing facilities, upwards of 100 dwellings, and numerous facilities appropriate to an urban area. Since the general conditions of life, and the specific patterns of affiliation of the Eskimo population differed somewhat between the two types of settlement, they will be dealt with separately below.

[10] The term village is being used in its spatial sense, not as an indication of legal status. By 1970 many villages had been incorporated as "cities" so that they could qualify for certain types of government aid. Some of these "cities" barely exceeded 100 in population.

Villages

In 1970 there were 25 villages within the area defined here as Northwest Alaska, with a total population of 5,062 according to the census taken in that year (U. S. Bureau of the Census 1970a :Table 2). Of the 25, 17 had populations of less than 200 people, 5 had populations between 201 and 400, and just 3 had populations between 401 and 500. In all cases, the figures include Whites in a village when the census was taken; but with rare exception, Whites constituted a very small portion of a village population.

The U. S. Census data are not detailed enough to provide anything more than general indications of the organizational situation in the villages. More useful are the results of a household census of 14 villages carried out in 1969 by the Northwest Economic Development and Planning Council (1969). Comparable data for a fifteenth village were acquired at the same time by Charles Amsden (1969), so that it is possible to present here information on household size for a sample of 15 of the 25 villages in Northwest Alaska. The data refer exclusively to the native portion of the population, including people considered residents of the village who were away when the count was made.[11]

Data on household size in the sample of villages are presented in Table 11. Average household size was slightly under 6, suggesting a modest decrease from the traditional average of 7. The gross figures for 1969 are slightly misleading, however, because of the relatively large number of houses occupied by single individuals. If we exclude the 45 single-person households from consideration, we are left with 3,017 people living in 471 households in the 15 sample villages. The result is an average household size of 6.4.

The general situation with respect to domestic family *structure* in the villages for the end of the recent period is summarized in Table 12.[12] Slightly more than 80% of the Eskimo population belonged to conjugal family households (many of which

[11] The major discrepancies between the U. S. census data and my own can be accounted for on this basis.

[12] For roughly comparable data, see Gubser (1965:346–352) and Milan (1964:83–95).

TABLE 11   Household Size in 15 Northwest Alaskan
Eskimo Villages, 1969 [a]

Village	No. of Eskimo Households	Total Eskimo Pop.	Average Household Size	Maximum Household Size	Minimum Household Size
Ambler	29	158	5.4	11	1
Anaktuvuk Pass	25	133	5.7	11	1
Buckland	14	98	7.0	14	1
Deering	16	79	4.9	10	1
Diomede	11	70	6.4	13	2
Elim	32	185	5.8	13	1
Kivalina	31	170	5.5	11	1
Kobuk	13	60	4.6	14	1
Koyuk	22	155	7.0	16	1
Noatak	47	258	5.5	13	1
Noorvik	62	432	7.0	14	1
Point Hope	59	381	6.5	13	1
Selawik	79	431	5.5	13	1
Shungnak	27	150	5.6	12	1
Wainwright	49	302	6.2	13	1
OVERALL	516	3,062	5.9	16	1

[a] Data from Amsden (1969) and the Northwest Economic Development and Planning Board (1969).

were very large).[13]   Roughly 10% of the population belonged to extended family households of one sort or another (and some of these were also fairly large).   The balance, constituting

[13] Interestingly, the term *amilraqtuyaat*, which traditionally referred to the members of a very large *local family*, had come to denote a very large household composed of a marital pair with a large number of offspring.

TABLE 12 Household Composition in 15 Northwest
Alaskan Eskimo Villages, 1969 [a]

Family Type		Composition	No. of Households	% of Households
Conjugal	1.	Conjugal pair and un-married children (if any)[b]	423	82
Extended	2.	Conjugal pair, married children, unmarried children, and grandchildren (if any)[b]	24	5
	3.	Adult siblings, spouses, and children (if any)[b]	9	2
	4.	Unmarried adult siblings and children (if any)[b]	10	2
	5.	Other combinations	5	1
Individuals	6.	Widower living alone	5	1
	7.	Widow living alone	12	2
	8.	Other adults living alone [c]	28	5
		TOTALS	516	100

[a] Data from Amsden (1969) and the Northwest Economic Development and Planning Board (1969).

[b] Natural and adopted children treated as equivalent.

[c] Divorced individuals not distinguished from never married individuals.

approximately 8% of the population, was in one-person households. Variation in the size of domestic units depended primarily on the number of children per conjugal pair; in traditional times variation had depended primarily on how many conjugal pairs lived together in the same house.

The census data were collected in terms of households, hence relate exclusively to the domestic family situation. But *local* families continued to operate in villages in Northwest Alaska in 1969, and the operation of kin relationships in the village cannot be understood without reference to them. Since quantitative data for several villages are lacking, the topic will be pursued through detailed analysis of a single case. For convenience, the village will be called "Aulik"; the relevant time period is the mid-1960's.

Aulik Village

In the mid-1960's, Aulik was one of the 17 Northwest Alaskan villages in which the population was below 200 people. It had a school, a store, two churches, a national guard armory, and an all-weather airstrip. Its inhabitants were dependent on hunting and fishing for most of their nutrition, and on seasonal employment and welfare for cash.

The 162 people of Aulik were distributed among 29 households, making for an average household size of nearly 6 people. Of the 29 households, 22 were organized in conjugal family units, and five in extended family units; two of the dwellings were occupied by single individuals. But the houses were not distributed randomly over the village site, nor was their location dictated solely by local topography. Instead, most of the houses were built in clusters, each of which was the residential domain of a local family; only four households in the entire village were not involved in local family organizations. Many of the local families in Aulik were small in size and simple in structure compared to their traditional counterparts. They also had been replaced by the domestic family unit as the primary focus of solidarity. Local families were nonetheless viable kinship units, membership in which made life a great deal more comfortable than it was in domestic families whose members had to operate essentially on their own.

The composition of Aulik local Family A is indicated in Figure 21. A small unit of only 9 members, it illustrates the fact that the size and composition of recent *local* families were becoming identical to those of a traditional *domestic* family unit. The organization represented in the diagram was simply an extended family whose members were distributed between two adjacent dwellings. Actually, the members of this particular unit were very closely related to those in local family C. There

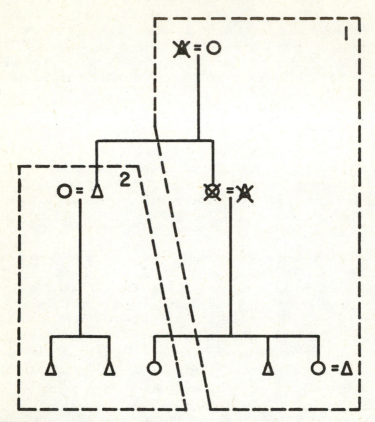

FIGURE 21   Diagram showing the composition of Aulik local family A, mid-1960's.

had been some conflict between the individuals involved, however, so they chose to construct their houses somewhat apart
from each other, and to operate in terms of different local
family organizations.

The composition of local family B is indicated in Figure 22.
Structurally this was a simple extended family involving three
brothers, their mother, their spouses, and their children. However, there were so many children that the members could not
all fit into the same dwelling. The old woman could not stand
the noise in any of her sons' houses, so they built a little house
for her, and her favorite grandchild moved in to look after her.

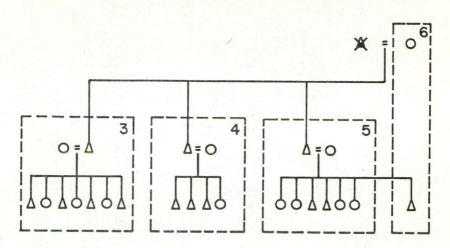

FIGURE 22   Diagram showing the composition of Aulik local family B, mid-1960's.

Aulik local family C is represented in Figure 23.   In terms of numbers, this was a large unit involving 58 members.   Thirty-seven of these were children below marriageable age, so the number is misleading as an indicator of structural complexity.

The composition of one other Aulik local family (D) is illustrated in Figure 24.   At first glance this appears to have been the most complex unit in the village.   Actually, it was just another extended family.   It was built around a single line of descent; only the people in Household 14 were involved in it by virtue of ties other than those of descent or of marriage to someone in that line.

The two other local families that existed in Aulik in the mid-1960's were both simple extended families whose members lived in two dwellings.   In both cases, one dwelling was occupied by representatives of a senior generation and their unmarried children, while the other was occupied by a married son, his wife, and children.   The simplicity of these units obviates the need for diagrammatic representation.

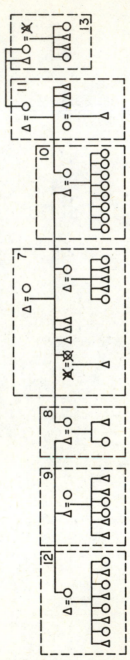

FIGURE 23   Diagram showing the composition of Aulik local family
C, mid-1960's.

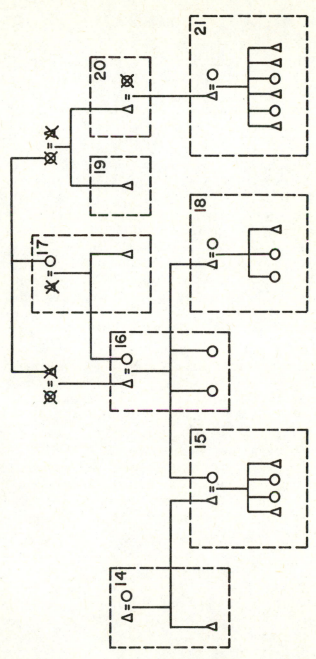

FIGURE 24 Diagram showing the composition of Aulik local family D, mid-1960's.

Communities

Communities, like domestic and local families, continued to operate in the village setting during the recent period. Indeed, it would appear that, as local family units decreased in size and in significance in daily affairs, and as the population became increasingly sedentary, community organizations became progressively more important as foci of solidarity in Northwest Alaska.

Eskimo communities were composed of a set of local families during the recent period, as they had been in traditional times. The members of the different local families in a village were inter-related in terms of both marital and descent ties, probably to a greater extent than they had been traditionally because of their much smaller size. The separate social centers of the traditional local family units had been supplanted during the intermediate period by organizations permitting wider involvement. The most important of these were churches and stores, but the school and the village council also served to integrate all of the inhabitants of a village at the community level.

The local family components of each community continued to operate as kin-based factions, between or among which much of the intra-village conflict occurred. However, the lines between these factions were not as sharply drawn as they had been traditionally, and kin-based factionalism generally was being rapidly exceeded in volume and bitterness by the church-based variety. At the start of missionary activities in Northwest Alaska late in the 19th century, the various denominations divided up the country in such a way that most villages contained only one church. The practice seems to have been abandoned during the 1950's, and representatives of several denominations, some of them new to the Northwest Alaskan area, went into many villages to compete for members. Conversions took place primarily at the domestic family level, a situation that led to considerable conflict at the local family level. During the intermediate period, the (one) village church had served as a major unifying factor in village life; by 1970, (the two or more) churches had become the most divisive force in practically every village in Northwest Alaska.

Towns

The three towns of Barrow, Kotzebue, and Nome had a combined population of 6,288 in 1970 (U. S. Bureau of the Census 1970a).[14] The residents of these three settlements thus comprised about 55% of the total population of Northwest Alaska. Even if one makes the extreme assumption that 40% of the total town population included in the census was White, there must have been almost as many Eskimos in these three centers in 1970 as there were in all 25 villages put together.

Data directly comparable to those presented for the villages unfortunately are not available. The most detailed study of native life in one of these towns was conducted in Kotzebue in the summer of 1965 by Valene Smith. On the basis of a census of 238 Eskimo households, she asserts flatly that the "contemporary Eskimo family is nuclear, including a husband, wife, and unmarried children" (Smith 1966:68). To rephrase her predominantly demographic statement in social terms, the overwhelmingly predominant form of domestic organization in Kotzebue in 1965 was a conjugal family.

My own, less systematic, observations of the residential situation in Kotzbue in 1969–70 confirm Smith's analysis. Furthermore, my data indicate that local family units (which Smith does not mention) although present, were rapidly decreasing in size and importance. Instead of building their houses next door to one another, as people still did in the villages, closely related townsfolk were beginning to build houses at dispersed points throughout the settlement. This trend, slightly less developed in Barrow, quite a bit more advanced in Nome, was the result of three factors: (1) less freedom of choice in the towns, (2) immigration, and (3) changes in affiliation strategy. Each of these factors will be discussed separately.

A primary cause of the decline of local family units in the towns was the simple fact that, by 1960 (much earlier in Nome), townspeople simply had little freedom of choice as to where they

[14] A comprehensive description of Nome during the relevant time period was written by Alaska Consultants (1968a), and a similar account of Kotzebue was prepared by the Alaska State Housing Authority (1971). Other useful information on these settlements is contained in Hippler (1969, 1970), and V. Smith (1966).

could live. By this time the land had been surveyed and divided into lots, and in Kotzebue and Nome most of the lots were owned by Whites.[15]   Much of the townsite was already occupied, if not by family dwellings, then by stores, schools, hotels, hospitals, and the like.   People had exactly three options open to them: (1) they could purchase vacant lots at the periphery of the town, (2) they could buy or rent lots with houses already on them, or (3) they could build their houses well away from town, on some un-surveyed piece of land.   The third option is scarcely relevant in the present discussion since it in effect involved the creation of a brand new settlement, one that was not part of the town at all. The second option, which involved the occupation of a house in an already established neighborhood, severely limited the opportuni-ty for relatives to live next door to one another since a physically adequate house at the right place rarely became available just when the "right" people had the wherewithall to purchase it.   In short, only the option of settling on the periphery of the town provided a real possibility for local family residence since it was only here that close relatives could buy adjacent lots and build houses on them.   This did happen from time to time, but the de-sire to be closer to the stores, to work, or to one's church tended to outweigh this particular possibility.

The second basic factor in the decline of local family units in the towns had to do with the process by which these settlements reached their 1970 population levels.   Without going into the rather complex and quite different demographic and social histories of these three settlements, it is accurate to say that the major proportion of the 1970 native populations of each of them consisted of first or second generation migrants from several other districts (v. Alaska State Housing Authority 1971:18; Hippler 1970; Ray 1967:391–392; Smith 1966:64).   Most of the migrants had come in domestic family units, most of which were of the conjugal, rather than extended, variety.   They thus began life in the towns on a neodomestic basis, and, because of the other factors involved, never found it convenient or necessary to try to establish local family units subsequently.

A change in affiliation strategy characterized by a rapidly in-creasing emphasis on activities in terms of non-kin organizations

[15] Kotzebue was surveyed in either 1952 (Alaska State Housing Authority 1971:95) or 1955 (V. Smith 1966:119); Nome was surveyed in 1905 (Alaska Consultants 1968a:91); Barrow was surveyed in 1947 (Sonnenfeld 1957:500).

was the third factor leading to the decline of local family units in the towns.   In the *villages*, major subsistence efforts by males were carried out either on an individual basis or in terms of kin-based hunting and fishing crews even in 1970; there were few opportunities for women to work outside the home.   In the *towns*, however, subsistence efforts required wage employment, and there were at least some job opportunities for both men and women.   With rare exceptions these were in terms of non-kin organizations: stores, hotels, hospitals, airlines, and the like. The situation offered few advantages for the development of local family units, and maximum advantage to be gained by living close to one's place of work.   For the unemployed the situation was less clear, but for most the desire to be close to a movie theater, a church, or a local hang-out seemed to outweigh the wish to be near relatives.   In short, Eskimo strategies of affiliation in the three towns of Northwest Alaska resulted in an affiliation pattern that increasingly approached the general North American model as the years of the recent period progressed.

Community organizations scarcely existed in either Nome or Kotzebue.   This was the case for at least three reasons.   First, although both locations had been traditional occupation sites, no organizational continuity between traditional and recent times had been maintained on those sites.   In both cases, there had been periods of little or no occupation before the settlements that eventually grew into the modern towns were established. Secondly, both towns had been founded by Whites, and had been largely White dominated subsequently.   Although the latter situation was beginning to change by 1970, particularly in Kotzebue, the effective separation of the townspeople into Native and White segments made the operation of a community organization very difficult.   Finally, the Eskimo populations of both towns were derived from many different districts.   Regional prejudice had so far prevented the development of community organizations even among the Eskimo segment of the population.

The situation in Barrow was quite different than it was in either Kotzebue or Nome.   This location too had been a traditional habitation site, but, in contrast with the other two, a degree of organizational continuity had been maintained there despite a tremendous turnover in population during the early and intermediate transitional periods.   Furthermore, although Whites had been importantly involved in local affairs virtually without interruption since the early 1880's, they had never dominated the situation as thoroughly as they had in the other two places. Finally, during the recent period, at least, there was effective native leadership in Barrow, and a very strong feeling among the general population of involvement in a community that was evolving under Eskimo rather than White direction. Indeed, although such things are difficult to measure, Barrow in the 1960's may well have been the location of the most highly integrated community organization that operated in any Northwest Alaskan settlement during the entire time period covered by this study.

8

Summary and Conclusions

The traditional Northwest Alaskan Eskimos were organized in terms of twenty societies. Each of these societies consisted of a number of interrelated domestic and local families which, together, constituted a social network in which the major structural units (i. e., families) were connected to one another by means of several types of kinship ties. Each network, as a system, was characterized by (1) a high level of endogamy, (2) a distinct yearly cycle, (3) an association with a particular territory, (4) an association with regional dialect of the Inupik language, and (5) a number of other but less easily specified distinctive features (e. g., regionally specific taboos, clothing styles). But despite the fact that each society was an autonomous social system, all twenty were very similar to one another in basic structure.

In this study I have described in detail a particular portion of the similarities among the traditional societies, namely, those relating to the kinship system. At the most general level, these common features included the following:

(1) A basic set of 27 kin relationships, each of which was ideally characterized by distinctive membership criteria, content, sentiment, or strength, or some combination of the four.

(2) An ethical standard in which an overwhelming emphasis was placed on kinship ties in an individual's strategies of affiliation.

(3) Two basic patterns of interconnecting most of the 27 relationships into the dominant operating units of daily life, these being domestic and local families.

(4) A number of mechanisms for changing the *personnel* involved in a kin organization without affecting the *structure* of that organization.

The distribution of these features throughout Northwest Alaska made it possible to ignore minor regional differences in kinship phenomena and to focus instead on the general pattern.

The traditional situation in Northwest Alaska began to change during the mid-19th century, when whalers, explorers, and other outsiders began to have a significant impact on native life. I have described the effect of these changes on Eskimo kinship in terms of three broad temporal spans, the early (1850–1890), intermediate (1890–1940), and recent (1940–1970) transitional periods. During the 120 years covered by the study, the twenty traditional societies ceased to exist as operating systems, and all of the Eskimos of Northwest Alaska became involved in United States society.

Within the kinship sphere, the major changes that occurred were the following:

(1) A few of the traditional kin relationships (particularly those associated with plural marriage) ceased to function, and all the rest were affected by changes in membership criteria, content, sentiment, and/or strength.

(2) There was a substantial reduction in the emphasis on kinship ties generally in strategies of affiliation.

(3) There was a considerable simplification in the *structure* of both domestic and local family units, but very little reduction in family *size*.

(4) The traditional mechanisms for changing personnel without affecting the structure of a kinship organization were either lost or greatly reduced in significance.

All of the above changes were in the direction of patterns prevailing in the United States as a whole.

The phenomena summarized above were described on practically every page of this volume, and detailed recapitulation of the familiar would be of little value. The material presented in this study relates to a number of broader conceptual and theoretical issues, however, and it is fitting to conclude by referring to them. Consistent with the perspective suggested by the subtitle of this volume, and presented more fully in Chapter Seven, the point of view underlying these concluding remarks will be that Eskimo kin relationships in general were *family* relationships in particular when they were actually in operation. Accordingly, the emphasis in what follows will be on the analysis of families, not on the analysis of kinship in the broadest sense of the term.

Family Analysis

I begin by noting that, although kinship analysis in the general sense has continued to flourish as a specialty within social/cultural anthropology during the third quarter of the twentieth century, family analysis as such has held a very minor place in the theoretical literature of the field. This claim is supported by an examination of three recent anthropological texts on kinship. In a volume edited by Graburn (1971), for example, only one chapter (20 pages) out of 16 (400 pages) is devoted specifically to families. Buchler and Selby (1958) are a bit more generous, but even so, in their volume of 13 chapters (317 pages), only two (50 pages) deal with family units as such. Finally, Fox's (1967) text does not include even one chapter devoted specifically to families; according to the index, the subject is discussed explicitly on only 29 out of 262 pages. In view of the extreme importance of families in the general operation of societies (Levy 1967, 1970) and in the formation of individual personalities (Hsu 1965, 1971), this modest coverage indicates a major weakness in the field as a whole.

Much of the recent anthropological literature on kinship has focussed on unilineal descent units, and on marital alliances between such units. Most of the reaction against this emphasis has taken the form of analyses of non-unilineal descent units (cf. Buchler and Selby 1968:85ff.; Fox 1967:146ff.; Graburn, ed., 1971:191ff.). But even here, the emphasis has been on descent units, not on families. Presumably, this interest reflects the fact that, in a great many societies, descent units of one kind or another are primary foci of solidarity. I do not question the importance of such units in the societies in which they occur, but it is appropriate to point out that, in many societies, descent units are *not* primary foci of solidarity. This fact, while obvious, is not trivial, for societies lacking lineages and clans are apparently different in a number of interesting respects from those in which such organizations hold a prominent place in the general social structure.

On a more specific level, I suggest that many entire kinship systems could be referred to accurately as "family-oriented" kinship systems. By "family-oriented" I mean that families, not some other kind of kinship organization, are the primary foci of kinship solidarity. The traditional Northwest Alaskan Eskimos and most mid-20th century North Americans, for example, operated in terms of systems of this type.

It would appear—and I hypothesize—that, in addition to the defining criteria, family-oriented kinship systems are characterized by a number of distinctive characteristics. Among them are the following: (1) very vague boundaries to recognized descent (in the general sense of "descent" indicated in Chapter Two), (2) an emphasis on bilaterally recognized descent; and (3) what Lévi-Strauss (1969:xxiii) has called a "complex marriage structure" (cf. Fox 1967:221ff.). In kinship systems of this kind, descent is not ignored, but it is not emphasized, and there are no organizations in which solidarity is specialized along descent lines. Instead, relationships based on descent constitute a social resource upon which individuals may draw for purposes of affiliation, but (except for the mother-infant relationship), they are not ties that individuals should or must emphasize for that purpose. Finally, I hypothesize that family-oriented kinship systems are relatively common in hunting-gathering societies, universal in highly modernized societies, and rare at intermediate levels of social complexity.

It is also possible, and I think it would be fruitful, to talk about family-oriented societies—as opposed to family-oriented kinship systems. A family-oriented society is one in which family units are not only the primary foci of solidarity within the kinship system, but the primary foci of solidarity in the society as a whole. The traditional Northwest Alaskan Eskimos operated in terms of societies of this type.

In addition to the defining criteria and the three characteristics listed above, I hypothesize that family-oriented societies are characterized by (1) an emphasis on complex family units, minimally including some combination of domestic and local families, and (2) considerable variation (in both time and space) with respect to family membership despite a high level of homogeneity in family structure. The former characteristic sharply differentiates this type of society from the kind in which there is a family-oriented kinship system, but in which non-kin units are at least the equivalent of families as foci of solidarity. The second characteristic is the one that gives family-oriented societies the peculiarly "amorphous" cast referred to earlier. Finally, I hypothesize that societies meeting the defining criteria of the type are common at the lower end of the scale of social complexity, rare at intermediate levels, and nonexistent at the top.

Several years ago Robert Pehrson (1959) made a plea for greater anthropological interest in what I am now calling "family-oriented societies." Subsequently, Albert Heinrich (1963a:357–377), remarking at length on the similarities between Northwest Alaskan Eskimo and Lappish social organization (particularly as described by Pehrson 1959, 1964), echoed the same theme. It would appear that very few anthropologists have heeded their call, despite the fact that Pehrson's paper has been reprinted at least twice. I now repeat their plea, suggesting that if *any* of the above hypotheses are tenable, then surely this type of system is worthy of greater anthropological attention than it has received in the past.

Levels of Family Organization

Those few anthropologists who have been concerned with families on a general conceptual or theoretical level have focused much of their attention on the specific type of organization known as the "nuclear family." This type of organization, consisting of relationships involving a married man and woman and their offspring, is reportedly included in all other varieties of family; indeed, it is said to be *the* foundation upon which all others are built.

George Peter Murdock (1949:2), the best known proponent of this point of view, has summarized it as follows:

> The nuclear family is a universal human social grouping. Either as the sole prevailing form of the family or as the basic unit from which more complex familial forms are compounded, it exists as a distinct and strongly functional group in every known society.

A few authors (e. g., Buchler and Selby 1968:24; Fox 1967:-37–40; Levy and Fallers 1959) have challenged this view on various empirical, theoretical, and methodological grounds, but the position expressed by Murdock is still held by a large number of social/cultural anthropologists. It is an issue of some importance here, since it has been claimed as recently as 1972 that "the nuclear family is the basic residential unit" in Eskimo societies (Guemple 1972a:84–85). Even more specifically, Albert Heinrich (1963a:85–86) has made this claim for the Eskimos of Northwest Alaska.

The attentive reader will have noticed that the phrase "nuclear family" did not appear even once in the descriptive chapters of the present study. It was not mentioned for the simple reason that I find the nuclear family concept virtually useless in understanding social organization in that area. I now address some further remarks to that point. By extension, I am contesting the broader claim that nuclear families are significant in all Eskimo societies, as well as in human societies generally, although my argument will focus exclusively on the material from Northwest Alaska. The procedure will be to take up each point made by Murdock in the above quotation and to analyze it in the light of information presented earlier in this volume.

Murdock's first claim is that nuclear families can be found in every society. The Northwest Alaskan data would certainly confirm this proposition, since there did exist, from time to time, organizations made up of marital, parent-child, and sibling relationships, and of no others. In addition, a set of relationships conforming to the definition of nuclear family could be *analytically* distinguished in virtually every domestic organization in Northwest Alaska. But the latter procedure would just about always leave a residual set of relationships, in addition to the "nuclear" set. These "satellite" relationships, one would have to suppose, were either there by accident, or else because of some sort of non-family kinship tie. The former possibility would, of course, be nonsense. The second alternative would be too unless one defined the general term "family" in such a way that it coincided with "nuclear family." In the latter case, of course, one could not talk logically about extended or polygynous "families." Unfortunately, most authors who have emphasized the importance of nuclear families have either failed to define "family" on a general level, i. e., in such a way that nuclear, extended, and polygynous (etc.) families would be logically possible categories, or else they have used the term inconsistently after they defined it. Neither approach is satisfactory.

The second element in Murdock's general statement is that the nuclear family is "basic." Now, what is meant by "basic?" One possibility, the one clearly implied in the above quotation, is that "basic" means "first in time." The Northwest Alaskan data would refute Murdock's thesis, given this interpretation. Young couples virtually always began their marital career in an extended family setting in traditional times, and most of them did during the recent period as well. However, other interpretations of "basic" are possible.

One alternative is that the *minimal* type of family unit conforms to the definition of nuclear. The Northwest Alaskan data would confirm the theory, given this interpretation of "basic," for the minimal family unit in traditional Northwest Alaska was indeed generally of this type. *It was also an arrangement that most people wanted to avoid,* for numerous reasons outlined in Chapter Six. I cannot conceive of a situation in which the traditional Eskimos would really want to operate in terms of such an organization. Even in times of extreme famine, when pressure was greatest to separate into very small groups, there were almost always aged parents or grandparents who had to be looked after, and the organizations in terms of which that obligation could be met were extended, not nuclear families.

One other possible interpretation of "basic" is that the various types of relationships in a nuclear family—parent-child, sibling, marital—were all strong, and further, that these three types were stronger than any other kind of kinship tie. Given this interpretation, Murdock's theory is partially supported by the Northwest Alaskan data. It is true that parent-child relationships were stronger than any others, and that sibling relationships ranked just behind them. But, the husband-wife (*ui-nuliaq*) relationship—critical in most conceptions of nuclear family—was weak in traditional times, ideally (and usually actually) ranking far below parent-child and sibling ties in precedence, and below most other consanguineal bonds as well.

The third point in Murdock's statement about the universality of nuclear families in human societies is that such organizations exist as "distinct groups" in every society. If, by "distinct groups" one means that an observer could easily determine who is related to whom in terms of marital, parent-child, and sibling ties, then I doubt very much that the traditional Northwest Alaskan data would support the proposition, although it is impossible to substantiate this claim definitively because of the time gap. If an observer had watched the members of a typical traditional local family (of, say 15–20 people) going through their daily routine, I suspect that he would have had a fair amount of difficulty sorting out the various relationships simply on the basis of what he could see. All of the children in such a unit would probably have interacted in terms of sibling ties, and many of the adults would have too—even if they had been cousins. Most of the adults would have treated all of the children in pretty much the same way (i. e, as if they had been their own offspring or grandchildren), and *vice versa*. The men would have spent very little time in the company of their wives. Even during meals, all the men would have congregated in one house (or *in the qazgi*), and all the women and little children would have gather together in another.

Only in a time of crisis would boundaries *within* a local family be more clearly drawn, but this would rarely divide the organization into a set of nuclear families. In the case of a feud, if there was any split at all, it would separate affines. Since that category included husbands and wives, a feud could result in the virtual destruction of nuclear families as operating units. In the case of famine, the division would often be along some kind of extended family lines. The latter issue can be clarified with a simple hypothetical example: if, in time of famine, nuclear families were supposed to separate; and if a

particular domestic family involved an aged couple, their adult
son, his wife, and offspring; with whom should the adult son
go when famine struck—his aged parents (nuclear family of
orientation), or his wife and children (nuclear family of procreation)? As the material in Chapter Four indicates, he would
be obliged to go with *all* of them. This meant keeping the extended family unit intact, an outcome inconsistent with the nuclear family premise.

The final point in Murdock's general theory about the universality of nuclear families is that the nuclear family is
"strongly functional" in every known society. If by "strongly
functional," he means that marital, parent-child, and sibling relationships have a high content level, then the Northwest Alaskan data would certainly support his claim. However, in traditional Northwest Alaska, there continued to be a high content
level in parent-child relationships even after the children had
had children of their own—thus presumably establishing separate nuclear families. Similarly, there continued to be a high
content level in sibling relationships even after siblings married
and had children—thus establishing separate nuclear families.

One can pose the question more succinctly with reference to
a hypothetical case. In a typical traditional domestic family
involving say, an aged woman, her two adult sons, their wives,
and offspring (numbering perhaps eight people), to how many
nuclear families would each adult son belong? If the answer is
"one," then the proposition is refuted, since ties with high content would cross nuclear family boundaries, regardless of whether the "one" is the son's family of orientation or the son's family
of procreation. If the answer is "two," then the proposition is
confirmed. But the second conclusion would amount to saying
that an extended family really consists of two (or more) nuclear
families with overlapping membership, and that it does not
exist as an entity in its own right. And that, I suggest, would
be to impose a theory upon the facts in the least fruitful way
possible.

In sum, we can say that the Northwest Alaskan data confirm
the theory that the nuclear family is universal—since nuclear
families did indeed occur there. But if one is trying to understand how Eskimo societies (or individuals) operated in this
area, the notion of "nuclear family" is not very helpful. Indeed,

I can think of no concept that does more to obscure the situation than this one. I cannot help but suspect that, given comparable data from many other societies, the same conclusion would be in order.

Instead of wasting time worrying about the universality of the nuclear family, I suggest that a greater understanding of social organization would result if greater attention were paid to the two types of family unit I defined in Chapter Seven, namely, domestic and local families. In that chapter I tried to show that, if one wants to understand what kinship is all about in Northwest Alaska, these two concepts are extremely useful. I now wish to raise the possibility of using them more extensively in cross-cultural analysis.

The existence of domestic and local families has not been explicitly recognized in the anthropological literature, despite the fact that descriptions of both types of organization abound; the second type in particular is rarely if ever treated *as a form of family*. Much of the literature focusing specifically on such units discusses them under the heading of "bands." For example, in the volumes on *Man the Hunter* (Lee and DeVore 1968b) and *Band Societies* (Damas, ed., 1969), several authors (e. g., Damas 1968a; 1969a; Helm 1968, 1969; Leacock 1969) describe in detail organizations of the same general type that I dealt with in Chapter Seven. As I noted earlier, however, given my definition of "family," it would be inconsistent to refer to the smaller unit as a "family" and to the larger unit as a "band." Now I go a step further and suggest that it would appear useful to distinguish between kinship units, called "families," and nomadic residential units, called "bands."

Empirically, local family membership in hunting-gathering societies often seems to coincide with band membership. However, the two will not coincide by definition—given my definitions—but according to the nature of the empirical case. As Damas (1968a, 1969a, 1969c) has shown for the three Central Eskimo Societies, the degree of coincidence between band and local family membership can vary even between neighboring societies whose members share a common cultural heritage. By separating organizational and residential units, this conceptual distinction should facilitate the discovery of both similarities and differences among hunting-gathering societies throughout the world.

The conceptual distinction between "band" and "local family" also makes it possible to apply the latter notion to several kinds of societies, not just to those of the hunting-gathering type. *Any* society in which households of relatives are normally situated close together may contain organizations usefully analyzed in terms of the domestic/local family distinction. Since such societies are quite common, investigation of this possibility may uncover cross-cultural similarities which have not been recognized clearly before.

Changes in Family Structure

It is fitting to terminate this volume with a few comments on the subject of change. During the course of this book I described the process whereby the twenty family-oriented societies of the traditional Northwest Alaskan Eskimos were absorbed by the United States, a society which is not family oriented, but which does have a family-oriented kinship system. During the transition, the structurally complex domestic and local families of the traditional period gradually gave way to simpler forms of organization. In this process of structural simplification, the Eskimos participated in the trend in which family systems everywhere were approaching "some variant of the conjugal family system" (Goode 1963:368). In addition, and perhaps ironically, by the end of the recent period, the Northwest Alaskan Eskimos were closer to operating in terms of an "Eskimo type" of kinship system (cf. Heinrich 1963a:245–248) than they had been at any other period in their recorded history.

At the general level, there appear to have been three main factors involved in guiding changes in family structure along the particular course they took in Northwest Alaska. First, and most obvious, was the acquisition of general (White) North American values regarding all facets of life, including kinship structures. To some extent these new standards were imposed by force (as in the case of divorce and remarriage), or through strong pressure from missionaries (as in the case of polygamous and co-marital unions). More important over the long run, however, were the more subtle acculturative forces associated with White controlled schooling and mass media of communication (particularly radio, movies, and magazines), and direct personal experiences by Eskimos of the Whiteman's way of life during visits outside of Northwest Alaska.

The second major factor involved in changes in family structure was the great increase in average number of offspring per marital pair. In this development the medical revolution of the recent period held a prominent place, but it cannot be considered the whole explanation until both the fact and the causes of the (apparent) low fertility of traditional times have been established more thoroughly than they have been at the time of this writing. In any case, the demographic transition had profound social consequences, affecting not only gross changes in family structure, but also the membership, content, sentiment, and strength of practically every one of the relationships in the entire system.

The third and final factor in the trend toward conjugal family units in Northwest Alaska was the increasing importance of non-kin ties in both basic and intermediate strategies of affiliation. The need for a cash income was probably the critical factor here, since the people who could pay cash for the goods and services that the Eskimos could produce were for the most part non-Eskimo, hence non-kin. As the general level of native affluence increases in Northwest Alaska, as it was beginning to in the 1960's, there may be a slowing down or even a temporary reversal of this trend; but the Eskimos were too thoroughly integrated into general United States society by 1970 for the process to stop for very long.

Despite the great changes in family structure which occurred during the period covered by this study, the majority of individuals in the villages of Northwest Alaska continued in 1970 to operate in terms of both domestic and local family units. In addition, as I have pointed out before, during the 1960's large numbers of kin relationships which had lain dormant for years were being discovered and activated, re-uniting relatives throughout the entire length and breadth of Northwest Alaska. In short, change is not extinction; indeed, change often functions to prevent that very outcome. Therefore, just because Eskimo family relationships changed to meet the altered conditions of life, it should not be concluded that they ceased to operate altogether. Having predicted in 1965 the very rapid demise of a

Northwest Alaskan village, only to find it thoroughly rejuvenated just two years later (and still going strong in 1970), I have learned from experience that caution is in order on predictions of this kind. During efforts to analyze my own error in judgement, I realized that the traditional Eskimos had been notable for their ability to modify their life style in order to cope with the changing problems of survival; their descendents in the recent period were simply applying the traditional approach to the new situation—and they were doing so quite successfully.

*

References

Aberle, David, *et al.*
  1950 "The Functional Prerequisites of a Society." *Ethics* 60:-
         100–111.

Adams, Colin
  1971 "Flexibility in Canadian Eskimo Social Forms and Be-
         havior: A Situational and Transactional Appraisal." In
         D. L. Guemple, ed., *Alliance in Eskimo Society: Proceed-
         ings of the American Ethnological Society, 1971, Supple-
         ment*, pp. 6–16. Seattle: University of Washington Press.

Alaska Consultants
  1968a *Nome Comprehensive Development Plan.* Anchorage, Alas-
          ka: Alaska State Housing Authority.
  1968b *Teller Comprehensive Development Plan.* Anchorage, Alas-
          ka: Alaska State Housing Authority.

Alaska Magazine
  1973 "From Ketchikan to Barrow," *Alaska Magazine* 39(1):60
         [Note on locations of people enrolling in Alaska Native
         Claims Settlement Act].

Alaska State Housing Authority
  1971 *Kotzebue, Alaska. Comprehensive Development Plan.* Pre-
         pared for the City of Kotzebue by the Alaska State Hous-
         ing Authority. Anchorage, Alaska.

Aldrich, Herbert L.
  1889 *Eight Months in Arctic Alaska and Siberia with the Arc-
         tic Whalemen.* Chicago: Rand McNally & Co.

Amsden, Charles
[1969] [Census data for Anaktuvuk Pass, 1969] Personal Communication.

Anderson, H. Dewey, & Walter Crosby Eells
1935 *Alaska Natives: A Survey of their Sociological and Educational Status*. Stanford, California: Stanford University Press.

Armstrong, Terence
1971 "Regional Sub-divisions of Alaska." *Polar Record* 15(97):- 544–546.

Balikci, Asen
1967a "Female Infanticide on the Arctic Coast," *Man* 2(4):- 615–215.
1967b *The Netsilik Eskimo*. Garden City, New York: Natural History Press.

Bancroft, Hubert H.
1959 *History of Alaska 1730–1885*. (Original Publication 1886.) New York: Antiquarian Press.

Barnes, J. A.
1961 "Physical and Social Kinship." *Philosophy of Science* 28 (3):296–299.
1964 "Physical and Social Facts in Anthropology." *Philosophy of Science* 31(3):294–297.

Barth, Fredrik
1964 *Nomads of South Persia. The Basseri Tribe of the Kamseh Confederacy*. London: Allen & Unwin.

Beattie, J. H. M.
1964 "Kinship and Social Anthropology." *Man* 130:101–103.

Bee, J. W., & E. R. Hall
1956 *Mammals of Northern Alaska, on the Arctic Slope*. University of Kansas, Museum of Natural History, Miscellaneous Publication No. 8. Lawrence, Kansas.

Beechey, F. W.
1831 *Narrative of a voyage to the Pacific and Bering's Strait to cooperate with the Polar Expedition performed in His*

Beechey, F. W. (Cont.)

Majesty's Ship 'Blossom' . . . *in the years 1825, 1826, 1827, and 1828.* 2 Vols. London: H. Colburn & R. Bentley.

Befu, Harumi

1964 "Eskimo Systems of Kinship Terms—Their Diversity and Uniformity." *Arctic Anthropology* 2(1):84–98.

Bender, Donald B.

1967 "A Refinement of the Concept of Household: Families, Co-residence, and Domestic Functions." *American Anthropologist* 69:493–504.

Black, Robert F.

1958 "Lowlands and Plains of Interior and Western Alaska." In Howel Williams, ed., *Landscapes of Alaska: Their Geologic Evolution*, pp. 76–81. Berkeley & Los Angeles: University of California Press.

Britton, Max E.

1967 "Vegetation of the Arctic Tundra." In H. P. Hansen, ed., *Arctic Biology*, pp. 67–130. Corvallis: Oregon State University Press.

Brower, Charles D.

n.d. "The Northernmost American: An Autobiography." [Unedited manuscript for his 1942 book; in the Stefansson Collection, Dartmouth College Library, Hanover, New Hampshire.]

1942 *Fifty Years Below Zero.* New York: Dodd, Mead and Co.

Buchler, I. R.

1966 "On Physical and Social Kinship." *Anthropological Quarterly* 39:17–25.

Buchler, I. R., & H. A. Selby

1968 *Kinship and Social Organization. An Introduction to Theory and Method.* New York: The MacMillan Co.

Burch, Ernest S., Jr.

1966 "Authority, Aid and Affection. The Structure of Eskimo Kin Relationships." Unpublished Ph.D. thesis, Depart-

Burch, Ernest S., Jr. (Cont.)
ment of Anthropology, University of Chicago, Chicago, Illinois.

1970a   "The Eskimo Trading Partnership in North Alaska: A Study in 'Balanced Reciprocity.'" *Anthropological Papers of the University of Alaska* 15:49–80.

1970b   "Marriage and Divorce among the North Alaskan Eskimos." In Paul Bohannan, ed., *Divorce and After*, pp. 152–181. Garden City, New York: Doubleday & Co.

1971   "The Nonempirical Environment of the Arctic Alaskan Eskimos." *Southwestern Journal of Anthropology* 27(2):-148–165.

1972   "The Caribou/Wild Reindeer as a Human Resource." *American Antiquity* 37:339–368.

1974   "Eskimo Warfare in Northwest Alaska." *Anthropological Papers of the University of Alaska* 16(2): 1–14.

Burch, E. S., Jr. & Thomas C. Correll
1972   "Alliance and Conflict: Inter-Regional Relations in North Alaska." In D. L. Guemple, ed., *Alliance in Eskimo Society. Proceedings of the American Ethnological Society, 1971, Supplement*, pp. 17–39. Seattle: University of Washington Press.

Cantwell, John C.
1887   "A Narrative Account of the Exploration of the Kowak River, Alaska, under the direction of Capt. Michael A. Healy." In M. A. Healy, *Report of the Cruise of the Revenue Marine Steamer "Corwin" in the Arctic Ocean in the Year 1885*, pp. 21–52. Washington, D. C.: Government Printing Office.

Carrasco, Pedro
1963   "The Locality Referent in Residence Terms." *American Anthropologist* 65(1):133–134.

Chance, Norman A.
1960a   "Culture Change and Integration: An Eskimo Example." *American Anthropologist* 62(6):1028–1044.

1960b   "Investigation of the Adjustment of the Eskimos at Barter Island, Alaska, to Rapid Cultural Changes." *Arctic* 13(3):205.

1963   "Notes on Cultural Change and Personality Adjustment among the North Alaskan Eskimo." *Arctic* 16(4):264–270.

Chance, Norman A. (Cont.)

1964   "The Changing Role of Government among the North Alaskan Eskimo." *Arctic Anthropology* 2(2):41–55.

1965   "Acculturation, Self-Identification, and Personality Adjustment." *American Anthropologist* 67(2):372–393.

1966   *The Eskimo of North Alaska.* New York: Holt, Rinehart & Winston.

Chance, Norman A., & Dorothy A. Foster

1962   "Symptom Formation and Patterns of Psychopathology in a Rapidly Changing Alaskan Eskimo Society." *Anthropological Papers of the University of Alaska.* 11(1):32–42.

Chance, Norman A., & John Trudeau

1963   "Social Organization, Acculturation and Integration among the Eskimo and the Cree: A Comparative Study." *Anthropologica* 5(1):47–56.

Chang, Kwang-Chih

1962   "A Typology of Settlement and Community Patterns in some Circumpolar Societies." *Arctic Anthropology* 1(1):-28–41.

Collier, Arthur

1902   "A Reconnaissance of the Northwestern portion of Seward Peninsula, Alaska." *U. S. Geological Survey Professional Paper*, No. 2.

Correll, Thomas Clifton

1972   "Ungalaqlingmiut: A Study in Language and Society." Unpublished Ph.D. thesis, Department of Anthropology, University of Minnesota.

Damas, David

1963   *Igluligmiut Kinship and local Groupings: A Structural Approach.* National Museum of Canada Bulletin No. 196. Ottawa.

1964   "The Patterning of the Iglulingmiut Kinship System." *Ethnology* 3(4):377–388.

1968a   "The Diversity of Eskimo Societies." In R. B. Lee & I. DeVore, eds., *Man the Hunter*, pp. 111–117. Chicago: Aldine Publishing Co.

1968b   "The Eskimo." In C. S. Beals, ed., *Science History, and Hudson Bay*, Vol. 1, pp. 141–172. Ottawa: Queen's Printer.

Damas, David (Cont.)

1969a　"Characteristics of Central Eskimo Band Structure." In D. Damas, ed., *Contributions to Anthropology: Band Societies*, pp. 116–134. Ottawa: National Museum of Canada Bulletin 228.

1969b　"Environment, History, and Central Eskimo Society." In D. Damas, ed., *Contributions to Anthropology: Ecological Essays*, pp. 40–64. Ottawa: National Museums of Canada Bulletin 230.

1969c　"Locality, Lineality, and Settlement Type." In D. Damas, ed., *Contributions to Anthropology: Ecological Essays*, pp. 154–159. Ottawa: National Museums of Canada Bulletin 230.

1972　"The Structure of Central Eskimo Associations." In Lee Guemple, ed., *Alliance in Eskimo Society: Proceedings of the American Ethnological Society, 1971, Supplement*, pp. 40–55. Seattle: University of Washington Press.

Damas, David, ed.

1969　*Contributions to Anthropology: Band Societies*. National Museum of Canada Bulletin 228.

Dunning, R. W.

1962　"An Aspect of Recent Eskimo Polygyny and Wife-Lending in the Eastern Arctic." *Human Organization* 21(1):17–20.

1964　"A Note on Adoption among the Southampton Island Eskimo." *Man* 62(2):163–167.

Edmonds, H. M. W.

1966　"The Eskimo of St. Michael and Vicinity as Related by H. M. W. Edmonds," Dorothy Jean Ray, ed. *Anthropological Papers of the University of Alaska* 13(2):1–143.

Environmental Science Services Administration

1970　"Local climatological data. Annual Summary with Comparative Data: 1969. Unalakleet, Alaska." U. S. Department of Commerce, Environmental Science Services Administration, Environmental Data Service.

Fay, Francis H.

1957　"History and Present Status of the Pacific Walrus Population." *Transactions of the 22nd North American Wildlife Conference*, pp. 431–443. Washington, D. C.: Wildlife Management Institute.

REFERENCES

Federal Field Committee for Development Planning in Alaska
   1968   *Alaska Natives and the Land.* Washington, D. C.: U. S. Government Printing Office.

Firth, Raymond
   1957   *We, the Tikopia. A Sociological Study of Kinship in Primitive Polynesia. Second ed.* New York: Barnes & Noble.
   1963   "Bilateral Descent Groups: An Operational Viewpoint." In I. Schapera, ed., *Studies in Kinship and Marriage, dedicated to Brenda Z. Seligman on her 90th Birthday,* pp. 22–37. London: Royal Anthropological Institute.

Foote, Don Charles
   1959   "The Economic Base and Seasonal Activities of some Northwest Alaskan Villages: A Preliminary Study." Report for Bioenvironmental Studies of Project Chariot, Atomic Energy Commission (Unpublished ms.).
   1964a   "American Whalemen in Northwestern Arctic Alaska." Arctic Anthropology 2(2):16–20.
   1964b   "Changing Resource Utilization by Eskimos in Northwestern Arctic Alaska, 1850–1962." Paper read before the section on the Arctic and Sub-Arctic, VII International Congress for the Science of Anthropology and Ethnology. Moscow. U. S. S. R.
   1965   "Exploration and Resource Utilization in Northwestern Arctic Alaska before 1855." Unpublished Ph.D. thesis, Department of Geography, McGill University, Montreal, P.Q.
   1966   "Human Geographical Studies in Northwestern Arctic Alaska. The Upper Kobuk River Project, 1965. Final Report." Montreal (mimeographed).

Foote, Don Charles, & Alan Cooke
   1960   "The Eskimo Hunter at Noatak, Alaska: Winter, 1960, by Don Charles Foote; Summer, 1960, by Alan Cooke." Report for Bio-Environmental Studies of Project Chariot, Atomic Energy Commission. Unpublished ms.

Foote, Don Charles & H. Anthony Williamson
   1961   "A Human Geographical Study in Northwest Alaska." Final Report of the Human Geographical Studies Program, United States Atomic Energy Commission, Project Chariot. Unpublished ms., Cambridge, Mass.

Foote, Don Charles, & H. Anthony Williamson (Cont.)
1966   "A Human Geographical Study." In N. J. Wilimovsky & J. N. Wolfe, eds., *Environment of the Cape Thompson Region, Alaska,* pp. 1041–1107. Oak Ridge, Tennessee: United States Atomic Energy Commission.

Fortes, Meyer
1959   "Primitive Kinship." *Scientific American* 200(6):147–158.
1962   "Introduction." In Jack Goody, ed., *The Developmental Cycle in Domestic Groups,* pp. 1–14. Cambridge: Cambridge University Press.
1969   *Kinship and the Social Order. The Legacy of Lewis Henry Morgan.* Chicago: Aldine Publishing Co.

Fox, Robin
1967   *Kinship and Marriage. An Anthropological Perspective.* Hamondsworth, England: Penguin Books.

Franklin, Sir John
1828   *Narrative of a Second Expedition to the Shores of the Polar Sea in the Years 1825, 1826, and 1827.* London: J. Murray.

Freeman, Milton M. R.
1971a   "The Significance of Demographic Changes Occurring in in the Canadian East Arctic," *Anthropologica* 13(1–2):-215–236.
1971b   "A Social and Ecologic Analysis of Systematic Female Infanticide among the Netisilik Eskimo." *American Anthropologist* 73(5):1011–1018.

Fried, Morton
1967   *The Evolution of Political Society. An Essay in Political Anthropology.* New York: Random House.

Gabrielson, I. N., & F. C. Lincoln.
1959   *The Birds of Alaska.* Washington, D. C.: Wildlife Management Institute.

Gellner, Ernest
1957   "Ideal Language and Kinship Structure." *Philosophy of Science* 24(1):235–242.
1960   "The Concept of Kinship." *Philosophy of Science* 27(1):-187–204.

Gellner, Ernest (Cont.)
1963 "Nature and Society in Social Anthropology." *Philosophy of Science* 30(3):236–251.

Giddings, James Louis, Jr.
1952 "Observations on the 'Eskimo Type' of Kinship and Social Structure." *Anthropological Papers of the University of Alaska* 1(1):5–10.
1956 "Forest Eskimos," *University Museum Bulletin* 20(2):1–55.
1961 *Kobuk River People.* University of Alaska Studies of Northern Peoples No. 1. College, Alaska.
1967 *Ancient Men of the Arctic.* New York: Alfred A. Knopf.

Goode, William J.
1963 *World Revolution and Family Patterns.* New York: The Free Press of Glencoe.

Graburn, Nelson H. H.
1969 *Eskimos without Igloos. Social and Economic Development in Sugluk.* Boston: Little, Brown, & Co.

Graburn, Nelson, H. H., ed.
1971 *Readings in Kinship and Social Structure.* New York: Harper & Row.

Green, Paul, aided by Abbe Abbott
1959 *I am Eskimo—Aknik My Name.* Juneau: Alaska Northwest Publishing Co.

Greist, Henry W.
n.d. "Seventeen Years with the Eskimo." Unpublished ms. in the Stefansson Collection, Dartmouth College Library, Hanover, N. H.

Grinnell, J.
1901 *Gold Hunting in Alaska.* Chicago: Cook & Co.

Gryc, George
1958a "Arctic Slope." In Howell Williams, ed., *Landscapes of Alaska: Their Geologic Evolution,* pp. 119–127. Berkeley & Los Angeles: University of California Press.
1958b "Brooks Range." In Howell Williams, ed., *Landscapes of Alaska: Their Geologic Evolution,* pp. 111–118. Berkeley & Los Angeles: University of California Press.

Gubser, Nicholas J.
1965 *The Nunamiut Eskimos: Hunters of Caribou.* New Haven: Yale University Press.

Guemple, D. L.
  1961   *Innuit Spouse Exchange.* Chicago: Department of Anthropology, University of Chicago.
  1965   "Saunik: Name Sharing as a Factor Governing Eskimo Kinship Terms." *Ethnology* 4(3):323–335.
  1972a "Eskimo Band Organization and the D. P. Camp Hypothesis," *Arctic Anthropology* 9(2):80–112. University of Wisconsin Press.
  1972b "Identity, Relationship, and Kinship in Eskimo Society." Paper read at the 1972 meeting of the American Anthropological Association, Toronto, Ontario.
  1972c "Kinship and Alliance in Belcher Island Eskimo Society." In Lee Guemple, ed., *Alliance in Eskimo Society: Proceedings of the American Ethnological Society, 1971, Supplement,* pp. 56–78. Seattle: University of Washington Press.

Hansen, Henry P., ed.
  1967   *Arctic Biology, 2nd ed.* Corvallis: Oregon State University Press.

Hanson, F. Allan
  1971   "Nonexclusive Cognatic Descent Systems: A Polynesian Example." In Alan Howard, ed., *Polynesia: Readings on a Culture Area,* pp. 109–132. Toronto: Chandler Publishing Co.

Harrison, Gordon S., & T. A. Morehouse
  1970   "Rural Alaska's Development Problem," *Polar Record* 15(96):291–299.

Heinrich, Albert Carl
  1950   "Some Present-day Acculturative Innovations in a Nonliterate Society." *American Anthropologist* 52(2):235–242.
  1955a "An Outline of the Kinship System of the Bering Straits Eskimos." Unpublished M.A. thesis, Department of Education, University of Alaska.
  1955b "A Survey of Kinship Forms and Terminologies found among the Inupiaq-speaking Peoples of Alaska." Unpublished Ms. in the University of Alaska Archives, College, Alaska.
  1960   "Structural Features of Northwestern Alaskan Eskimo Kinship." *Southwestern Journal of Anthropology* 16(1):-110–126.

Heinrich, Albert Carl (Cont.)

1963a "Eskimo-type Kinship and Eskimo Kinship: an Evaluation and a Provisional Model for Presenting the Evidence Pertaining to Inupiaq Kinship Systems." Unpublished Ph.D. thesis, Department of Anthropology, University of Washington.

1963b "Personal Names, Social Structure, and Functional Integration." *Department of Sociology, Anthropology and Social Welfare, Montana State University, Anthropology and Sociology Papers*, No. 27. Missoula, Montana.

1969 "Social Integration and Personal Names in an Eskimo Group." *The Journal of Karnatak University—Social Sciences* 5:1–14.

1972 "Divorce as an Alliance Mechanism among Eskimos." In Lee Guemple, ed., *Alliance in Eskimo Society: Proceedings of the American Ethnological Society, 1971, Supplement*, pp. 79–88. Seattle: University of Washington Press.

Heinrich, Albert C., & R. Anderson

1968 "Co-affinal Siblingship as a Structural Feature among some Northern North American Peoples." *Ethnology* 7 (3):290–295.

1971 "Some Formal Aspects of a Kinship System." *Current Anthropology* 12(4–5):541–548 (with comments, pp. 548–557).

Helm, June

1965 "Bilaterality in the Socio-territorial Organization of the Arctic Drainage Dene." *Ethnology* 4(4):361–385.

1968 "The Nature of Dogrib Socioterritorial Groups." In R. B. Lee & I. DeVore, eds., *Man the Hunter*, pp. 118–125. Chicago: Aldine Publishing Co.

1969 "Remarks on the Methodology of Band Composition Analysis." In D. Damas, ed., *Contributions to Anthropology: Band Societies*, pp. 212–217. National Museum of Canada, Bulletin No. 228.

Helm, June, & D. Damas

1963 "The Contact-Traditional All-Native Community in the Canadian North: The Upper Mackenzie 'Bush' Athapaskans and the Igluligmiut." *Anthropologica* 5(1):9–21.

Hennigh, Lawrence

1966 "Control of Incest in Eskimo Folk-tales." *Journal of American Folklore*, April-June, pp. 356–369.

Hennigh, Lawrence (Cont.)

1970 "Functions and Limitations of Alaskan Eskimo Wife Trading." *Arctic* 23(1):24–34.

1972 "You have to be a Good Lawyer to be an Eskimo." In Lee Guemple, ed., *Alliance in Eskimo Society. Proceedings of the American Ethnological Society, 1971, Supplement*, pp. 89–109. Seattle: University of Washington Press.

Hippler, Arthur E.

1969 *Barrow and Kotzebue: An Exploratory Comparison of Acculturation and Education in two large Northwestern Alaska Villages.* Minneapolis; Training Center for Community Programs, in Coordination with the Office of Community Programs, Center for Urban and Regional Affairs.

1970 *From Village to Town: An Intermediate Step in the Acculturation of Alaska Eskimos.* Minneapolis: Training Center for Community Programs, in coordination with the Office of Community Programs, Center for Urban and Regional Affairs.

Hoebel, E. Adamson

1954 *The Law of Primitive Man.* Cambridge: Harvard University Press.

Homans, George Caspar

1960 *English Villagers of the Thirteenth Century.* New York: Russell & Russell.

Honigmann, John, & Irma Honigmann

1959 "Notes on Great Whale River Ethos." *Anthropologica* 1(1–2):106–121.

Hooper, C. L.

1881 *Report of the Cruise of the U. S. Revenue Steamer "Thomas Corwin" in the Arctic Ocean, 1880.* Washington: U. S. Government Printing Office.

Hopkins, J. P., & D. M. Hopkins

1958 "Seward Peninsula." In Howell Williams, ed., *Landscapes of Alaska: Their Geologic Evolution*, pp. 104–110. Berkeley & Los Angeles: University of California Press.

Howe, G. P.

1909 "Medical Notes on Northern Alaska." In Ejnar Mikkelsen, *Conquering the Arctic Ice*, Appendix III. London: W. Heinemann.

Hsu, Francis L. K.
  1965 "The Effect of Dominant Kinship Relationships on Kin and
         Non-kin Behavior: A Hypothesis." *American Anthropolo-
         gist* 67(3):638–661.
  1971 "A Hypothesis on Kinship and Culture." In F. L. K. Hsu,
         ed., *Kinship and Culture* pp. 3–29. Chicago: Aldine Pub-
         lishing Co.

Hughes, Charles Campbell
  1963 "Review of James W. VanStone: Point Hope: An Eski-
         mo Village in Transition." *American Anthropoliogist*
         65(2):452–454.
  1965 "Under Four Flags: Recent Culture Change among the
         Eskimos." *Current Anthropology* 6(1):3–69.

Hultén, Eric
  1968 *Flora of Alaska and Neighboring Territories.* Stanford
         University Press.

Ingstad, Helge
  1954 *Nunamiut: Among Alaska's Inland Eskimos.* London:
         George Allen & Unwin, Ltd.

Jenness, Diamond
  1918 "The Eskimos of Northern Alaska: A Study in the Effects
         of Civilization." *Geographical Review* 5(2):89–101.
  1929 "Little Diomede Island, Bering Strait." *Geographical Re-
         view* 19(1):78–86.
  1957 *Dawn in Arctic Alaska.* Minneapolis: University of Min-
         nesota Press.
  1962 *Eskimo Administration: I. Alaska.* Arctic Institute of
         North America, Technical Paper No. 10, Montreal, P.Q.

Johnshoy, J. Walter
  1944 *Apauruk in Alaska: Social Pioneering among the Eskimos.*
         Philadelphia: Dorrance & Co.

Kleinfeld, Judith
  1971 "Visual Memory in Village Eskimo and Urban Caucasian
         Children." *Arctic* 24(2):132–138.

Klengenberg, Christian
  1932 *Klengenberg of the Arctic.* Tom MacInnes, ed., Toronto:
         Alden Press.

Knapp, Edward J.
  1905 "Twelve Months at Point Hope." *The Spirit of Missions*, November 1905, pp. 873–877.

Kotzebue, Otto von
  1821 *A Voyage of Discovery into the South Sea and Beerings Straits . . . 1815–1818. . . .* 3 vols. London: Longman, Hurst, Rees, Orme, & Brown.

Lantis, Margaret
  1947 *Alaskan-Eskimo Ceremonialism.* Seattle: University of Washington Press.

Larsen, Helge, & Froelich Rainey
  1948 *Ipiutak and the Arctic Whale Hunting Culture.* Anthropological Papers of the American Museum of Natural History, Vol. 42.

Leach, E. R.
  1958 "Concerning Trobriand Clans and the Kinship Category 'tabu.'" In Jack Goody, ed., *The Development Cycle in Domestic Groups*, pp. 120–145. Cambridge: Cambridge University Press.

Leacock, Eleanor
  1969 "The Montagnais-Naskapi Band." In D. Damas, ed., *Contributions to Anthropology: Band Societies.* National Museum of Canada Bulletin No. 228, pp. 1–17.

Lee, Richard B.
  1968 "What Hunters do for a Living, or, How to Make Out on Scarce Resources." In R. B. Lee and I. DeVore, eds., *Man the Hunter*, pp. 30–48. Chicago: Aldine Publishing Co.

Lee, Richard B., & I. DeVore, eds.
  1968a "Analysis of Group Composition." In R. B. Lee and I. DeVore, eds., *Man the Hunter*, pp. 150–155. Chicago: Aldine Publishing Co.
  1968b *Man the Hunter.* Chicago: Aldine Publishing Co.
  1968c "On Ethnographic Reconstruction." In R. B. Lee and I. DeVore, eds., *Man the Hunter* pp. 146–149. Chicago: Aldine Publishing Co.
  1968d "Problems in the Study of Hunters and Gatherers." In R. B. Lee and I. DeVore, eds., *Man the Hunter*, pp. 3–12. Chicago: Aldine Publishing Co.

Lee, Richard B., & I. DeVore, eds. (Cont.)
1968e "Resolving Conflicts by Fisson." In R. B. Lee and I. De-Vore, eds., *Man the Hunter*, p. 156. Chicago: Aldine Publishing Co.

Lévi-Strauss, Claude
1969 *The Elementary Structures of Kinship. Revised Edition.* Boston: Beacon Press.

Levy, Marion J., Jr.
1952 *The Structure of Society.* Princeton, New Jersey: Princeton University Press.
1965 "Aspects of the Analysis of Family Structure." In Ansley J. Coale, *et al., Aspects of the Analysis of Family Structure,* pp. 1–63. Princeton University Press.
1966 *Modernization and the Structure of Societies: A Setting for International Affairs.* 2 vols. Princeton, N. J.: Princeton University Press.
1967 "Family Structure and the Holistic Analysis of Societies." In Samuel Klausner, ed., *The Study of Total Societies,* pp. 162–176. New York: Frederick A. Praeger.
1970 "Some Hypotheses about the Family." *Journal of Comparative Family Studies* 1(1):113–131.
1971 "Notes on the Hsu Hypotheses." In F. L. K. Hsu, ed., *Kinship and Culture,* pp. 33–41. Chicago: Aldine Publishing Co.

Levy, Marion J., Jr., and L. A. Fallers
1959 "The Family: Some Comparative Considerations." *American Anthropologist* 61(4):648–651.

Lounsbury, Floyd G.
1965 "Another View of the Trobriand Kinship Categories." In E. A. Hammel, ed., *Formal Semantic Analysis.* Published as *American Anthropologist* 65(5), Part 2, pp. 142–185.

Lundsgaarde, H. P., & M. G. Silverman
1972 "Category and Group in Gilbertese Kinship: An Updating of Goodenough's Analysis." *Ethnology* 11(2):-95–110.

Mair, Lucy
1965 *An Introduction to Social Anthropology.* Oxford: Clarendon Press.

Maguire, Rochefort
    1854   "Report on the Proceedings of Her Majesty's Discovery
            Ship 'Plover,' Commander Rochefort Maguire." In *Great
            Britain, Admiralty Papers, Relative to the Recent Arctic
            Expedition on the Search for Sir John Franklin and the
            Crews of the H.M.S. 'Erebus' and 'Terror,'* Part XIII,
            pp. 169–186. London: Eyre & Spottiswoode.

Malinowski, B.
    1930   "Kinship." *Man* 30:19–29.

Manville, Richard H., & S. P. Young
    1965   *Distribution of Alaskan Mammals.* Bureau of Sport Fish-
            eries and Wildlife, Circular 211. Washington, D. C.:
            U.S. Government Printing Office.

McElwaine, Eugene
    1901   *The Truth about Alaska, the Golden Land of the Midnight
            Sun.* Published by the author.

McPhail, J. D., & C. C. Lindsey
    1970   *Freshwater Fishes of Northwestern Canada and Alaska.*
            Fisheries Research Board of Canada, Bulletin 173. Ottawa.

Mikkelsen, Ejnar
    1909.   *Conquering the Arctic Ice.* London: W. Heinemann.

Milan, Frederick A.
    1964   "The Acculturation of the Contemporary Eskimo of Wain-
            wright, Alaska." *Anthropological Papers of the University
            of Alaska.* 11(2):1–95.
    1970a   "A Demographic Study of an Eskimo Village on the North
            Slope of Alaska." *Arctic* 23(2):82–99.
    1970b   "The Demography of an Alaskan Eskimo Village." *Arctic
            Anthropology* 7(1):26–43.
    1970c   "Preliminary Estimates of Inbreeding Levels in Wain-
            wright Eskimos." *Arctic Anthropology* 7(1):70–72.

Morgan, Lewis Henry
    1871   *Systems of Consanguinity and Affinity of the Human
            Family.* Washington: Smithsonian Contributions to
            Knowledge.

Murdoch, John
    1892   *Ethnological Results of the Point Barrow Expedition.*
            Ninth Annual Report of the Bureau of American Ethnology,
            1887–1888. Washington.

Murdock, George Peter
1949 *Social Structure.* New York: MacMillan.

National Center for Health Statistics
1971 "Provisional Statistics. Annual Summary for the United States, 1970. Births, Deaths, Marriages, and Divorces." *Monthly Vital Statistics Report,* Vol. 19, No. 13. Rochville, M. D.: National Center for Health Statistics, Health Services and Mental Health Administration.

Needham, Rodney
1960 "Descent Systems and Ideal Language." *Philosophy of Science* 27(1):96–101.
1962 "Genealogy and Category in Wikmunkan Society." *Ethnology* 1:233–264.

Nelson, Edward William
1899 *The Eskimo About Bering Strait.* Bureau of American Ethnology, 18th Annual Report (1896–97), Part 1. Washington, D. C.

Nelson, Richard K.
1969 *Hunters of the Northern Ice.* Chicago: University of Chicago Press.

Northwest Economic Development and Planning Board
[1969] [Census data for 14 villages in Northwest Alaska.] Kotzebue: Northwest Economic Development and Planning Board, Affiliate of Alaska Federation of Natives. (Courtesy of Daniel Lisbourne, Executive Director.)

Ostermann, H.
1952 *The Alaskan Eskimos, as Described in the Posthumous Notes of Dr. Knud Rasmussen.* H. Ostermann, and E. Holtved, eds. Report of the Fifth Thule Expedition, 1921–24. Vol. X, No. 3. Copenhagen.

Oswalt, Wendell
1967 *Alaskan Eskimos.* San Francisco: Chandler Publishing Company.

Parker, Seymour
1964 "Ethnic Identity and Acculteration in two Eskimo Villages." *American Anthropologist* 66:325–340.

Pehrson, Robert N.
1959 "Bilateral Kin Groupings as a Structural Type." In Morton H. Fried, ed., *Readings in Anthropology*. Vol. II *Readings in Cultural Anthropology*. New York: Thomas Y. Crowell.
1964 "The Bilateral Network of Social Relations in Könkämä Lapp District." *Samiske Samlinger*, Bd. VII.

Petroff, Ivan
1884 *Report on the Population, Industries and Resources of Alaska*. Tenth Census of the United States, 1880. Washington: Government Printing Office.

Porter, Robert
1893 *Report on the Population and Resources of Alaska at the Eleventh Census: 1890*. Government Printing Office.

Pospisil, Leopold
1964 "Law and Societal Structure among the Nunamiut Eskimo." In Ward H. Goodenough, ed., *Explorations in Cultural Anthropology. Essays in Honor of George Peter Murdock*, pp. 395–431. New York: McGraw-Hill Book Company.

Pospisil, Leopold, & William S. Laughlin
1963 "Kinship Terminology and Kindred among the Nunamiut Eskimos." *Ethnology* 2(2):180–189.

Radcliffe-Brown, A. R.
1950 "Introduction." In A. R. Radcliffe-Brown and Daryll Forde, eds., *African Systems of Kinship and Marriage*, pp. 1–85. London: Oxford University Press.

Rainey, Froelich
1941 "Native Economy and Survival in Arctic Alaska." *Applied Anthropology* 1(1):9–14.
1947 "The Whale Hunters of Tigara," *Anthropological Papers of the American Museum of Natural History* 41(2):231–283.

Rasmussen, Knud
1934 "Adjustment of the Eskimos to European Civilization, with special emphasis on the Alaskan Eskimos." *Proceedings of the 5th Pacific Scientific Congress, Victoria and Vancouver, B. C., 1933*, vol. 4, pp. 2889–2891. Toronto.

Ray, Dorothy Jean
1964 "Nineteenth Century Settlement and Subsistence Patterns in Bering Strait." *Arctic Anthropology* 2(2):61–94.

Ray, Dorothy Jean (Cont.)

1966 "Introduction." In "H. M. W. Edmonds' Report on the Eskimos of St. Michael and Vicinity," D. J. Ray, ed., pp. 7–22. *Anthropological Papers of the University of Alaska* 13(2):1–143.

1967 "Land Tenure and Polity of the Bering Strait Eskimos." *Journal of the West* 6(3):371–394.

n.d. "The Bering Strait of Alaska, 1650–1900." Unpublished Manuscript.

Ray, Patrick Henry

1885 "Ethnographic Sketch of the Natives." In P. H. Ray et al., *Report of the International Polar Expedition to Point Barrow, Alaska*, pp. 37–60. Washington: Government Printing Office.

Rogers, George W.

1968 "Alaska's Native Population as an emerging Political Force." *Inter-Nord* 10:148–150.

1969 "Party Politics or Protest Politics: Current Political Trends in Alaska." *Polar Record* 14(91):445–458.

1971 "Alaska Native Population Trends and Vital Statistics, 1950–1985." *I.S.E.G.R. Research Note*, November, 1971. Fairbanks, Alaska: University of Alaska Institute of Social, Economic, and Government Research.

Rosse, Irving C.

1883 "Medical and Anthropological Notes on Alaska." In *Cruise of the Revenue-Steamer Corwin in Alaska and the N. W. Arctic Ocean in 1881*, pp. 5–53. Washington: James Anglim & Co.

Ruel, M. J.

1962 "Genealogical concepts or 'category' words? A study of Banyang kinship terminology." *Journal of the Royal Anthropological Institute*, Vol. 92, Part. 2, pp. 157–176.

Saario, Doris J., & Brina Kessel

1966 "Human Ecological Investigations at Kivalina." In Norman J. Wilimovsky and John N. Wolfe, eds., *Environment of the Cape Thompson Region, Alaska*, pp. 969–1039. Oak Ridge, Tennessee: United States Atomic Energy Commission.

Savage, Jay M.
    1969   *Evolution.* *2nd ed.*, New York: Holt, Rinehart and Winston.

Schneider, David M.
    1964   "The Nature of Kinship." *Man* 64(217):180–181.
    1965a   "American Kin Terms and Terms for Kinsmen: A Critique of Goodenough's Componential Analysis of Yankee Kinship Terminology." In E. A. Hammel, ed., *Formal Semantic Analysis*, pp. 288–308. Special Publication of the American Anthropological Association. Published as *American Anthropologist*, Vol. 67, No. 5, Part 2.
    1965b   "Kinship and Biology." In Ansley J. Coale, *et al.*, *Aspects of the Analysis of Family Structure*, pp. 83–101. Princeton, N. J.: Princeton University Press.
    1972   "What is Kinship all About?" In Priscilla Reining, ed., *Kinship Studies in the Morgan Centennial Year*, pp. 32–63. Washington, D. C.: The Anthropological Society of Washington.

Searby, Harold W.
    1968   "Climates of the States. Alaska." U. S. Department of Commerce, Environmental Science Services Administration, Environmental Data Service, *Climatography of the United States*, No. 60–49. Washington, D. C., September, 1959. Revised and reprinted, May, 1968.

Seeman, Berthold
    1853   *Narrative of the Voyage of H.M.S. 'Herald,' During the Years 1845–51, Under the Command of Captain Henry Kellett, R.N., C.B.*, 2 vols. London: Reeve & Co.

Senungetuk, Joseph E.
    1971   *Give or Take a Century. An Eskimo Chronicle.* San Francisco: The Indian Historian Press.

Sherwood, Morgan
    1965   *Exploration in Alaska 1865–1900.* New Haven: Yale University Press.

Simpson, John
    1875   "Observations on the Western Eskimo, and the Country they Inhabit: From Notes taken during two Years at Point Barrow." In *A Selection of Papers on Arctic Geography and Ethnology*, pp. 233–275. London: Royal Geographical Society.

Simpson, Thomas
1843 *Narrative of the Discoveries on the North Coast of America; effected by the Officers of the Hudson's Bay Company During the Years 1836–1839.* London: R. Bentley.

Smith, Philip S., & J. B. Mertie
1930 *Geology and Mineral Resources of Northwestern Alaska.* U. S. Geological Survey Bulletin 815.

Smith, Valene
1966 "Kotzebue: A Modern Eskimo Community." Unpublished Ph.D. thesis, Department of Anthropology, University of Utah, Salt Lake City.
1968a "In-Migration and Factionalism: An Eskimo Example." Paper presented at the Annual Meetings of the American Anthropological Association, Seattle, November 24, 1968.
1968b "Intercontinental Aboriginal Trade in the Bering Straits Area." Paper presented at the VIII International Congress of Anthropological and Ethnological Sciences. Tokyo.

Solecki, Ralph
1951 "Archeology and Ecology of the Arctic Slope of Alaska." In *Smithsonian Institution Annual Report* for 1950, pp. 469–495. Washington, D. C.: U. S. Government Printing Office.

Sonnenfeld, J.
1957 "Changes in Subsistence among the Barrow Eskimo." Unpublished Ph.D. thesis, Department of Geography, Johns Hopkins University.

Spencer, Robert F.
1954 "Forms of Cooperation in the Culture of the Barrow Eskimo." *Science in Alaska. Proceedings of the Third Alaskan Science Conference,* pp. 128–130. College, Alaska.
1958 "Eskimo Polyandry and Social Organization." *Proceedings of the Thirty-Second International Congress of Americanists,* pp. 539–544. Copenhagen: Munksgaard.
1959 *The North Alaskan Eskimo: A Study in Ecology and Society.* Smithsonian Institution, Bureau of American Ethnology Bulletin 171. Washington: Government Printing Office.
1967/68 "Die Organization der Ehe unter den Eskimo Nordalaskas." *Weiner Völkerkundliche Mitteilungen,* XIV/XV J.G., N.F., BD. IX/X. Vienna: 1967/68.

Spencer, Robert F. (Cont.)

1968 "Spouse Exchange among the North Alaskan Eskimo." In Paul Bohannon and John Middleton, eds., *Marriage, Family, and Residence,* pp. 131–146. New York: Natural History Press.

1972 "The Social Composition of the North Alaskan Whaling Crew." In D. L. Guemple, ed., *Alliance in Eskimo Society: Proceedings of the American Ethnological Society, 1971, Supplement,* pp. 110–120. Seattle: University of Washington Press.

Stefansson, Vilhjalmur

1909 "Northern Alaska in Winter." *Bulletin of the American Geographical Society* 41(10):601–616.

1914 *The Stefansson-Anderson Arctic Expedition of the American Museum: Preliminary Ethnological Report.* Anthropological Papers of the American Museum of Natural History, Vol. 14, Part 1.

1951 *My Life With the Eskimo.* New York: The Macmillan Co.

1956 "Causes of Eskimo Birthrate Increase." *Nature* 178(4542):-1132.

Stoney, George M.

1900 *Naval Explorations in Alaska.* Annapolis, Md. U. S. Naval Institute.

Stuck, Hudson

1920 *A Winter Circuit of our Arctic Coast.* New York: Charles Scribners Sons.

Swadesh, Morris

1951–52 "Unalliq and Proto-Eskimo I.–V." *International Journal of American Linguistics* 17:66–70, 18:25–34, 69–76, 166–171, 241–256.

Thornton, Harrison Robertson

1931 *Among the Eskimos of Wales, Alaska, 1890–93.* Baltimore: The Johns Hopkins Press.

United States Bureau of the Census

1913 "Alaska. Number of Inhabitants, and Composition and Characteristics of the Population." In *Thirteenth Census of the United States,* Vol. III, pp. 1127–1153.

United States Bureau of the Census (Cont.)

1915   *Indian Population in the United States and Alaska, 1910.* Washington: U. S. Government Printing Office.

1960   *Historical Statistics of the United States, Colonial Times to 1957.* Washington, D. C.: U. S. Government Printing Office.

1961   "U. S. Census of Population: 1960. General Population Characteristics, Alaska." Final Report PC(1)–3B. Washington, D. C.: U. S. Government Printing Office.

1963   *Eighteenth Decennial Census of the U. S. Census of Population 1960.* Vol. 1. *Characteristics of the Population,* Part 3 "Alaska." Washington, D. C.: U. S. Government Printing Office.

1965   *Historical Statistics of the United States, Colonial Times to 1957; Continuation to 1962, Revisions.* Washington, D. C.: U. S. Government Printing Office.

1970a *1970 Census of the Population, Advance Report. Final Population Counts, Alaska.* U. S. Department of Commerce, Bureau of the Census, Document No. PC(VI)–3. Washington: U. S. Government Printing Office.

1970b *Statistical Abstract of the United States, 1970.* 91st edition. Washington, D. C.: U. S. Government Printing Office.

VanStone, James W.

1957   "The Autobiography of an Alaskan Eskimo." *Arctic* 10 (4):195–210.

1958   "An Eskimo Community and the Outside World." *Anthropological Papers of the University of Alaska* 7(1):-27–38.

1960   "A Successful Combination of Subsistence and Wage Economics on the Village Level." *Economic Development and Cultural Change* 8(2):174–191.

1962   *Point Hope: An Eskimo Village in Transition.* Seattle: University of Washington Press.

1964   "Some Aspects of Religious Change Among Native Inhabitants in West Alaska and the Northwest Territories." *Arctic Anthropology* 2(2):21–24 (1964).

Wells, Ensign Roger, and John W. Kelly

1890   "English-Eskimo and Eskimo-English Vocabularies, preceded by Ethnographical Memoranda concerning the Arctic Eskimos in Alaska and Siberia." *Bureau of Education, Circular of Information* No. 2. Washington, D. C.

Weyer, Edward Moffat, Jr.
  1962 *The Eskimos: Their Environment and Folkways.* Hamden,
        Conn.: Archon Books. (Reprint of Yale University Press
        edition of 1932.)

Wiggins, I. L., & J. H. Thomas
  1962 *A Flora of the Alaskan Arctic Slope.* Arctic Institute of
        North America, Special Publication No. 4. Toronto: Uni-
        versity of Toronto Press.

Williams, Howel, ed.
  1958 *Landscapes of Alaska: Their Geologic Evolution.* Berke-
        ley and Los Angeles: University of California Press.

Williamson, H. Anthony
  1961 "The Founding and Early Years of Noatak Village." In
        Don Charles Foote and H. A. Williamson, "A Human
        Geographical Study in Northwest Alaska. Final Report
        of the Human Geographical Studies Program, United States
        Atomic Energy Commission, Project Chariot," pp. 77–86,
        Cambridge, Mass.: Mimeo.

Willmott, W. E.
  1960 "The Flexibility of Eskimo Social Organization." *Anthro-
        pologica,* ns. 2(1):48–59.

Woodburn, James
  1968 "Stability and Flexibility in Hadza Residential Groupings."
        In R. B. Lee and I. DeVore, eds., *Man the Hunter,* pp.
        103–110. Chicago: Aldine Publishing Co.

Woolfe, Henry D.
  1893 "The Seventh or Arctic District." In R. P. Porter, *Report
        on Population and Resources of Alaska.* Eleventh Census
        of the United States, 1890. Washington: U. S. Government
        Printing Office.

Wrong, Dennis H.
  1963 "The Oversocialized Concept of Man in Modern Sociology."
        In Neil J. Smelser and William J. Smelser, eds., *Personality
        and Social Systems,* pp. 68–79. New York: John Wiley
        and Sons, Inc.

Index